QUALITATIVE DATA ANALYSIS WITH NVIVO

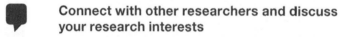
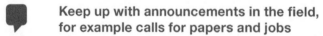

SECOND EDITION

QUALITATIVE DATA ANALYSIS WITH NVIVO

PAT BAZELEY & KRISTI JACKSON

Los Angeles | London | New Delhi
Singapore | Washington DC

Los Angeles | London | New Delhi
Singapore | Washington DC

SAGE Publications Ltd
1 Oliver's Yard
55 City Road
London EC1Y 1SP

SAGE Publications Inc.
2455 Teller Road
Thousand Oaks, California 91320

SAGE Publications India Pvt Ltd
B 1/I 1 Mohan Cooperative Industrial Area
Mathura Road
New Delhi 110 044

SAGE Publications Asia-Pacific Pte Ltd
3 Church Street
#10-04 Samsung Hub
Singapore 049483

Editor: Jai Seaman
Editorial assistant: Anna Horvai
Production editor: Ian Antcliff
Proofreader: Jonathan Hopkins
Copyeditor: Richard Leigh
Marketing manager: Ben Griffin-Sherwood
Cover design: Lisa Harper
Typeset by: C&M Digitals (P) Ltd, Chennai, India
Printed and bound by MPG Printgroup, UK

Library of Congress Control Number: 2012952715

British Library Cataloguing in Publication data

A catalogue record for this book is available from
the British Library

ISBN 978-1-4462-5655-8
ISBN 978-1-4462-5656-5 (pbk)

Contents

Figures

Tables

About the authors

Pat Bazeley (PhD, Macquarie University) provides research training and consulting through her company, Research Support P/L, to academics, graduate students and practitioners from a wide range of disciplines in universities and government agencies both within Australia and internationally. Additionally, she has a part-time appointment as Associate Professor in the Centre for Primary Health Care and Equity at the University of New South Wales. Since graduating in psychology she has worked in community development, project consulting and in academic research development. Her experience with research design and methodology broadly across the social sciences includes over 20 years of providing training in the use of QSR software for qualitative and mixed methods research. Her research and publications focus on qualitative and mixed methods data analysis, and on the development and performance of researchers.

Kristi Jackson (MEd, University of Vermont) was Vice President of an evaluation research firm in Denver, Colorado until 2002, when she founded Queri, a qualitative research consulting company. Queri provides assistance to large entities (e.g., the Centers for Disease Control and Prevention, the National Institutes of Health, and the US Government Accountability Office) as well as many small, nongovernmental organizations in rural and urban settings. Her conference presentations and published papers often focus on the implications of the growing importance of qualitative data analysis software, and she is currently studying conceptualizations of qualitative research transparency among researchers who do and do not use this genre of software. In her 17 years of experience as an evaluation researcher, she served as principal investigator, co-investigator or advisor on a diverse array of qualitative research projects, primarily in education and health.

Preface to the second edition

Since the publication of the first edition of this book, the world of qualitative data analysis has changed yet again. The tools in NVivo have adapted to the increasing popularity of mixed methods research, research involving use of multimedia, and the greater involvement of teams in qualitative projects. They have adapted, as well, to a world-wide increase in the digitization of data and new modes of digital communication, for example, through social media sites such as Facebook, LinkedIn, Twitter and YouTube. While the impact of these advancements in the software required additions to this book, another wave of change also informs this edition. Where the emphasis in early qualitative data analysis software was on coding as a primary strategy, this emphasis is progressively shifting to provision of tools to facilitate thinking, linking, writing, modelling and graphing in ways that go beyond a simple dependence on coding. As a response to these many developments, in this edition we include new chapters on working with multimedia sources, datasets from surveys, and data from social media sites; using NVivo for your literature review; ways to leverage visualizations to explore your data and communicate your findings; and on strategically using NVivo in the context of team research.

One of the consequences of our need to include new material in this edition of the book, compared to the first, is a subtle shift in focus from approaches to undertaking a qualitative project in the context of one or another methodological approach, supported by NVivo, to a more direct focus on the tools NVivo provides and how these can support qualitative research more generally. For readers who found the first edition helpful methodologically as well as technologically and who notice the change (and for others who would benefit from help with methods), Pat offers the extended alternative of a book dedicated to providing down-to-earth help for researchers working with qualitative data, *Qualitative Data Analysis: Practical Strategies* (Sage, 2013). Each book is, in many ways, a companion to the other. Our primary goal in this book remains, however, to help you *thoughtfully* make use of the software as you apply it strategically to your data.

Qualitative data analysis software, and NVivo in particular, has become increasingly flexible in adapting to the demands of modern research projects. An unfortunate but unavoidable consequence of increasing flexibility is increased complexity. QSR International, the developers of NVivo, have responded by providing guidance for users in various forms – video tutorials, webinars, and extensive, detailed on-line Help – all of which are extremely valuable if you know what to ask for, and for stimulus in using the software. They are less helpful in providing guidance as to what tools to choose for a particular research problem, and in guiding the user through the strategies needed to work right through a research task without becoming lost in the multiple options available.

The multiplicity of approaches to analysis of qualitative data poses particular problems not only for writers of Help files and tutorials, but also for a book of this nature, with the purpose of walking you through a project: How best to organize and sequence the tasks and the introduction of different tools? As there is no standard pathway through a project, we don't expect everyone to work straight through this book. Nevertheless, the book is organized along broad sequential stages in working from raw data through conceptualization to strategies for analysis. We attempt, therefore, to take you right through a series of actions to complete necessary steps along the most common pathways travelled with each primary tool, source of data, or approach, but you will need to step forward or back at various times to find the instruction, suggestions or discussion *you* most need for particular points in *your* project. At the same time, at each step we point you to where you might find additional ideas and assistance in case your journey requires a digression or raises a complication.

Following the chapter-by-chapter sequence will take you through all the elements you need to consider: this might be the best general approach for someone new to the software. Those who already have some knowledge of the software from earlier versions might use the brief description of each chapter or the table of contents to identify where they might find the major discussion of a particular topic within the chapters. A more detailed index is provided, of course, at the end of the book. A companion website (www.sagepub.co.uk/bazeleynvivo) accompanies the book, providing you with access to sample data, additional technical help, links to useful resources, and updates to information in this book. The Help files provided by QSR are both detailed and comprehensive, and they are always updated as the software is updated. They can be consulted, therefore, to resolve any discrepancies between our instructions or screen shots and the software that might result from ongoing updates to the software.[1]

---

[1] The current version of the NVivo software, at the time of writing, was version 10 for Windows. Check the companion website also for supplementary notes to assist with features changed or added in later versions.

Chapter outline

Chapter 1: Perspectives: Qualitative computing and NVivo – Settle in with a little grounding in the history and relevance of this genre of software to help you prepare for the journey. After considering the potential advantages and disadvantages of using software for this type of work, we take you on a gentle tour of an existing database to start putting things into perspective.

Chapter 2: Starting out, with a view ahead – Start a project in NVivo well before collecting or constructing data if you can. Begin with a question and your thinking around that question, or perhaps with a theory. Craft an early model of these ideas, add some literature (or any source material), and start writing memos. Create links to help trace the connections in these early ideas. By starting your project in NVivo earlier rather than later, you will lay a sure foundation for working with data and verifying the conclusions you draw from them.

Chapter 3: Designing an NVivo database – Prepare for the work ahead by reflecting on what a 'case' might be in your research and tie this to the strategies you employ as you prepare your data. While the software supports a wide range of text, audio, video, picture, spreadsheet and web page formats, you can do things to prepare the data (text-based files in particular) to maximize the benefit of some of the software tools you might use later.

Chapter 4: Coding basics – Discover the day-to-day activities of reflecting on the data and coding as you work through your first sources. Connect this coding process with the strategies you learned for memoing and linking, as ideas take shape. Observe and manage your use of inductive and deductive coding strategies as you learn the basics of creating codes (nodes) and coding.

Chapter 5: Going on with coding – Go beyond the basics to start developing a coding *system* designed to address your research questions. Learn to move nodes, combine and rename them. Consider different conceptual approaches to creating the system and learn some tips to keep you from creating a voluminous, chaotic coding structure. Experiment with automated coding strategies (the auto code and text-mining tools) before taking steps to review your coding by standing back and then coming close.

Chapter 6: Cases, classifications and comparisons – Learn how to store demographic and other kinds of quantitative information as attributes of cases. Learn different ways of entering these into your project, and how to use them to make comparisons and examine patterns in your data.

Chapter 7: Working with multimedia sources – Seriously consider why you might or might not want to use audio, video, images and web pages as material in your project and prepare yourself for a host of methodological considerations. Then learn how to capture, import, code and link this material and examine the way it exports as either Word or html files.

Chapter 8: Adding reference material to your NVivo project – Understand the opportunities and hazards associated with importing and coding pdf files, and see how to import material from bibliographic databases and web pages. Consider the many different reasons why you might use reference material and push your thinking beyond a basic literature review.

Chapter 9: Datasets and mixed methods – Explore the new ways you can combine data types in NVivo, in particular through the use of structured questionnaires, web surveys, and social media that typically contain both forced-choice and open-ended fields. Learn how to prepare, import, code and sort such data, and read an assortment of examples to get you thinking further about different types of data and the rationale for using them in NVivo.

Chapter 10: Tools and strategies for visualizing data – Apply the visualization tools in NVivo to think through your cases, concepts, relationships and theories. Models, charts, graphs and diagrams can also be used to display your results and communicate findings, and while in the software they also provide you with direct access to the data they represent.

Chapter 11: Using coding and queries to further analysis – Consider the corpus of these sophisticated search tools and the various ways you can use them to search for relationships and patterns in the data. This might be the culmination of your analytic journey, or you might experiment with a few queries early on in the project. Learn the framework for the overall structure and purpose of the queries, before turning to other chapters where a contextually grounded example of each of the seven queries is located.

Chapter 12: Teamwork with NVivo – Dive into the exciting and challenging experience of team research and learn how NVivo can help with organizing team activities and framing the analytical process. Some tools in NVivo are specifically designed for team research and others should be addressed anew in the context of team research. Practical help includes strategies for tracking team member contributions, ways of coding as a team, combining copies of databases and comparing the coding of different researchers.

Acknowledgements

We are pleased to specifically acknowledge the original developers of the software, Lyn and Tom Richards, who launched both of us on this journey back in the early 1990s. While we learned and changed from our interactions with other researchers through the years, the entire journey would never have started without Lyn and Tom, their enthusiasm, and especially their vision for qualitative research evidenced in the intellectual foundation of NVivo. More recently, we owe thanks to the many staff members at QSR, especially Marcus Ogden for his tireless responses to our enquiries and suggestions. The march ahead with new ways of thinking about qualitative data is also due to the many dedicated researchers around the world who continue to explore, advance, challenge and discuss the role of software in qualitative research. While we owe a great deal to the collective work of our colleagues and the stimulation of our clients, there are too many to mention specifically. Know that we are thankful for the many ideas you provide in our ongoing conversations; they most certainly helped shape this book. We are indebted, too, to the team at Sage, especially Jai Seaman and Anna Horvai, for their encouragement and support for this second edition of this book.

Writing about constantly evolving software is always time pressured. This collaboration of two long-term teachers of research using software has been built on a shared perspective on what software can and cannot do, and how best to use software to support research. On a more personal level, it has been built on mutual respect, tolerance and good humour. Each of us learned from the other, made demands on the other, and supported the other. For Pat, after a long and intense period of solo writing, this has been a refreshing experience. This collaboration made this revision possible, with friendship surviving a tight time frame not only intact but strengthened: thank you, Kristi!

Starting farther back in her own voyage, Kristi would also like to acknowledge her parents, Buzz and Lainie: thank you for preparing me with perhaps the most important provision for the ongoing journey – endless encouragement to pursue my interests. I also thank one very dedicated and talented Pat Bazeley for such a happy collaboration.

1

Perspectives: Qualitative computing and NVivo

Perspective influences the way we approach any new experience – including the way we approach the use of software for qualitative analysis. The history of qualitative data analysis software (QDAS) has influenced the current trajectory of software development, and this history is also linked to current researcher perceptions of advantages and disadvantages of software. Depending on when current qualitative research experts chose to adopt (and in some cases subsequently abandon) QDAS, they have different understandings of the purpose and applicability of software tools. Many of us who use, teach and write about QDAS encounter both positive and negative claims regarding the software that are obsolete but have survived as part of the discourse among qualitative methods instructors and scholars. In this chapter we place some of the claims and counterclaims in perspective before providing you with a brief exploration of how NVivo, as one example of QDAS, can assist analysis of qualitative data.

In this chapter:

- Discover how the use of software can support you in doing qualitative research.
- Understand the historical context and ongoing development of this type of software.
- Consider issues and objections people have raised about the use of software for qualitative research.
- Begin with a tour of an existing database to understand the overall composition of the software.

Qualitative research purposes and NVivo

Researchers engage in projects involving interpretation of unstructured or semi-structured data for a variety of reasons. These might include exploration, description, comparison, pattern analysis, theory testing, theory building, or evaluation. Methodologists routinely urge researchers to assess the fit between purpose and method, with the choice to use a qualitative approach being determined by the research question and purpose, rather than by prior preference of the researcher (Maxwell, 2013; Richards & Morse, 2012). Qualitative methods will be chosen in situations where a detailed understanding of a process or experience is wanted, where more information is needed to determine the boundaries or characteristics of the issue being investigated, or where the only information available is in non-numeric (e.g., text or visual) form. Such investigations typically necessitate gathering intensive and/or extensive information from a purposively derived sample.

How NVivo supports qualitative analysis

QSR International, the developers of NVivo, promise only to provide you with a set of tools that will *assist* you in undertaking an analysis of qualitative data. The use of a computer is not intended to supplant time-honoured ways of learning from data, but to increase the effectiveness and efficiency of such learning. NVivo was developed by researchers, and continues to be developed with extensive researcher feedback to support researchers in the varied ways they work with data. The efficiencies afforded by software release some of the time used to simply 'manage' data and allow an increased focus on ways of examining the meaning of what is recorded. The computer's capacity for recording, sorting, matching and linking can be harnessed by researchers to assist in answering their research questions from the data, without losing access to the source data or contexts from which the data have come. In some instances, researchers reported that the software opened up new ways of seeing their data they missed when managing the information without software.[1]

The average user of any software program typically accesses only a small portion of its capabilities; this is no doubt true for users of NVivo also. If you are using NVivo for a small descriptive project, you can work without having

---

[1] Examples include exploring multiple meanings in the data (L. Richards, 2002), challenging researcher assumptions and first impressions of the data (Garcia-Horta & Guerra-Ramos, 2009), becoming aware of gaps in the collected data (Wickham & Woods, 2005), revisiting data with a new conceptual lens (Sin, 2007), fending off an uncritical reification of method (Ozkan, 2004), reflecting on the social construction of evidence (Kaczynski & Kelly, 2004), and unpacking some of the tacit views of research transparency among qualitative researchers (Jackson, 2009).

to learn complex procedures, but if you are undertaking complex analytical tasks, you can find the additional tools you need. Choices about what tools to use and how to use them are entirely up to you.

Using NVivo during the analysis of qualitative data will help you:

- Manage data – to organize and keep track of the many messy records that go into making a qualitative project. These might include not just raw data files from interviews, questionnaires, focus groups or field observations, but also published research, images, diagrams, audio, video, web pages, other documentary sources, rough notes and ideas jotted into memos, information about data sources, and conceptual maps of what is going on in the data.
- Manage ideas – to organize and provide rapid access to conceptual and theoretical knowledge generated in the course of the study, as well as the data that support it, while at the same time retaining ready access to the context from which those data have come.
- Query data – to ask simple or complex questions of the data, and have the program retrieve from your database all information relevant to determining an answer to those questions. Results of queries are saved to allow further interrogation, and so querying or searching becomes part of an ongoing enquiry process.
- Visualize data – to show the content and/or structure of cases, ideas, concepts, sampling strategies, timelines, etc., at various stages of the interpretive process, and to visually represent the relationships among these items in a range of (often interactive) displays.
- Report from the data – using contents of the qualitative database, including information about and in the original data sources, the ideas and knowledge developed from them, and the process by which these outcomes were reached.

There is a widely held perception that use of a computer helps to ensure rigour in the analysis process. In so far as computer software will find and include in a query procedure, for example, every recorded use of a term or every coded instance of a concept, it ensures a more complete set of data for interpretation than might occur when working manually. There are procedures that can be used, too, to check for completeness, and use of a computer makes it possible to test for negative cases (where concepts are *not* related). Perhaps using a computer simply ensures that the user is working more methodically, more thoroughly, more attentively. In these senses, then, it can be claimed that the use of a computer for qualitative analysis can contribute to a more rigorous analysis. Even so, human factors are always involved, and computer software cannot turn sloppy work into sound interpretations, nor compensate for limited interpretive capacity by the researcher. As much as 'a poor workman cannot blame his tools', good tools cannot make up for poor workmanship.

If you are coming to NVivo without first meeting qualitative methodology or methods, then you are strongly advised to read some general texts such as Bazeley (2013), Flick (2009), Maxwell (2013), Patton (2002), Richards (2009), Richards and Morse (2012), or introductory texts from within your own discipline. Then use the recommended reading lists in those texts to further explore the methodological choices available to you. Qualitative methods are a rich, diverse, and complex sphere of knowledge and practice. Be careful about adopting the first approach you encounter (e.g., ethnography or phenomenology) as the only approach, or assuming that because you are working from data up that you are doing grounded theory. Learn about the relevant methodological debates regarding data collection, management and interpretation before fully framing your research.

Perhaps surprisingly, the tools described in this book are 'method-free', in so far as the software does not prescribe a method but rather supports a wide range of methodological approaches. Different tools will be selected or empha-sized and used in alternative ways for a variety of methodological purposes.

> We reiterate that no single software package can be made to perform qualitative data analysis in and of itself. The appropriate use of software depends on appreciation of the kind of data being analyzed and of the analytic purchase the researcher wants to obtain on those data. (Coffey & Atkinson, 1996: 166)

There are, nevertheless, some common principles regarding the most effective use for many of the tools, regardless of methodological choices. For example, the labels used for coding categories will vary depending on the project and the methods chosen, but the principles employed in structuring those categories into a branching coding system are common to many methods where coding takes place. These common principles allow us to describe in general how you might use the various tools. It is then your task to decide how you might apply them to your project.

The evolution of qualitative data analysis software

Alongside the various strands of qualitative methods applied and refined in the 1980s, university faculty from Australia, Germany, and North America began independently developing software programs to facilitate the analysis of quali-tative data. The developers of these software programs believed that a primary purpose of their enterprise was to facilitate data management and promote the rigour of qualitative research.[2]

Initially, these early developers were working in isolation, unaware of paral-lel developments by other researchers (Davidson & di Gregorio, 2011; Fielding, 2008). After networks of researchers began informally sharing their experi-ences with software in qualitative analysis, the first Surrey Research Methods conference was held at the University of Surrey in the UK in 1989. This

---

[2] For detailed discussions on the purpose and evolution of NUD*IST and NVivo, see Richards and Richards (1994) and T. Richards (2002).

conference established a dialogue between developers and early users (Fielding & Lee, 2007).

By 1990, Renata Tesch was able to catalogue over 26 qualitative analysis software packages. These were mostly MS-DOS or Unix based at the time, although she also discussed other platforms. She framed their capabilities in terms of the qualitative approaches they were intended to support – structural analysis, content analysis, interpretational analysis, text retrieval, and theory-building. In the conclusion to her book, Tesch candidly acknowledged that the rapid pace of software development (combined with the time that elapses between conceptualizing and distributing a book) meant her book was already out of date.

This sentiment helps explain the creation, in 1994, of the Computer Assisted Qualitative Data AnalysiS (CAQDAS) networking project in the UK (http://caqdas. soc.surrey.ac.uk). By establishing an internet presence and a location where more recent advancements could be posted without the delays of paper publishing, the CAQDAS site became a cutting-edge source of information about qualitative software, without formal financial ties to any developer. This project was funded for many years by the UK Economic and Social Research Council (ESRC). Shortly thereafter, Weitzman and Miles (1995) produced comprehensive comparison tables of the range of tools provided in 24 programs available at the time.

Common tools across current programs include the ability to write memos and track ideas, index or code data with thematic or conceptual labels, add demographic or other categorical information for the purpose of comparing subgroups, run searches to examine constellations or patterns, develop visual models or charts, and generate reports or output from the data. Lewins and Silver (2007) provided a good overall map of these common tools and the common research activities they support.

These software programs became collectively known as qualitative data analysis (QDA) software (Yuen & Richards, 1994), also commonly referred to as QDAS.[3] For the most part, program developers promoted and sold their own products via their own start-up companies, and they offered training in how to use the software. Although the early presence of these programs represented a great diversity of features, purposes and software platforms, the software development trajectory since then has become fairly typical (Norman, 1998). The early diversity of programs and their notable limitations in handling only a narrow methodological approach or data type gave way to programs containing more features. This allowed for more diverse applications through any one

---

[3] Because the acronym CAQDAS often conflates the collaborative networking project in the UK with the genre of software, we prefer the term QDA software or QDAS to refer to the software and we reserve CAQDAS for the collaborative network.

software program. A few products took the lead around 2005, some have fallen by the wayside, and as of today the CAQDAS networking site provides reviews of only nine qualitative analysis programs.

To more fully investigate the influence that different QDAS options have on the research process, and to re-examine whether the choice of one of the current programs over another has an influence over the research findings, organizers of the Netherlands Association for Qualitative Research (KWALON) designed a comparative investigation (Evers, Silver, Mruck, & Peeters, 2011). Experts in several of these software packages (ATLAS.ti, Cassandre, MAXQDA, NVivo, and Transana) independently analysed a common set of data. These participants were in widespread agreement that they came up with very similar conclusions regarding the primary research questions and that the impact of a particular QDAS in analysing the data was negligible. This corroborates the claims by Gilbert, di Gregorio, and Jackson (2013) that over the last 20 years QDAS software has simultaneously become more comprehensive, more applicable to a diverse range of methodologies, and more homogeneous.

Issues raised by using software for qualitative data analysis

'Tools extend and qualitatively change human capabilities' (Gilbert, 2002: 222). Users of NVivo's tools can face opposition from those who express doubts about using software for analysis of qualitative data, or who simply have an aversion to technological solutions. Nonetheless, the development of software tools (and technology in general) has a significant impact on how research is done. The constantly expanding use of the web to provide access to data is now extending and changing the range of qualitative source data as well as the structure of surveys and survey samples. The advent of social networking will have an as yet unknown influence on social research and method. Historically, the widespread use of tape recorders in interpretive research changed both the level and kind of detail available in raw material for analysis, and as video recording became more common, data and method changed again.

Given this context, it is dangerous to adopt a simplistic understanding of the role of QDAS. Tools range in purposes, power, breadth of functions, and skill demanded of the user. The effectiveness with which you can use tools is partly a software design issue because software can influence your effectiveness by the number or complexity of steps required to complete a task, or by how information is presented to the user. It is also a user issue because the reliability (or trustworthiness) of results obtained depends on the skill of the user in both executing method and using software. The danger for novices using a sophis- ticated tool is that they can 'mess up' without realizing they have done so (Gilbert, 2002).

Historically, the use of QDAS has facilitated some activities (such as coding) and limited others (such as seeing a document as a whole or scribbling memos alongside text). In so doing, early computer programs somewhat biased the way qualitative data analysis was done. Historically, also, qualitative researchers were inclined to brand all 'code-and-retrieve' software as supporting grounded theory methodology – a methodology which has become rather ubiquitously (and inaccurately) associated with any data-up approach – with the implication that if you wanted to take any other kind of qualitative approach, software would not help.[4]

Concerns about the impact of computerization on qualitative analysis have most commonly focused around four issues:

- the concern that computers can distance researchers from their data;
- the dominance of code-and-retrieve methods to the exclusion of other analytic activities;
- the fear that use of a computer will mechanize analysis, making it more akin to quantitative or 'positivist' approaches; and
- the misperception that computers support only grounded theory methodology, or worse, create their own approach to analysis.

Closeness and distance

Early critiques of QDAS suggested that users of software lost closeness to data through poor screen display, segmentation of text, and loss of context, thereby risking alienation from their data. Despite enormous changes in technology and in software, these attitudes persist in some communities of practice. The alternative argument is that the combination of full transcripts and software can give too much closeness, and so users become caught in 'the coding trap', bogged down in their data, and unable to see the larger picture (Gilbert, 2002; Johnston, 2006).

Qualitative software was designed on the assumption that researchers need both closeness and distance (Richards, 1998): closeness for familiarity and appreciation of subtle differences, but distance for abstraction and synthesis, and the ability to switch between the two. Closeness to data – at least as much as can be had using manual methods – is assisted by enlarged and improved screen display, improved management of and access to multiple sources and

---

[4] Kelle (1997) traced the assumption that programs were written to support grounded theory to the need for a methodological underpinning for analysis, and grounded theory is one of the few methodologies where authors have been prepared to be explicit about what it is they actually do in analysis – although, as Kelle goes on to point out, 'a closer look at the concepts and procedures of Grounded Theory makes clear that Glaser, Strauss and Corbin provide the researcher with a variety of useful heuristics, rules of thumb and a methodological terminology rather than with a set of precise methodological rules' (1997: paragraph 3.4).

types of data, rapid retrieval of coded text and easy ability to view retrieved segments of text in their original context. Other tools are designed to provide distance, for example, tools for modelling ideas, interrogating the database to generate and test theory, or summarizing results. These take the researcher beyond description to more broadly applicable understanding. Tacking back and forth between the general and the specific, exploiting both insider and outsider perspectives, is characteristic of qualitative methods and contributes to a sophisticated analysis.

Domination of code and retrieve as a method

The development of software for textual data management began when qualitative researchers discovered the potential for text storage and retrieval offered by computer technology. Hence, early programs became tools for data storage and retrieval rather than tools for data analysis, because that was what computers were best able to do. The few programs that went beyond retrieval to facilitate asking questions about the association of categories in the data, particularly non-Boolean associations such as whether two concepts occurred within a specified level of proximity to each other, were less rather than more common, and in these early stages were given special status as second-generation 'theory-building' programs (Tesch, 1990).

Computers removed much of the drudgery from coding (cutting, labelling and filing); they also removed the boundaries which limited paper-based marking and sorting of text.

> When recoding data involves laborious collation of cut-up slips and creation of new hanging folders, there is little temptation to play with ideas, and much inducement to organize a tight set of codes into which data are shoved without regard to nuance. When an obediently stupid machine cuts and pastes, it is easier to approach data with curiosity – asking 'what if I cut it this way?', knowing that changes can be made quickly. (Marshall, 2002: 67)

Simply making coding more efficient was not, in itself, a conceptual advance from manual methods of data sorting. Criticism that segments of text were removed from the whole, creating a loss of perspective, was frequently levelled at computer software (apparently without recognition that cutting up paper did the same thing, with even greater risk of not having identified the source of the segment). Fears were expressed that computers would stifle creativity and reduce variety as code and retrieve became the dominant approach to working with data.

Most problematically, the facility for coding led to what Lyn Richards commonly referred to as 'coding fetishism' – a tendency to code to the exclusion of other analytic and interpretive activities, which biases the way qualitative research is done, and which often contributes to a report that comprises only 'themes from the data'. Prior to the development of computer software for coding, more emphasis was placed on reading and rereading the text as a whole, on noting ideas that were generated as one was reading, on making links between passages of text, on reflecting on the text and recording those reflections in journals and memos, and on drawing connections seen in the data in 'doodles' and maps. Improvements in the memoing, linking, and modelling tools within current qualitative software now provide ample capacity for these approaches to analysis, allowing the user to strike a balance between coding and reflecting and linking as they work with data.

Computers and mechanization

Fears that the computer, like HAL in Arthur C. Clarke's *Space Odyssey* series, might take over the decisions and start controlling the process of analysis stem in part from the historical association of computers with numeric processing. Adding to that concern is the computer's capacity to automate repetitive processes or to produce output without making obvious all the steps in the process.

There are software programs designed to automate the coding process entirely, using complex dictionaries and semantic rule books to guide that process, but these are specifically designed for quantitative purposes, and the results of their coding are generally interpreted through the use of statistics with minimal recourse to the original text. Keyword searches within *qualitative* analysis will almost always be preliminary to or supplemental to interactive coding of the data, if they are used at all.

Automated coding processes have a place in handling routine tasks (such as identifying the speakers in a focus group, or what question was being answered), in facilitating initial exploration of texts, or in checking thoroughness of coding. These remove drudgery without in any way hindering the creativity or interpretive capacity of the researcher. They do not substitute for interpretive coding that still needs to be done interactively (live on screen).

One of the goals of this book is to ensure that researchers using NVivo understand what the software is doing as they manipulate their data, and the logic on which its functions are based – just as artisans need to understand their tools. Such metacognitive awareness ensures researchers remain in control of the processes they are engaging in and are getting the results they think they asked for (Gilbert, 2002). More aware, creative, and adventurous users can experiment with new ways of using NVivo's tools to work with their data, just as the good artisan knows how to make his or her tools 'sing' to produce a creative piece of work.

Homogenization of qualitative approaches to analysis

Primarily in the early literature on QDAS, software was talked about as if it promoted a narrow view of qualitative methodology (Coffey, Holbrook, & Atkinson, 1996). Some current scholars express their concern that unguided novices might still view software as having its own method (Hutchison, Johnston, & Breckon, 2009; Johnston, 2006), while software experts critique the simplified views of software portrayed by individuals without QDAS expertise (Carvajal, 2002; Gilbert et al., 2013; Jackson, 2003; MacMillan & Koenig, 2004).

The oversimplification of qualitative methods has occurred and continues to occur whether software is involved or not. Researchers talk about 'doing qualitative' as if to imply there is just one general approach to the analysis of qualitative data. While there are some generally accepted emphases, different approaches to qualitative analysis are shaped by differences in foundational philosophies and understandings of the nature of social reality, the nature of the questions being asked, and the methodological approaches adopted. Researchers must integrate their chosen perspective and conceptual framework into their choices regarding what tools they will use, what and how they might code, and what questions to ask of the data. *This is the role of the researcher whether or not they use software.*

Exploring an NVivo project

Throughout this book we will be illustrating the principles and activities being discussed with examples from a number of our own projects, those undertaken by colleagues or students, projects from the literature, and some practice-informed vignettes. To give you an overview of the tools available for working in an NVivo project and of what you might be working towards, we will start by taking a look at the sample project that comes with the software. Because this is a moderately mature project, these instructions are not designed to show you how to make a start on working in your NVivo project, but rather what will become possible as you progress through your analysis.

As you read these instructions and others in later chapters, you will encounter a number of special icons:

▶ indicates these are steps (**actions**) for you to follow.
✓ indicates a **tip** or series of tips – handy hints to help you through.
! indicates a **warning** – ignore at your peril!
? indicates where to find this topic or tool in the **Help** files. Access NVivo Help by clicking on the question mark near the top right-hand side of the screen when NVivo is open. NVivo Help also provides a glossary, should you come across unfamiliar terms (you might also check for these in the index of this book as it will point you to where they are described).

In presenting instructions, we have adopted a number of conventions:

- Ribbon tabs are in **bold italic text**. Group names within the ribbon are in *italic text*.
- The three main views in the interface (*Navigation*, *List*, and *Detail*) are in *italic text*.
- Source names and node names are written in *italics*.
- Words that are copied from the screen as part of a click instruction are in **bold**.

Installing the software

If you don't already have the software on your computer, then your first step to using NVivo will be to install either a fully licensed or a trial version on your computer. These are available through the QSR website: www.qsrinternational. com.[5] Use the free *Getting Started* guide to find minimum computer requirements and detailed instructions for installing the software. Basically, insert a disk or double-click the downloaded software and follow the steps as they appear on screen after launch. It is likely that you will be required, as part of this process, to install several supporting programs prior to installing NVivo itself: the installation wizard will guide you through the necessary steps.

Once you have completed the installation, if you own the software, or your institution has a site licence, you will need to have available the licence number that came with your software or is available through your institution. Whether you are using a licensed version or the 30-day trial (a fully functional version of the program that operates on your computer for 30 days without a licence key), you will need to activate the software before you can begin to use it. Activation can be done via the internet, or, if necessary, by phone or email. In addition, the first time you launch the software after installation, you will be asked for your name and initials. This prompt for the current user occurs once only, unless you change the default option to always 'Prompt for user on launch' (**File > Options > ☑ Prompt for user on launch**). More about the potential need to change this default is in Chapter 12 on teamwork.

- ✓ In order to keep using NVivo beyond the 30-day trial period, you do not need to uninstall the trial and reinstall the software. All you will need is to enter and activate a new licence key to extend your existing version. (Click **File > Help > Extend License** to enter your new licence key.)
- ✓ Unless you just downloaded the software from the QSR website, you might also go to **File > Help > Check for Software Updates** to ensure you have the latest version on your computer.
- ✓ If you have an earlier version of NVivo on your computer, you do not need to remove it before installing the latest version of NVivo. If, however, you have more than one

---

[5] Our instructions regarding installation, user passwords, etc. pertain to the standalone version of the software; if you are using NVivo Server you should access the NVivo Help files for alternative installation instructions.

version of NVivo on your system, your computer will default to open the most recent software, even if you launch from a project created in an earlier version. NVivo will then walk you through the steps to convert your older project so it can be used in the new version. As a result, you will have two copies of the same project in two different versions of the software; naming them carefully will help avoid confusion later.

!   If you convert a project to the new version of NVivo, you cannot reopen or resave that copy of the project in an earlier version of the software.

?   When you first open the software, view the video tutorials, accessed via **File > Help > NVivo Tutorials**. These provide a demonstration of the various elements in an NVivo project, using data from the *Environmental Change* sample project.

▶   Alternatively (or as well), work through the instructions below as an introduction to NVivo using the *Environmental Change* data.

The *Environmental Change Down East* project

The *Environmental Change Down East* project explores the attitudes of individuals in 13 communities in an area of North Carolina known as 'Down East'. The goal of the data collection and analysis was to foster dialogue among stakeholders (residents, land developers, legislators, business owners, etc.) regarding community planning, land use, and sustainable development.

Throughout the book, you will find illustrative examples drawn from the *Environmental Change Down East* project (referred to here as the *Environmental Change* project) and from Pat's *Researchers* project. These sample projects provide material on which you can explore the software and practise using it. The *Environmental Change* project accompanies every licence as an embedded sample project and is installed (by default) in Public Documents\NVivo Samples. It is available also for download from the QSR International website via a link from the companion website for this book. The *Researchers* project is also available from the companion website. It comprises focus groups, extracts from interviews, and some other sources designed to help answer the questions of what brings people to engage in research, and what it is about their experience that keeps them researching.

Open a project

When you double-click on the NVivo icon to open the software, NVivo opens to the Welcome window, with options (at the left of the window) to create a new project or to open an existing project. The **My Recent Projects** list contains the five most recently opened projects on your computer. If you want to open a project that is on your computer, but not on the list, you will need to click on **Open Project** and then navigate to locate the project. Opening a project takes you into the project workspace from which you can access all the software tools.

▶   Open the *Environmental Change* project by clicking on its title in the Welcome screen, *or*, if it isn't listed, go to **Open Project** and look for it in the NVivo Samples folder in your Public Documents library.

The project workspace

Figure 1.1 illustrates the workspace and its components for the *Environmental Change* project.

A **ribbon** with nine standard tabs (formerly known as menus) spans the top horizontal position in NVivo (e.g., **Home**, **Create**, **External Data**), with supplementary tabs that open when the researcher is active in media, modelling, or any other special purpose tool. Items available in the ribbon can be available or greyed out, depending on which part of a project is active. Within each tab of the ribbon, groups help to organize the many options. For instance, if you select the **Home** tab, you will find group names in grey text along the bottom of the ribbon, including *Workspace, Item, Clipboard.* We will direct you to a group within a ribbon to help you quickly identify the correct icon or option.

Within the main screen, there are three areas, or views, where you will begin working, depending on your task.

- From the *Navigation View* you can choose which component (Sources, Nodes, Classifications, etc.) of the project you wish to access. Here, in addition to the sub-folders provided in the software, you can further organize items in your project into folders and subfolders.
- The *List View* provides a list of the contents in a selected folder. Most importantly, items such as an interview transcript can be accessed from this view, and new contents such as a focus group transcript or an image can be added in this view.
- The *Detail View* shows the actual content of an opened item, so that you can work with it by examining, coding, linking, memoing, etc.

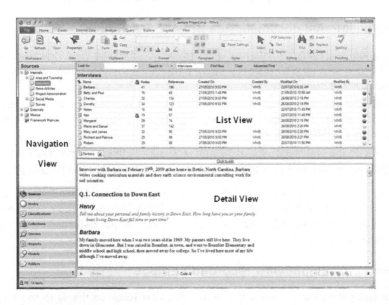

Figure 1.1   The NVivo workspace showing the ribbon, and *Navigation, List* and *Detail Views*

In each of these views, a context-sensitive menu can be accessed by right-clicking.

✓ Whenever you're not sure what to do or where to look for an action when you are working in NVivo, ensure your mouse pointer is pointing directly to the relevant item on your screen, and try right-clicking as a first option to find what you want. Right-click options change, depending on what you are pointing to.

As you explore NVivo using the *Environmental Change* project, you will gain some appreciation of how NVivo can assist with organizing and analysing your data. Sources are neatly filed; cases are identified with demographic and other details; ideas are recorded and appropriately linked to their sources; descriptive material and evidence for emerging understanding and ideas are captured using codes; codes are organized to facilitate querying the data so that research questions might be clarified, developed and answered; and for those who like to work visually, emerging understanding can be explored in models and charts.

Explore sources in NVivo

The workspace will first open to show **Sources** in the *Navigation View*, and will default to the **Internals** folder. There are several types of Internals stored in the *Environmental Change* project: these are organized into subfolders designed to assist with data management. The following activities show you how to open and look at the materials, but it is simply a gentle tour. Instructions are provided later in the book regarding the steps needed to import, edit, code, and link your sources.

View an internal document (the project description)

▶ The top-level folder for *Internals* is already selected. In *List View*, double-click on *Overview of Sample Project* to open it in *Detail View*. Read this for additional detail about the sample data.

▶ Note the use of heading styles in this (and other) sources. The level of heading is indicated in the **Home** ribbon, *Styles* group. Heading styles can be added or changed at different levels.

▶ Click on the first line of the document. You will see this is in Heading 1 style.

▶ Click on the line that says *Introduction* and you will see this is in Heading 2 style.

✓ Headings break the text into parts. If you are unfamiliar with headings, you can learn more about them in Microsoft Word or NVivo Help files. You can ask NVivo to code across (or within) your sources to collect all the data marked by a particular heading level.

View a project interview recorded as video

▶ In *Navigation View*, expand the **Internals** folder (click on the +) to see further folders for various document sources (e.g., Area and Township, Interviews, and News Articles).

▶ To see the list of project interviews, select **Sources > Internals > Interviews**.

▶ In *List View*, select any interview and double-click to open it in *Detail View*.

▶ Double-click on *Betty and Paul* to see a video record of an interview.

▶ From the **Media** ribbon, you can select **Play** to hear and watch the video. Click **Stop** after you look at a sample of the file.

▶ To close *Betty and Paul* (and any other interviews you opened) click on the ×️ next to their names in the tab.

View an internal dataset

A ***dataset*** is a table that holds the kind of information you would generate from a structured survey with both open and closed questions.

▶ In *Navigation View*, select **Sources > Internals > Survey**.

▶ In *List View,* double-click on *Survey Responses*.

▶ This dataset was imported from an Excel file. As you scroll across it, you will see it contains some columns with nominal, ordinal or interval data, and several columns with open-ended responses.

▶ Use the tab on the right margin of the *Detail View* to see the data in **Form** view rather than **Table** view.

NVivo allows you to automatically code much of the information in a dataset. You can then, additionally, interactively code the detail within people's open-ended responses.

View an internal picture

▶ In *Navigation View*, select **Sources > Internals > Area and Township**.

▶ In *List View*, double-click on *Competing water uses*.

▶ To the right of the picture, click on the number 1 next to the first row of text to illuminate the part of the image associated with this observation.

✓ If you need to enlarge the image in the *Detail View*, try using the zoom tool at the bottom right-hand side of the screen (within the NVivo window).

▶ If you need more room, go to **View** ribbon, *Window* group and uncheck **Docked**. Wait, and the *Detail View* will open in a new window. This is especially helpful if you have two monitors (you can view your project on one screen, and whatever is in *Detail View* on the other screen).

View social media data

▶ In *Navigation View*, select **Sources > Internals > Social Media**.

▶ In *List View*, double-click on *Cartaret County on Twitter*.

This dataset was collected with NCapture. NCapture is a browser extension for Internet Explorer or Google Chrome that accompanies NVivo. It is designed to

(Continued)

(Continued)

capture data from Facebook, LinkedIn, YouTube and Twitter and convert these data sources for use in NVivo.

Closing items in *Detail View*

▶ To close any item you have opened during the tour so far, click on the × next to the name of the item in the *Detail View* tab.

Trace the links from internal sources

As you read through the Overview document, notice some of the text is coloured or highlighted (Figure 1.2). These markers indicate links to other items.

▶ Return to *Navigation View* > **Sources** > **Internals**, then to *List View* and double-click on the *Overview of Sample Project*.

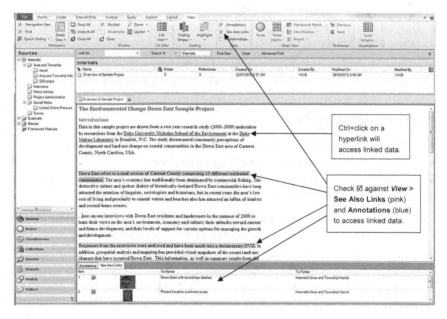

Figure 1.2   Viewing hyperlinks, 'see also' links, and annotations from an internal source

Hyperlinks to external items

▶ In the first paragraph of the *Overview*, blue underlined text indicates the presence of a **hyperlink** to an external item. Ctrl+click on <u>Duke Marine Laboratory</u> to access the linked webpage.

See also links to internal items

In the fourth paragraph of the *Overview*, a pink highlight indicates that a ***see also link*** has been created.[6] See also links take you to other items (text, images, video, models) or to portions of internals that relate to the marked text.

▶ Go to the ***View*** ribbon, *Links* group > ☑ **See Also Links**. The linked items become visible at the bottom of the screen. In this instance, three aerial photographs of the region have been linked to the text.

▶ Click on the pink highlight, then double-click on the associated number to open the linked item.

Annotations on text

In the seventh paragraph, blue highlighting indicates an ***annotation.*** Annotations are comments, reminders, or reflections on the text.

▶ Go to the ***View*** ribbon, *Links* group > ☑ **Annotations.** The linked annotation is now visible at the bottom of the screen.

▶ Click on the blue highlight and the associated comment will be highlighted.

▶ Click on the number next to an annotation at the bottom of the screen, and the related passage will turn from a light blue to a darker teal.

▶ Close *Overview of Sample Project* and any associated items in *Detail View*.

Linked memos

Notes and thoughts related to a document (or node) are recorded in its linked ***memo***.

▶ Return to *Navigation View* > **Sources** > **Internals** > **Interviews**.

The names of the people who were interviewed will show in *List View*. An icon to the right of the document name in *List View* indicates that the document has a linked memo (e.g., for *Ken* in the *Interviews* folder).

▶ Hover (hold the mouse pointer) over the document name, right-click and select **Memo Link** > **Open Linked Memo**, or use **Ctrl+Shift+M** on your keyboard.

There are further memos stored in the **Memos** folder under *Navigation View* > **Sources**.

Explore nodes and coding

Nodes provide the storage areas in NVivo for references to coded text. Each node serves as a container for everything that is known about one particular concept or category. Nodes can be used also as a tool to organize qualitative data in particular ways, to be discussed later.

(Continued)

---

[6] We recognize, but have learned to live with, the awkward grammatical construction 'see also links' creates. We hope you will be able to as well!

(Continued)

Nodes for concepts and categories coded from the data

▶ In *Navigation View*, click on **Nodes**. The *List View* will open to display nodes stored at the top level in the Nodes folder. This top-level folder contains, in general terms, the kinds of categories, concepts and themes that the researcher deems important within the data.

▶ In *List View* click on the + next to one of these top-level nodes to expand it to show the subnodes below.

▶ Double-click on a subnode to see the coded data in the *Detail View* below (Figure 1.3). The source of each passage is identified.

▶ View the context from which a selected passage came using the right-click menu: **Right-click > Coding Context > Broad;** or **Right-click > Open Referenced Source** (Figure 1.3).

▶ Create a new node by selecting some text from a source or an existing node: **Right-click > Code Selection > Code Selection At New Node (Ctrl+F3),**

Figure 1.3　Nodes, with referenced text and context menu, and showing retrieved (Broad) context for Charles's statement about local identity

name the new node and click **OK**. Your new node will show at the top level of the node hierarchy (double-click on your new node to see the passage you coded).

Tracing links from nodes

▶ Note that the node *Community\Connection to Down East\Local identity* has a memo symbol next to it. **Right-click > Memo Link > Open linked memo** (or **Ctrl+Shift+M**) to see the notes made about the way people talked about local identity.

▶ Note also that many of the notes are shaded pink, indicating the presence of see also links. If you click on the *View* ribbon, *Links* group > **See Also Links**, you will be able to read the specific passages that prompted the researchers' comments.

Nodes to organize and manage data

In *Navigation View*, the subfolders under **Nodes** organize and manage data. These include *Places and People* where all data for each individual location and for each separate person in the project are stored, and *Autocoded Responses* for everyone's responses to each question asked.

▶ From the *Navigation View*, select **Nodes > Places and People**, and from the *List View*, select **Interview Participants** to see the list of people who were interviewed. Double-click on *Barbara* and see all the qualitative data she contributed to the project. If Barbara was interviewed twice, you would first see the content of Barbara's initial interview, and then the contents of her second interview as you scrolled down the page.

▶ While in the *Detail View* for this case, go to the **View** ribbon and choose **Coding Stripes > Nodes Most Coding** to see the nodes coded most often for this case.

▶ Hover over the coding density bar (the vertical stripe with segments in different shades of grey) to see a list of nodes coding the adjacent text (Figure 1.4).

The heading styles used in the interview transcripts made it possible to auto code everyone's responses to the structured questions asked in these interviews.

▶ Select **Nodes > Autocoded Responses**, and in *List View*, **expand + Autocoded Interview Questions**.

▶ Double-click on *Q.1. Connection to Down East*. All of the exchanges in response to Question 1, throughout the interview data, have been gathered here, based on auto coding the questions.

(Continued)

(Continued)

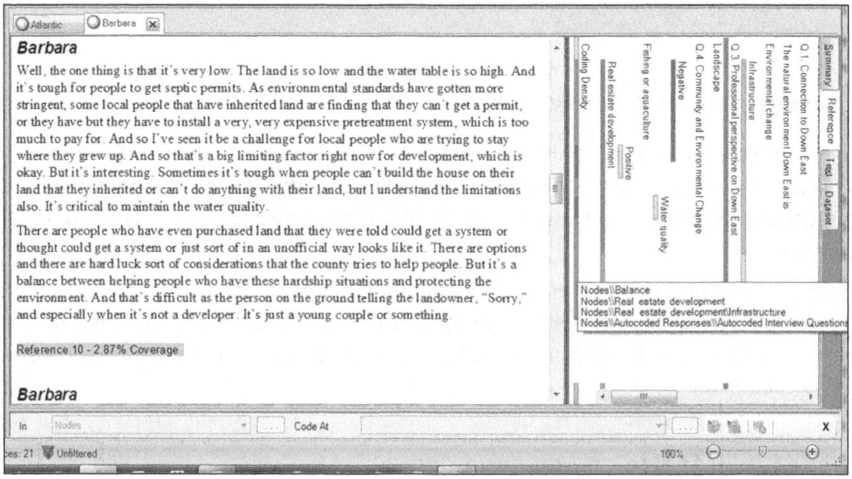

Figure 1.4   Coding density and coding stripes showing nodes coded on Barbara's text

Explore classifications and attributes

Participants have **attribute values**, that is, a record of demographic and quantitative data known about them that is relevant to everything they say. This is recorded separately from coding of passages within their text. Attribute values are used primarily to assist in comparing data across subgroups in your research.

▶ View the attribute values linked to a participant by going to the *Navigation View* and selecting **Nodes > Places and People**.

▶ In *List View*, expand **+ Interview Participants** > *Barbara*. **Right-click > Node Properties** (or **Ctrl+Shift+P**). Click on the **Attribute Values** tab in the Node Properties dialogue to see the assigned values.

Classifications help to organize the structure of your attributes and values. You can have different types of cases, and in this sample data we see *people* as well as *places*. Some attributes will pertain to people (e.g., age, gender) and some will pertain to places (e.g., median parcel size, total population). The classifications area organizes these different attributes and values according to the kinds of cases for which they are relevant. Remember that information about the cases (people and places) has been stored in nodes, to allow for multiple sources of information for any particular case.

▶ In *Navigation View*, go to **Classifications > Node Classifications**. You will see data organized in two ways: by participant (Person) and by Places (sites where participants lived).

▶ Expand **+ Person** to see a list of attributes relevant to participants. Double-click on an attribute (e.g., **Township**) and then on the **Values** tab to see how an attribute is set up.

Attribute values for all participants can be viewed (and modified) in the ***Classification Sheet***. They can be entered one at a time, or they can be imported from a spreadsheet or created from a dataset.

▶ Select **Person, Right-click > Open Classification Sheet**. To change a value in any cell, choose from the drop-down list for that cell.

View sets (in Collections)

Sets in NVivo contain shortcuts to any nodes and/or any documents, as a way of holding those items together without actually combining (merging) their content. They are used primarily as a way of gathering items for use in handling queries, reports or models, or simply as a way of indicating that these items 'hang together' in some way (perhaps conceptually or theoretically).

▶ In *Navigation View,* select **Collections** to see a list of **Sets**. Click on *Nodes for coding comparison* to see the items in the set shown in *List View.*[7]

Review queries

Queries store questions you want to ask of your data. Queries might be about the occurrence of a word or words, about patterns of coding, comparison of groups, or some combination of these elements. They can be created and run once, or stored to use again with more data, or with a variation. ***Results*** hold the data found by the query to help you answer your questions; they can be stored alongside the queries.

▶ In *Navigation View*, select **Queries**.
▶ In *List View*, **Right-click** on *Word Frequency Query in interviews* > **Query Properties** to see how a simple word frequency query was set up.
▶ Click on **Run**. The results will open in *Detail View*.
▶ Click on the tabs at the very right-hand margin of your screen (**Summary, Tag Cloud, Tree Map, Cluster Analysis**) to see different ways of viewing these results.
▶ Double-click a word from the **Summary** tab to see all instances of this word found by the query.
▶ Now look at a more complex query. In *List View*, **Right-click** on *Attitude about environment by longevity Down East* > **Query Properties** to see how it was set up, and click on **Run**. The results will appear as a matrix with counts of passages coded (coding references) in each cell. Double-click a cell to see the text. Later you will learn how to obtain other kinds of information from the matrix result.

(Continued)

---

[7] In this project, sets were used in a very limited way only.

(Continued)

Check some predefined reports

Reports provides predefined output types. It is also possible to customize a report. Many of the reports provide a topographical view of the data only, such as a list of nodes. Some provide content.

▶ In *Navigation View*, select **Reports**.

▶ In *List View*, double-click on **Node Summary Report**.

▶ Check next to **Node Hierarchical Name** (Figure 1.5), then **Select > Balance > OK > OK**.

The report will show various statistics about how often the node was used to code text.

▶ In *List View* double-click on **Coding Summary by Node Report**.

▶ Check the first filter option, **Select > Balance > OK > OK**.

The report will contain all text coded at that node.

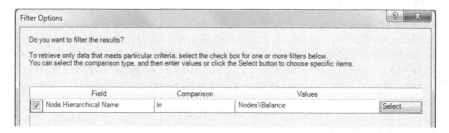

Figure 1.5   Filter options for a report

Explore models and visualizations

And finally (for now), ***models and visualizations*** display ideas about the relationships between project items.

View a model

▶ In *Navigation View*, select **Models**. Double-click on **Geographic units used in this project**.

▶ To obtain a fuller view of the model on a separate screen, go to the ***View*** ribbon and uncheck **Docked**, or use your zoom tool on the bottom right-hand side of the NVivo window.

Experiment with visualizations

▶ Go back to **Nodes** in *Navigation View*. Click and drag to select all the nodes under *Natural environment*. **Right-click > Visualize > Cluster Analysis of Nodes**.

The visual shows which nodes are most similar based on words used in the coded text. Change the number of clusters to 4, and experiment with other ways of visualizing this information from the options in the *Cluster Analysis* ribbon.

Save changes

While you were looking at the sample project, you were warned that it was 15 minutes since the project was last saved, and asked if you wanted to save changes made to the project. This is NVivo's way of making sure you are regularly saving changes to your project, in case of power failure or freezing. When you are working on your own project, it is strongly recommended that you save each time you are asked, unless you are simply experimenting, do not want to save your changes, or you are in the middle of an Undo operation.

Close the project by selecting **File > Close** or, if you want to quit working in NVivo for the time being, choose to **Exit**.

Overview: what's in an NVivo project?

An NVivo project typically comprises:

- data records (e.g., transcriptions, field notes, other documents, video, audio, photographs, web pages);
- records of your thinking about the data (memos);
- nodes to store coded references to your data (so you can retrieve all you know about a topic, idea, case or relationship);
- variable-type information (attribute values) relating to sources or cases in your study (e.g., demographic details, responses to categorical or scaled questions, dates);
- records of and results from interrogative queries conducted on your data; and
- models showing relationships between items in your project.

All of these are held in a single database-style file, which, if the file location options have not been changed, will be located in the **Documents** area of your computer.

2

Starting out, with a view ahead

Something in your social or working environment excites interest, and investigation begins. You might start in the library or by observing 'the field', perhaps with some exploratory discussions with relevant people or with reflection on personal experience. Right from the start, you will find tools in NVivo that will support your work as you explore possibilities, refine questions, and think through project design.

The tools you use and the habits you develop early will become integral to your work *throughout* your project. Analysis is as much about reflecting on data and making connections across data as it is about categorizing and manipulating data in codes. You will find, therefore, that journals, memos and links will become essential to the quality of your analysis.

In this chapter:

- Start to frame your research project.
- Start working in the software: create a project with a model, memo, and source document.
- Create links in the database using annotations, see also links and hyperlinks.
- Discover ways in which these tools might be extended to build a web of data within and across your project items.

Exploring the research terrain

A research project begins well before you gather data. Thought and planning at this stage will do much to ensure a smoother process of data collection and a deeper and more meaningful interpretation of those data.

Develop questions

Qualitative research often begins with a vaguely defined question or goal. It may well begin 'with a bit of interesting "data"' (Seale, Gobo, Gubrium, & Silverman, 2004: 9). Visualization techniques (concept maps) and thought experiments can help to clarify what might be useful questions (Bazeley, 2013; Maxwell, 2013). Your initial explorations serve to refine your question, so more deliberate ('purposive') data gathering can occur. These explorations become part of your data, and can be managed within NVivo.

Record these starting questions as you set out. In NVivo, you create a research journal to record them. They will help you to maintain focus as you work, and then later to evaluate the direction you are taking. Keep notes about any random (or less random) thoughts you have around those questions as you read, discuss, observe, or simply reflect on issues as they arise, and date these. Keeping a record will allow you to keep track of your ideas and to trace the path those ideas have taken from initial, hesitant conceptualization to final, confident realization.

Identify assumptions

Previous knowledge is a prerequisite to gaining understanding:

> Qualitative researchers who investigate a different form of social life always bring with them their own lenses and conceptual networks. They cannot drop them, for in this case they would not be able to perceive, observe and describe meaningful events any longer – confronted with chaotic, meaningless and fragmented phenomena they would have to give up their scientific endeavour. (Kelle, 1997: paragraph 4.2)

But previous knowledge brings with it assumptions about what you might find. Rather than deny their existence, you should recognize them, record them, and become aware of how they might be influencing the way you are thinking about your data – only then can you effectively control (or at least, assess) that impact. Maxwell (2013) recommends creating a 'researcher identity memo' to explore personal goals, recognize assumptions and draw on experiential knowledge. So, add to your research notes, or create a conceptual model that captures what you are *expecting* to see.

Explore existing data

Data relevant to your project often exist before you make or locate new data. Consider the possibilities of:

- Starting with observations of yourself and of others – field notes or diary records will play a significant early role. Adapt the instructions for creating a project journal (below) to create documents in which to record your observations.
- Starting with data already in the public sphere such as newspapers, novels, radio, internet, or archived data (Silverman, 2010). These can provide valuable learning experiences as you master both software and analysis strategies.
- Starting with literature. The belief that an inductive approach to inquiry requires researchers to come to their data without having been influenced by prior reading of the literature in their field and without bringing any theoretical concepts to the research is generally no longer seen as feasible, nor is it broadly supported. Strauss and Corbin (1998: 47) declared: 'Insights do not happen haphazardly; rather they happen to prepared minds during interplay with the data.' In many fields, qualitative researchers are expected to gain a firm grasp of the relevant literature, and for university-based research, prior understanding of the literature on the topic is an essential element of a funding application or doctoral research proposal.

Explore the terrain with software

Your project begins from the time you start asking questions – from the thought that X might be something interesting to investigate. This is also a good time to start using software!

- Early use of software ensures you don't lose precious early thoughts. Indeed, sketching ideas and writing even rough notes will help to clarify thinking as you plan your project.
- Starting early, if you are still learning software, will give you a gentle introduction to it and a chance to gradually develop your skills as your project builds up. This is better than desperately trying to cope with learning technical skills in a rush as you become overwhelmed with data and the deadline for completion is looming.
- Starting with software early acts as a reminder that data collection and data analysis are not separate processes in qualitative approaches to research. So start now!

Several of NVivo's tools are useful to most researchers at this beginning point.

- ▶ Create a model to identify and show what you already know, to point to what you still need to know, and to assist in identifying steps on the pathway to finding out.
- ▶ Create a new blank document as a project journal within NVivo, to become an ongoing record of questions, ideas, and reflections on the project.
- ▶ Import some literature or other existing data and annotate it or reflect on it in a journal or memo.

Setting up a project

First you need to have a project created in the software![1]

Creating a project in NVivo

▶ From the base of the Welcome window that appears when you open the program, select the **New Project** button.

▶ Type in a **Title** to briefly describe your project. It can be more than one word. Notice NVivo assigns a matching file name to the project (Figure 2.1).

▶ Choose whether or not to create a log of your actions in this project. (You can see what a project event log looks like by opening the *Environmental Change* project and selecting *File* > **Info** > **Open Project Event Log**.)

✓ Unless you change the program's default file locations (***File*** > **Options** > **File Locations**), NVivo will elect to store your project in your Documents folder.

✓ When you make a backup copy of the project, you are likely to change the file-name that is seen in Windows Explorer (e.g., by adding a date to it), but the title of the project will remain the same.

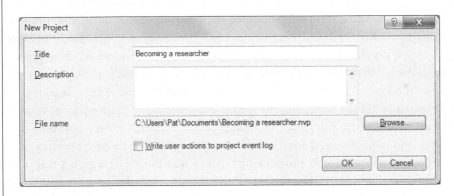

Figure 2.1   Creating a new project

One or many projects?

Your research project may have a number of components with data generated from different sources (rural and urban; companies A, B and C), with

---

[1] Details of name and location can be changed later if needed.

data from different phases of the project (pilot phase and main data collection; wave 1, 2, and 3 of interviews), or with data of different types (literature, observations, interview transcripts, a dataset, pictures or video, web pages). NVivo provides data management tools that allow you to compare or isolate different components within your project. What this means in practice is that it is best to incorporate *all* those components into a single NVivo project, rather than make separate projects for each component. Having everything together in one NVivo project will allow you to gather together everything you know on any topic, regardless of source, and to make instant comparisons across different sources, phases, types of data, or cases. If you wish, you will still be able to interrogate just one component of the data by placing relevant sources within a specific folder for documents or cases, or by identifying that component as belonging to a defined set. (Chapters 3 and 6 will show you how to create and use folders, sets, and classifications to manage your data.)

Create a model

Sketching your ideas about your project at this stage is a particular way of journaling what you think it is you are asking or doing – great for those who prefer to think and work visually and beneficial even for those of us who sometimes struggle to work visually. Maxwell (2013) argues strongly for creating an early concept map to help clarify the conceptual framework or theoretical underpinning of a study. In NVivo, concept maps, flow charts, or purely exploratory diagrams can be created using the modelling tool, and are generically referred to as models. Put any concepts or categories contained in or implied by your questions in a model, and note observed associations or explore possible theoretical links.

Models serve multiple purposes during a qualitative research project, as outlined in Chapter 10. For now, use the NVivo modeller to map your starting point and the assumptions you are bringing to the project, making a diagram of the concepts, relationships or patterns you *expect* to find. This will assist with clarifying your research questions and planning your data collection.

If you find it a struggle to develop a concept map, then try some of Maxwell's (2013: 62) suggestions:

- Think about the key words you use in talking about the topic, or in things you've already written about your research.
- Take something you've already written and map the implicit theory within it.
- Take one key concept or term, and think of all the things that might be associated with it.
- Ask someone to interview you about the topic, then listen to the tape and note the terms used.

Creating a simple model

▶ In *Navigation View*, select **Models**.

▶ **Right-click** in the empty space available within the *List View* > **New Model**. Provide a **Name** for the new model > **OK**. An area for working will be created in *Detail View*.

▶ To create more working space, in the **View** ribbon, *Window* group > uncheck **Docked** and the *Detail View* will become a separate window which can be enlarged to fill the screen.

▶ If you want more space, close the Model Groups pane: **Model** ribbon, *Display* group > uncheck **Model Groups**.

▶ In the **Model** ribbon, click on a *Shape* to add it to the model. Double-click on the shape to name it > **OK**.

▶ Move the shapes to where you want them, by dragging them to another location in the grid. Multiple selections can be moved at the same time so their spatial relationships are preserved. Items can be resized, or the shape can be extended in one or other direction by selecting the shape in the model and selecting and dragging the dots on the perimeter.

▶ Modify the font, colour and/or line thickness of a selected shape or line in the **Home** ribbon, *Format* group.

▶ Add connectors to show links between shapes (Figure 2.2). Select the first item for the linked pair. Use Ctrl+click to select the second item (dots will

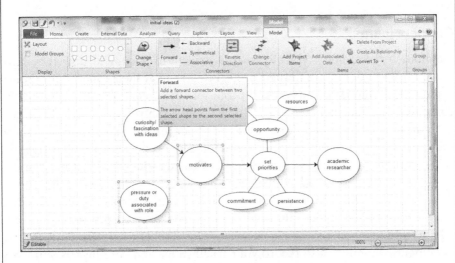

Figure 2.2 Adding a connector to a conceptual map

(Continued)

(Continued)

be visible around the perimeter of both shapes). In the **Model** ribbon, click on the type of connector that best describes the relationship between the two items. If you create a one-way arrow that is pointing the wrong way, select it and click on **Model** ribbon, *Connectors* group > **Reverse Direction** to fix it.

▶ To archive a copy of the model for your records while you preserve a dynamic copy to keep working on, **Right-click > Create As Static Model**. Use the same name, but add a date to the end.

! If you return to your dynamic model to add to or change it, you will need to click on **Click to edit** at the top of the grid to make those changes.

Record in your NVivo journal any insights gained as you were devising the model, such as questions prompted by doing it, or strategies you might need to employ for data-making or analysis. You could find it alerts you to the need to include particular people in your sample, or to explore a broader context. You might also find it useful, as you proceed, to create nodes to reflect the concepts you identified in the process of creating your model (**Right-click** on a named shape > **Convert to** > **Convert to New Project Item**). Later you can review the model to see how far your thinking has moved in response to gathering and working with data.

Create a journal

Qualitative researchers typically keep a journal to document how they have moved from initial forays in their project to arrival at their conclusions; hence some refer to the journal as an audit trail for the project. Lyn Richards (2009) compares the journaling process to keeping a ship's log with its careful account of a journey, and provides detailed suggestions about what might be recorded there. Without such a record, it will be difficult to keep track of when and how insights were gained and ideas developed, and it may be difficult to pull together the evidence you need to support your conclusions. Without it, precious, fleeting ideas will become forgotten as the data marches in, the next task is upon you, or the complexity of concepts begins to overwhelm you. Unlike the ship's log, however, the journal can be a private document: you might also record your frustrations and your joys as you work through your project. Perhaps the best advice of all, as you focus on ideas and your responses to them (rather than dry description), is to enjoy the journaling task – write freely without worrying about formality of style or 'correctness' of thoughts. Writing 'often provides sharp, sunlit moments of clarity or insight – little conceptual epiphanies' (Miles & Huberman, 1994: 74).

In NVivo a journal is simply a document, and it will always be available for modification as you are working in the project. In addition, you will be able to establish links ('see also' links) from your written ideas to specific data or other evidence which prompted or supports those thoughts. Additionally, you will be able to code the journal as you write it, making it easy to retrieve the ideas you generate on any topic – and this is something you can do with any other memo or document you create within your project. No more coloured tags hanging off the sides of pages to help you find those insightful ideas!

✓ Use NVivo's date and time stamp (**Ctrl+Shift+T**) on journal entries to help with the auditing process.

Creating a journal

The journal is a working document in the program as a kind of 'scratch pad' for ideas and thoughts. Because it stores reflections rather than observed or recorded data, you will create it within the Memos folder.

▶ Open *Navigation View* > **Sources** > **Memos.** In *List View* (in the white space), **Right-click** > **New Memo** (Figure 2.3).

▶ **Name** the memo, provide a **Description** and **Colour** if you wish (both of which can be changed later), and click **OK**. The name of the memo will now be visible in *List View* and a new blank document will open in *Detail View*.

✓ If you place an underscore at the beginning of a document name, for example **_Journal**, then it will always appear at the top of any alphabetically sorted list.

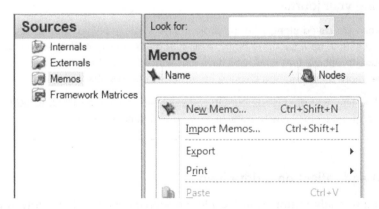

Figure 2.3 Creating a memo document to use as a journal

(Continued)

(Continued)

> This is especially useful for facilitating access to something like a project journal to which you will frequently return.
>
> ✓ If you have an existing electronic journal, you can import that, rather than creating a new one. In the empty space available in List *View*, **Right-click > Import Memos > Browse** to select the memo for importing.
>
> ✓ Use colours to group items visually, for example, to quickly identify the journal(s) you create about the project as a whole versus your memos about specific sources or nodes. Because there are only seven to choose from, you will not be able to add a different colour to every different item.

Writing in your journal

Working with your journal in the *Detail View*, you can now begin recording the questions, assumptions, or other ideas you are bringing to the project. The following prompts might help:

Why are you doing *this* project?
What do you think it's about?
What are the questions you're asking, and where did they come from?
What do you expect to find and why?
What have you observed so far?

> ▶ Use **Ctrl+Shift+T** to insert the date and time, or locate it on the *Home* ribbon, *Editing* group > **Insert** > **Insert Date/Time** (time stamps do not automatically become codes).
>
> ▶ From the **Home** ribbon, *Format* group, select fonts and use colour to add emphasis. (You cannot automatically code on the basis of colour.)

Saving your journal

Sources are saved along with the project as a whole in NVivo; that is, you do not save a source as a separate entity, even if you are closing it. If, however, you are anxious to ensure that what you have just written is not lost, then choose *File >* **Save** (more on saving and backing up at the end of this chapter).

> ! Next time you open your journal, you will need to click on **Click to edit** at the top of the *Detail View* to be able to write additional material.

Import and reflect on a data item

Now you're ready to import and explore a source document! For now, this could be an article or report; notes from your reading; the text of a preliminary interview; field notes from a site visit; the transcript of (or notes from) a conversation about your project with a colleague or your dissertation advisor or supervisor; or text from a web page.[2] In Chapter 3 we will explain in more detail the range of source types you can import, and things to be aware of when preparing and importing data for use in NVivo. For now, simply importing a text-based source of some sort will suffice. Text file types that can be imported include *.doc and *.docx (Word files), *.txt (text files), *.rtf (rich text files), and *.pdf (portable data format files).

When you import a source into NVivo, the program makes *a copy* of that source into its database, leaving the original where it was. Changes you make to the source in NVivo will not be reflected in the original copy, so it remains in the original location as a secure backup.

Importing and viewing a text-based document

▶ From *Navigation View* select **Sources**, and then **Internals**.

▶ If this is the first source you are importing, your *List View* will be empty. Right-click in the white space in *List View* to open the **Import Internals** dialogue (Figure 2.4).

▶ Select the type of file you wish to import (**Documents** or **PDFs** at this stage), then click on **Browse** to locate it. Select the file(s), click on **Open > OK**.

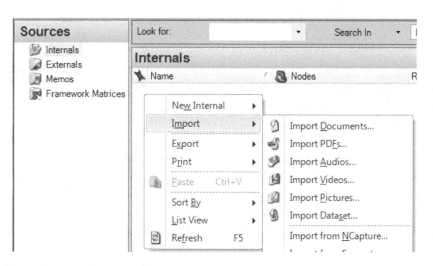

Figure 2.4   Importing a file as an internal source

(Continued)

---

[2] If the source is an interview or similar, we would suggest you substitute pseudonyms for any identifying names or places prior to importing it (use Replace in Word). If you use the pseudonym from the start, it will become as familiar to you as the real name, and it reduces the risk of breaking confidentiality.

(Continued)

✓ Use Shift+click or Ctrl+click to select more than one file (of the same type and location) when choosing sources for import.

▶ After you import the item, go to *List View*, double-click to select the document you imported.[3] The text will show in *Detail View*.

Your first reading of a document should be rapid but purposeful, directed but not bound by your research questions. The idea is to get a sense of the whole, so as you begin to identify specific points or issues in the data, you will see them in the context of the whole (see Bazeley, 2013: Chapter 4). Reading right through before you start coding is especially important if it is some time since you gathered this particular item of data, or if your recent work on it was piecemeal. Many people prefer to scribble on hard copy at this stage, on scrap paper, or in a notebook, but there is a real advantage in making notes on the computer – they don't get lost, and you have tools to help find particular bits within them.

Mark text with annotations

As you read (or later, as you code) in NVivo, you might annotate words or phrases in the text. Annotations in NVivo work rather like a comments field or a footnote in Word. Whereas the project journal and other memos are more useful for storing (often extensive) reflective thoughts and ideas from the text, annotations are useful for adding (usually brief) comments or reminders about a particular segment of text.[4] You might use annotations also to clarify an acronym, note the intonation of the voice at a point in the conversation, identify a translation or transcription problem, or comment on some aspect of the discourse. For example, when a coach referred to a celebrity in her study of sexual abuse in elite swimming, Joy Bringer used an annotation to note the significance of that reference to the conversation (Bringer, Johnston, & Brackenridge, 2006: 249). Annotations work best as reminders of things you need to be aware of whenever you read this bit of text.

---

[3] We recommend that you acquire the habit of selecting a project item by clicking on its icon rather than its name, to avoid accidentally selecting the name for editing.

[4] Annotations are limited to 1,024 characters in length.

Annotating text

▶ Select the passage to be annotated (usually short).

▶ **Right-click** (on the area you just highlighted) **> Annotations > New Annotation**.
A space for typing will open at the base of the *Detail View* (Figure 2.5).

▶ Type your annotation.

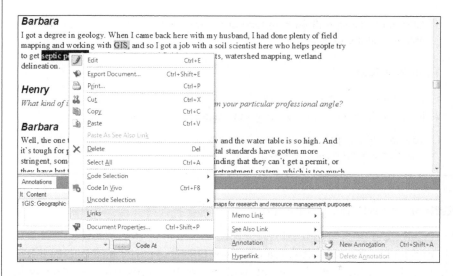

Figure 2.5   Creating an annotation

▶ Passages with an annotation will be indicated with a blue highlight. To bring
annotations into view or to turn them off, go to the ***View*** ribbon, *Links* group >
check or uncheck ☑ **Annotations**.

▶ Click anywhere in the blue highlighted text to see the matching comment at the
bottom of the screen, or click on a comment to see the associated highlight in
the text turn a darker blue.

✓ When the blue highlighted text that anchors an annotation is coded, the annotation will also be visible from the node view.

✓ The text of annotations can be searched for keywords (in a word frequency or
text query) but not coded. If you want to find particular comments later, either
code the blue anchor for the annotation or include a relevant keyword in the
comment.

Edit text and mark with colour

If you find an error in your text, you can switch to edit mode and correct it.[5] If you are reading on screen and an interesting expression or detail draws your attention, change the text to a colour so it stands out in retrievals or on later review. Then write a note in a memo or an annotation about *why* it appears significant.

Editing a source

▸ Click on **Click to edit** (in blue text) at the top of the *Detail View*. You are now able to edit the text.

To colour text

▸ Select the text to be coloured.

▸ From the **Home** ribbon, *Format* group, select a font colour.

! You cannot highlight behind the text with colour, and highlighting applied in a Word document does not import.

Reflect on text, using a memo

In NVivo, your project journal is recorded as a memo. Depending on the nature of your data, you might also create memos linked to particular sources. Memos often include a kind of 'discussion with yourself' as you explore ideas arising from your data. The memo for each document becomes an invaluable asset as it ties together the different threads of data for the case. Writing about your ideas avoids losing them when they fade from memory or become submerged in the morass of data. Because memos can be coded, searched and queried, later you will be able to locate your thoughts on a topic by asking the software to find just what you have written in memos on that topic.

A document memo might include:

- field notes generated after data collection, such as unrecorded comments, observations and impressions;
- a summary of the main points in the document, or notes about your overall impressions from the document;
- thoughts about the meaning or significance of things said or written in this particular document;
- reflections on a word or phrase;
- issues for further investigation and hunches to check out.

---

[5] If you plan to merge this source with another copy of the same source as part of combining two projects, then *do not edit it*. Editing will prevent NVivo from recognizing it as the same source, with the consequence that the two copies will not merge.

It doesn't matter if the typing or the grammar is rough, as long as you get the ideas down. If you can discuss some or all of the document with a colleague, the conversation is likely to strengthen your reflective thinking about the text and its interpretation – then add these thoughts to your notes. You can add further notes to your memo at any time.

Creating a linked source memo

Each internal source in NVivo can optionally be assigned one primary memo, that is, a linked document with additional observations, reflections and other materials relating to that source.

▶ Select the source in *List* (or *Detail*) *View*, **Right-click > Memo Link > Link to New Memo (Ctrl+Shift+K)**.

▶ Name the new memo and click on **OK**. The memo will open as an editable document in *Detail View*, ready for your text.

✓ An icon indicating that a memo exists for that source will be evident in *List View*. The actual memo will be located in the Memos folder.

✓ It is helpful in naming memos to make clear their primary relationship to a document. If you lose track of links or you link things unintentionally, then you can check and change them in *Navigation View* > **Collections** > **Memo Links**.

! You can attach only one *linked* memo to each source (to avoid unintentional creation of many small memo documents). Use *see also links* (discussed next) within the memo to link specific thoughts to specific segments of text in the source, and also to avoid problems associated with pasting quotes from the source into the memo.

Accessing and adding to a memo

▶ Select the source in *List* (or *Detail*) *View*, **Right-click > Memo Link > Open Linked Memo (Ctrl+Shift+M)**. The memo will open in *Detail View*.

▶ Click on **Click to Edit**, located at the top of the *Detail View*, or on the pencil icon in the Quick Access toolbar or *Home* ribbon, so you can type into the memo.

✓ If your thought has more general significance, it may be more appropriate to record it in the project journal, keeping the document's linked memo as a place for ideas arising specifically from this document.

Whether you decide to create a memo for particular sources in your project or simply use a general journal (in which you are careful to reference the sources that prompted your ideas) will be a matter of methodological choice and/or pragmatic decision-making and will vary from project to project. Individual document memos are not necessarily useful for all projects. For example, for data where responses are brief, it may be more useful to record a summary of key issues for each source (or case) in a single combined 'issues' journal, and to use a separate journal for reflecting on what you are learning from various cases and for noting common themes to explore. For any project dealing intensively with rich data for a small sample, however, the memo for each source becomes a valuable resource holding a reminder of key points learned, interpretive thoughts, and ideas to follow up in later analyses.

✓ Keep the memo open as you work through a document, so you can easily tab back and forth between it and the source.
✓ Memos can be combined or split at any time without losing associated information (as can any text-based source).
✓ To avoid anxiety about losing track of where you have recorded your ideas, we recommend you code the content of these memos, preferably as you are making them (once you have a coding system). This will ensure the ideas always turn up whenever you consider those topics in your project.

Link ideas with evidence, using a see also link

More often than not, the ideas you record in your journals or memos will relate to a particular segment of text, rather than a whole source. When you want to record something longer and more detailed and thoughtful than an annotation, and you want to retain the connection with the text that prompted the thought, a see also link will do it for you. A see also link will connect from a point (an anchor) in the text of the memo to selected text within a source document, so you can easily check the basis for the thoughts you are recording. Then, when you review your memo, you can also see the linked segment highlighted within its source context.

The see also link is one of the most useful tools in the program (and it's Kristi's favourite)! It provides a far better solution than copying and pasting text directly from a source document into a memo. Pasting text rather than the link is problematic, because (a) the segment has become disconnected from its identifying source and context, and (b) any coding on that text will be pasted with the text, generating double retrievals when you review the coding. A see also link identifies the source, provides context, *and* can be viewed or printed along with the text of your memo, to help you put together the argument you are developing for your article, report or thesis.

Create and view a see also link

Create the link

▶ In your source document, highlight and copy a passage that has prompted ideas you want to record.
▶ In the memo, write the thoughts related to the passage you have copied.

▶ Select some of the text you wrote to create an 'anchor' (a brief text passage) in the memo. **Right-click > Paste As See Also Link**.

When you click elsewhere in the memo, the anchoring text will show highlighted in pink to indicate the presence of a see also link. A tab at the base of the *Detail View* will indicate the location of the linked text.

View the linked text

▶ To bring see also links into view or to turn them off, go to the **View** ribbon, *Links* group > check or uncheck ☑ **See Also Links**.

▶ Click on the pink highlighted text, then double-click on the matching link at the base of the *Detail View*. The linked text will open, highlighted *in its original context* (Figure 2.6).

✓ Alternatively (or as well), you can make a link from the source to your reflective text in a memo.

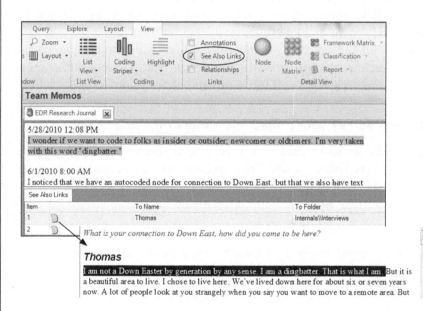

Figure 2.6 Viewing a see also link

Reporting from your source

The most useful type of report you can make from an internal data source or a memo is to export or print it with your annotations and links showing as endnotes.

Exporting or printing a source

▶ In *List View*, select the document or memo you want to print or export. **Right-click > Export** (or **Print**) **Document** (or **Memo**).

▶ Select the options you want from the Export (Print) dialogue > **OK**.

✓ Click Browse > Save as if you want it in a file type other than *.docx.

The text of the source will be printed or saved, with the content of see also links and annotations optionally provided as endnotes to the text.

Looking ahead: connecting a web of data

We point to the future here, more than the present, by showing how NVivo's tools for journaling, memoing, and linking can be extended, so you end up with a comprehensive understanding of your data and an audit trail for your project. The web of links you create in a project (and your reflections on those links) become an important antidote to the segmentation that can occur with coding (Maxwell & Miller, 2008). Some of these suggestions will become more meaningful as you learn more of the tools in NVivo, and you progress further in your project. They are relevant to all forms of data – text, pictures, video and audio.

Connecting across your project file – more on see also links

See also links do more than link evidence in source text to comments in memos. They are called *see also* links because, when you read or see *this* in a source, you should really check out (see also) *that* somewhere else in the project. There are two types of see also links, and each does something slightly different:

1 The first and most commonly used way of creating a see also link is to select a passage of text or part of a media file, copy it, then paste it elsewhere as a see also link – as described above. Use this method when you are linking a specific portion of one source to a specific portion of another source.
2 The second way of creating a see also link is to link a whole project item to an anchor within a source or a memo.

Examples of how you might apply the first type listed above (links to a portion of another source) include:

• Link interpretation of text to the passage that gave rise to the interpretation, as described earlier. In the *Environmental Change* project, this is evident when interpretations of what it means to be local (in the *Local identity and knowledge* memo) are linked to what was said in interviews.

- Identify questions or issues that you want to return to later. In the *Environmental Change* project this is evident in the *EDR Research Journal* (a memo written by Effie). If you open this memo, you will find a see also link connected to a portion of the interview with Thomas, where community newcomers are referred to as 'dingbatters'. Effie wants to return to this later to examine whether the designation should become a node or not.
- Use the capacity to create a see also link from one passage to another in the *same* document to point up contradictions in a narrative, or where one passage provides an explanation for or expansion of the other.
- Where the text illustrates something you read in the literature, create a see also link from that text to the relevant material in a reference document, such as a passage in a pdf article you imported.
- Communicate with and respond to other team members. In the *Environmental Change* project you will find an entry in the *WWS Research Journal* on 6/4/2010 where Wanda is responding to an observation Henry made in his *HGP Research Journal*.
- Eliminate the need to repeatedly articulate processes or protocols by adding see also links to point to where they have been described and/or used. In the *Environmental Change* project, the *Project protocol memo* contains such a link dated 5/15/2010 to the location where Wanda explains the process she used for assigning pseudonyms.
- Link across documents to build a sequentially ordered picture of an event or a life history through the eyes of one or more tellers, or to trace an evolving idea or saga. When a see also link is accessed, the linked item is opened with the selected passage highlighted. That passage might contain another link, allowing a further link in the web to be created.

Applications of the second type of see also link (links to the whole of another source) are less common:

- Create links in your memos to whole sources, nodes, models or other project items that illustrate or provide evidence for what you are reflecting on in the memo. For example, when you have explored an association within your data using a query, write about what you discovered in a memo with a link to the node that contains the stored results of the query.
- If you create a model, discuss it in a memo or journal, then link it to that discussion.

Creating a see also link to a whole project item

▶ In your journal or memo or other document, select text to act as an anchor for the see also link.

▶ On the selected text, **Right-click > Links > See Also Link > New See Also Link**.

▶ In the New See Also Link dialogue, **Select** the **Existing Item** to be linked and click on **OK**.

▶ The anchoring text will be highlighted in pink to indicate the presence of a linked item, and a tab in the *Detail View*, below the text of your source, will indicate the name and location of the linked item.

✓ View see also links as described earlier. If your exported or printed copy of the source or node includes a link to a whole item, the endnote for that link will include the name and location for that item, but not the content.

Connecting beyond your project file – hyperlinks

Perhaps your interviewee referred to a report that is on-line, or to an ongoing blog; the group discussion was based around a book or video; the emotion in the distraught mother's voice is best understood through a 'sound bite' from the original tape; or there is a cross-reference from an article you have imported to one that is on file but which you are not importing into your project. For such situations, hyperlinks allow you to make direct connections from a specific location within a source to items that are not in the project (on-line data or any digitally stored material on your computer), such as books or reports, pictures, web pages, video or audio files.[6] Use hyperlinks also to link from your journal to records of meetings with advisors, emails from colleagues, and other sources of influence on your developing thinking as well, as part of an audit trail for the project.

Create and view a hyperlink

▶ Click on **Click to edit** at the top of the *Detail View*, so the source you are working in can be edited. Select text to act as an anchor for the hyperlink.

▶ Hover over the selected text: **Right-click > Links > Hyperlink > New Hyperlink**.

▶ **Browse** the web to locate the URL or your filing system for the object to be linked. Click on **OK**.

▶ To view the link, **Ctrl+click** on the underlined blue text that marks the anchor for the link.

Looking ahead: keeping track of emerging ideas

Keeping track with journaling

Develop a routine of journaling as a way of keeping an audit trail of actions, reflections, spontaneous thoughts, and developing ideas relating to the topic of the research as a whole. A comprehensive audit trail, with its reflective content and links to evidentiary data, is a critical element in any qualitative project where the validity of conclusions has to be argued without the support of *p*-values and the like. The evidence it provides of the journey you have taken to reach your conclusions will therefore help you to argue and to write those conclusions.

---

[6] Many of these items can potentially be imported as data for the project where they can be linked using see also links. Use hyperlinks when you *don't* want to import the linked item.

Some researchers recommend setting up separate journals for different purposes in a project; others find it difficult to separate their random thoughts and
so they put everything in one journal. In the *Environmental Change* project, the
team members' individual journals (**Sources > Memos > Team Memos**) illustrate a broad mix of content, including records of changes made and reasons for
such changes, reflections on concepts and experimentation with ideas, and
reminders of things to do or conversations to have with colleagues (see especially
Wanda's research journal, *WWS Research Journal*). Separate general memos have
been created to document who has done what as each member of the team contributed to the project. In some projects you might find it useful to create an
additional journal to record reflections on methods, to debate theoretical issues,
to note points for a final report or, where there are a lot of brief project items,
simply to record a short summary of the main issue(s) raised by each item.

Adding to your journal

▶ Locate your journal in **Sources > Memos > [your journal]**. Double-click on its
  name in *List View* to open the journal.
▶ Click on **Click to edit** at the top of the *Detail View* for your journal, so you can
  write into it.
▶ Add further text, paste in pictures, and create links to other data, as desired or
  needed.

✓ Reference or link the source of any ideas you are adding, to assist later review.
✓ Code your journal so you can easily find and track your thoughts on particular
  topics.

Tracking concepts with node memos

When an idea about a category or concept attracts your attention, it can be more
appropriate to record those thoughts in a memo that will be linked with the
coding for that category or concept, rather than with a source or general journal.
Then, as your ideas develop, and later as you assess what you have learned and
check how this category relates to others, you can add to the memo, building it
in such a way – again, with links to evidence – that it can make a major contribution to your writing (part of a chapter, perhaps) for your project.

Creating a memo linked to a node that holds the coding you are writing
about is a parallel process to creating a memo linked to a source, that is, by
using the right-click menu in either *List View* or *Detail View* (see Chapter 4).
And again, the memo that is created will be stored in the Memos folder. Like
other sources, it can be searched or coded, to track cross-cutting ideas and
concepts.

Table 2.1 Memos, annotations and links – summary table*

	Journals (whole project memos)	Memos linked to a source	Memos linked to a node	See also links to specific content	See also links to entire items	Annotations	Hyperlinks
Primary use	Reflective memoing regarding the project as a whole; an audit trail that traces the development of the project, with links to examples and evidence	Notes regarding key issues in a source; field observations; a case summary; reflective thoughts about the source or parts of it	Reflective thoughts about the concept or case represented by the node; ideas for further analysis; summary of what has been learned about the concept	Link from a specific point in a source or node to specific content in another (or the same) source or node; e.g., use to track evidence, contradictions, link to connecting events or people in other sources	Link from a specific point in a source or node to the entirety of other relevant project items, including other sources, nodes, memos, sets, models, or query results	Notes that illuminate or briefly reflect on a specific part of a source (text, image, audio, etc.); like 'comments' in MS Word	Links from points within sources (internals, externals, memos), to non-project on-line items or websites
Visual cue on the screen	Listed in *List View* > Sources > Memos	Icon next to source in *List View*	Icon next to node in *List View*	Pink highlight on text	Pink highlight on text	Blue highlight on text	Underlined blue text
Can the content be coded?	Yes	Yes	Yes	NA The linked item may be coded already.	NA The linked item may be coded already.	No If you code the location where the annotation is anchored, you will see the annotation.	No If you code the anchor for the hyperlink, you will have access to the hyperlinked item.
Can the content of the linked material be searched for text?	Yes	Yes	Yes	No – only as part of the item from which it has come	No – only as part of the item from which it has come	Yes	No
How many can you have?	Unlimited	One linked memo per source	One linked memo per node	Unlimited	Unlimited	Unlimited	Unlimited
To create	*Create* ribbon > Memo	Select source or node: Memo Link > Link to New Memo; OR Ctrl+Shift+K		Copy portion to be linked, then select the anchor point and Paste as See Also Link	Highlight text in a source or node, Right-click > Links or select from the *Analyze* ribbon, *Links* or *Annotations* groups		
To view	*List View* > select the memo and double-click	Right-click source > Open Linked Memo; OR Ctrl+Shift+M		*View* ribbon > ☑ See Also Links	*View* ribbon > ☑ See Also Links	*View* ribbon > ☑ Annotations	Ctrl–click on blue underlined text

* Help item: About Links

Memos, annotations or links: which should it be?

So you can put things in perspective, Table 2.1 outlines the key features of memos, annotations, see also links, and hyperlinks, to help you gain a sense of when each might be most useful, and of the possibilities and limitations for each.

Saving and backing up your project

As you have been working, NVivo regularly asked if you wanted to save your work. There is no background autosaving in NVivo so, as we noted in Chapter 1, we would strongly recommend that you save each time you are asked, unless you are simply experimenting, do not want to save your changes, or you are in the middle of an Undo operation. Of course, you should always save as you exit the project as well.

For safety, you need backup copies, regularly updated, as a precaution against loss or drastic error. No matter how good your equipment, power failures or human intervention can make the program crash; no matter how confident you are, errors can occur; and no matter how thorough the programmers and testers have been, occasionally projects will become corrupted. Our recommendation is to make a backup on your working computer at the end of each day's work, and to copy that to another medium (a disk, memory stick, server, or cloud that is independent of that computer) on a regular basis. If you're cleaning out old files, a good housekeeping principle with backups is to keep the last known good copy – that means keep at least the last two backups, just in case the last one was corrupted as you saved it. You might also want to retain copies from important transition points, for example, before and after a major node restructuring, before and after combining the work of team members, or when you've developed key models or understandings of the project. These copies will help you write up the methods section of your final product. They can also help you prepare your final arguments to support your conclusions, as you can trace how your ideas developed and thus how you might convince a reader.

! Do not rely on automatic daily institutional backups unless you are sure these create a new copy each time – otherwise a good backup might be overwritten by a damaged file.

Backing up your project

While you are working in NVivo:

▶ Go to **File > Manage > Copy Project**. Locate and name the backup file. Be aware that in the process of copying your project, NVivo will close and then

(Continued)

(Continued)

reopen the project you are working on, in contrast to Save As in Word and many other programs (where you end up in the copy rather than the original). In the process, you will be required to save the current project before it closes, and it will reopen in the usual initial Sources view.

Alternatively, after you close your project:

▶ Go into Windows Explorer. Locate and copy the project, and paste it into a backup folder.

✓ So you can keep track of your backup files, always date them (this also overcomes the problem of duplicate names). We use an international date format (yymmdd) added to the name, so they sort in date order (from oldest to newest) in a file list or navigation dialogue.

3

Designing an NVivo database

NVivo was programmed with a high degree of flexibility. If elements of your qualitative research change over time as you come to new understandings about the data and about the setting, you will be able to rewrite, recode, reorder, reconfigure, redefine, revamp and reframe as necessary. A cogent plan has definite benefits, however, and so this chapter identifies those aspects of your database that warrant your attention early on. In this chapter we again urge you to focus on *your* research questions and the collection and construction of *your* data, to make sure the software is following rather than leading you. We provide conceptual and practical guidance that will allow you to move forward, anticipating your use of tools that will be covered in later chapters. If you are new to the program we ask you to trust that the advice we give in this chapter is based on a level of experience that you may not yet have.

In this chapter:

- Start thinking about what a 'case' may be in your research.
- Preview the ways you can leverage cases, attributes and values in NVivo to help you sort and compare items across different subgroups, because this will influence how you prepare your data.
- Consider suggestions about preparing and importing your data for NVivo in view of available strategies for management of data sources.

Qualitative data for your project

Different methodologies require different data and different ways of working with those data, but regardless of the choices, you are creating data for your project right from the time you start thinking about it. Already, in Chapter 2, you were recording ideas about your research. By talking with other researchers, people in the field, and perhaps through 'dialogue' with the literature, you were adding to those ideas.

These are all data that will supplement the specifically designed forms of data you will make or gather to inform the question(s) you are asking.

Moira interviewed backpackers who had been exposed to different cultures in their travels, in order to investigate their reactions when visiting those cultures where people experienced widespread poverty. Because she also travelled as a back-packer, including with some of those she interviewed, she also had a wealth of observational data and reflections in her travel diaries about her own emotional and intellectual responses to life in those countries. When she began to analyse her data, she realized that the notes in her diaries informed her understanding of many of the responses recorded in the interviews. Consequently, although it was not part of her original plan, she found it was valuable to add her diaries as data in her project.

By recording and selecting materials to inform your project, you make them into data. The problem for a project using qualitative data is not in generating data, which as Richards (2009) noted is 'ridiculously easy', but in making use-ful and manageable data records. Qualitative data records are often messy and large – an hour of interviewing, for example, can generate 25 pages or so of single-spaced text. Typically, also, data are complex, making them difficult to reduce; and data are contextualized, so that additional information about sources and the settings in which they were obtained is needed.

Most often, qualitative researchers think about working with transcribed records of interviews or focus group discussions, but not all interviews can be recorded, and not all data require full transcription. Consider also using com-ments added at the end of written questionnaires; records of observations; existing material such as media releases, nursing notes, web material, admin-istrative records, films and novels; or secondary sources obtained from quali-tative data archives. While NVivo is particularly appropriate for analysis of free-flowing texts, it is certainly not limited to that form of data. A complete list of the various formats for qualitative data that can be incorporated into an NVivo project can be found on the companion website, at www.sagepub.co.uk/bazeleynvivo. Although we focus on text-based data in this chapter to sim-plify our discussion about the basics of preparing to work in an NVivo project, many of the methods and strategies we describe will apply to data sourced from other media as well.

- Features related to working with media files will be covered in Chapter 7.
- The advantages and disadvantages of working with pdf files and a bibliographic data-base (EndNote, Zotero and RefWorks) are detailed in Chapter 8.
- Importing and using datasets (spreadsheet or database files containing both qualita-tive and quantitative fields) will be placed in a mixed methods context in Chapter 9.

Given the many different types of qualitative data now supported in NVivo, it is worth noting Coffey and Atkinson's (1996: 11) warning against making data 'in a spirit of careless rapture ... with little thought for research problems and research design'. Such enthusiasm tends to lead to the predicament of having 'all these data' and not knowing what to do with them. In similar vein to Maxwell (2013), they emphasized the necessity for an overall methodological approach which will link questions, design, data and analytic approaches, with each of these potentially subject to modification throughout the life of the project.[1]

Two ways of flagging qualitative data

Imagine you are reading a paper copy of an interview or a journal article, and this information represents some of the qualitative data you will consider during your analysis. Working on paper, you might create a bracket in the margin that surrounds the first paragraph and then flag the ideas in the paragraph using a few labels: *trust, loyalty,* and *happiness.* These will end up becoming codes later on in your analysis. We will look at coding in much more detail in Chapters 4 and 5, but for our present purpose this very simple example will suffice.

While reading this interview or article you also become aware that the entire document may warrant additional flags. For instance, if you are reading a woman's interview, or reading an article from 2011, you may want to flag the entire file as *female* or *2011,* respectively. Borrowing from our first image about creating a bracket around the first paragraph, you would draw a line down every page in the margin, and label it with *female* or *2011.* When you do this just for the paragraph, with labels such as *trust* or *loyalty,* you are coding a *portion* of the document with any relevant flags. With labels such as *female* and *2011,* you are coding the *entire document.* Eventually you could look at all the sources you bracketed with *female* and all the sources you bracketed with *male,* and sort them into two stacks. Then you could look through the female interviews, hunting for your bracket for *trust,* and then repeat this with the other stack, to compare with what the men said about trust. Through the years, researchers developed various complicated file management systems to facilitate sorting and comparing data in this way, always with limitations on what and how much was within reason to achieve.

While we use flags like *male* and *female* to sort data in this example, the flags need not be demographic categories. They could be any nominal, ordinal, or interval data, including Likert scale scores, respondent-identified personality traits, etc. You'll learn more about other examples for flagging the entire entity

---

[1] Chapter 2 of Bazeley (2013) details strategies for designing a qualitative project with requirements for analysis clearly in view, while Chapter 3 reviews strategies for managing qualitative data (with and without a computer), again, with a view to facilitating analysis.

(in this instance the entity is a person's transcript) in Chapter 6, but for now let's stay with our example of the demographic labels, *male* and *female*. At present, the important distinction is that some flags tend to be more specific to a portion of the data (e.g., *trust*), and some flags tend to pertain to the entire item (e.g., *female*). This could be true also of video, audio, photographic, and other kinds of data besides text, but for now we are using an example of a paper copy of a document.

When we consider this example of the two kinds of flags and move to handling them in a relational database such as NVivo, new opportunities arise that impact on both efficiency and complexity. Instead of taking a pen and drawing down each page of *Barbara's* interview to label her as *female*, you can instruct the computer to identify her not only as *female*, but also as someone born *Down East*, in her *40s*, and any other relevant factors – without missing bits or getting them mixed up. In relational databases, this process of adding flags such as *male* and *female* that pertain to entire sources tends to happen in a different location and with a different technical process than the more discrete coding of pieces of a document to *trust*, *loyalty*, or *happiness*. Nonetheless, the purpose and the outcome of adding flags for *male* or *female* is the same as if you were working on paper: a desire to create sorted piles according to subgroups, so that you can then compare what those different groups say about the flagged concepts of *trust*, *loyalty* and *happiness*.

Thinking cases

When you are sorting women into one pile and men into another pile, you are sorting cases. Use of the term 'case' in this context is not intended to imply that you are necessarily undertaking case study research. Rather, cases are employed in NVivo as a *unit of analysis* in a research study, and a study might involve cases of more than one type.

> In the sociological and anthropological literature, a case is typically regarded as a specific and bounded (in time and place) instance of a phenomenon selected for study. ... Cases are generally characterized on the one hand by their concreteness and circumstantial specificity and on the other by their theoretical interest or generalizability. (Schwandt, 1997: 12)

In the *Environmental Change* study, *Barbara* is a case, *Charles* is a case and *Dorothy* is a case. In this example, people are cases. Alternatively, you may be working in a project where policies are cases, geographical regions are cases, or less visible entities like mathematical theories are cases. This all depends on your research question, and it could also change as you analyse your data and realize that the case type you started with is not the case type you are currently interested in examining. You may initially be looking at individual people, thinking you'll compare men and women, and later decide that instead you want to focus on friendship clusters and compare insular and open clusters.

Even if you are doing a single case study (a methodology), you still might end up with multiple cases (a tool in NVivo).[2] For instance, if you are following a single Olympic athlete's journey to the summer games, you might be investigating this one person's experience, with each letter they write home to their family while they are in training being treated as a case. In this regard, when using NVivo you can easily sort the letters written to parents into one subgroup and the letters written to siblings in another and friends in another, so you can focus on a more detailed interpretation of the data (the content of the letters) and compare across these subgroups. It all depends on your research questions, and the data you collect to answer those questions. Your case structure in NVivo should follow your research design, not lead it.

Identifying your cases

Much has been written about selection of cases in qualitative work. Patton (2002) and Flick (2007) each give a thorough overview of the range of sampling and selection possibilities, as do a number of other qualitative authors. Case structures are often simple, but they can also be quite complicated. The main case unit(s) sometimes have illustrative cases embedded within them, for example, when a corporation is the case and one or more specific departments, or products, are illustrative cases within the study of that corporation (Yin, 2003). Alternatively, they might be layered, for example where schools, classes and the pupils in them are each treated as cases at different levels.

Yin (2003) warns to 'beware' cases which are not easily defined in terms of their boundaries – their beginning and end points. 'As a general guide, your tentative definition of the unit of analysis (and therefore of the case) is related to the way you have defined your initial research questions', and 'selection of the appropriate unit of analysis will occur when you accurately specify your primary research questions' (Yin, 2003: 23, 24). If your questions and conceptual framework are clear, it should take only minutes to define the case type (what kinds of units you are using) and thence the cases for the study (Miles & Huberman, 1994). Even if you do not intend to compare subgroups, you will benefit from understanding cases and how they help your work in NVivo.

---

[2] Some methodologists distinguish between theoretical and empirical cases (see Bazeley, 2013: Chapter 1).

Cases in NVivo

A case is a core structural element in NVivo. Each case unites *all* the different components of qualitative and quantitative data you have about that entity, that unit of analysis, in one place. Cases are incredibly flexible entities in three ways that are important for you to understand at the outset.

- First, you will be able to include just a single source, multiple sources, or portions of sources as data for each case. For instance, if you interview 30 people and as a result have 30 transcripts, generally these will be turned into 30 cases. Alternatively, a case could include several waves of data collection for a single person. You could also turn *portions* of a single document into a case, such as all the contributions an individual speaker makes to a focus group. Or you can use a combination of strategies. For example, some or all of your participants came to the focus group as well as completing one or more individual interviews, so you want their cases to contain their contributions to the focus group as well as their interviews.
- Second, each case might include only one kind of data, such as text in participant transcripts; or it could bring together information in multiple formats – in addition to an interview, you have photographs taken by the participant and videos of family celebrations.
- Third, you can combine related demographic and numeric (attribute) data with the text (or other qualitative data) for each case so that, for example, a flag such as *male* or *female* is applied to *all* data for the person who is that case, regardless of type, volume, or how many sources it is spread over.

Thus, for each case in NVivo, you are able to take advantage of the software's capacity to manipulate multiple data collection points, multiple formats of qualitative data, and quantitative as well as qualitative data.

In NVivo, cases are managed by creating case nodes, with each case node acting as the 'container' that holds all data, of all types, for each case, regardless of source.[3]

For an ethnographic study reviewing issues of research production and performance for academics in the arts, humanities and social sciences disciplines of a university, Pat created a case node for each member of academic staff, sorted by academic unit. Data for the study comprised administrative records of research funding received by each staff member and details of research publications produced by them (originally in two Excel spreadsheets), individually completed surveys, web profiles, media releases, field observations, interview notes, other official records, and incidental documentary sources. The case nodes brought

---

[3] This is an example of where nodes are used for organizational purposes, rather than for coding thematic content. As a consequence, you will store them in a folder to keep them separate from your thematic nodes (as you saw for the case nodes in the *Environmental Change* project in Chapter 1).

together data from all or part of the various documents, so she could instantly access everything she knew about a particular academic. Additionally, once all the data were coded for issues raised, and for the scholars' research areas (interpersonal violence, pedagogy of mathematics, or religious experience, for example), she could easily discover which academics were interested in which issues, whether there was sufficient interest in any particular topic to create a research group, and who might want to be part of such a group, including details of what their contribution might be.

Why does it matter now?

Cases and the case structure can be created at any time in your NVivo project. You can create a case structure before you import data; you can create cases as you import each source; or you can create cases and a case structure after data are imported, and even after all the data are coded (Chapter 6 details alternative methods for creating cases). Creating cases can be one of the first things or one of the last things you do in the database, with no negative effects on the analysis. Given this reality, why are we asking you to consider the issue of cases carefully before you begin?

What you primarily need to consider, at this planning and data preparation stage, is that the need to create a case structure can have implications for how you might best format the data in your sources, particularly for text-based data. Table 3.1 sets out the various possibilities. It is helpful to be aware of these issues even if your case structure is very simple. The second half of this chapter then provides guidance on the practical aspects of data preparation, particularly when you need to differentiate multiple speakers within a single source for the purpose of managing cases. It also details other factors to consider in preparing data that are independent of managing cases.

✓ Each source will remain intact throughout its NVivo journey, so you will never lose that important element of context, even if you divided its contents to create case nodes.
✓ Planning for cases and the attributes you will attach to each case has implications also for how you organize your coding system. Your flags for *male* and *female*, for example, can be rapidly applied to all relevant text yet they are kept right out of your coding system, making both attributes and coding more efficient and effective to use.

Planning for attributes

By now you will have realized that attributes (e.g., *age group*; *location*) and attribute values (e.g., *30s, 40s, 50s*; *rural, urban*) are intimately related to cases. We will be discussing attributes in detail in Chapter 6, but in the meantime, while you are preparing your data, we offer the following suggestions:

Table 3.1 Formatting strategies to facilitate case construction from different types of sources

Structure of data sources	What qualitative data will be included in each case node? (in addition to demographic and/or numeric attribute data)	Formatting requirements when preparing data, for most efficient handling of cases (other methods applied later will be much slower)
Each file (e.g., text of an interview, a video, a picture) contains all the data for one case only.	One source only.	No special formatting required, although it is useful to distinguish the text of different speakers (interviewer and interviewee) with some form of identifier at the beginning of each paragraph or by using headings.
Multiple sources for each case, where each source is related to one case only, e.g.: the same person has been interviewed several times; your information comes from different people associated with a single case; or you have different types of data, such as an interview and a picture, for each case.	Multiple sources.	No special formatting required within each file, but ensure that each file for a particular case has a common root name. Then, where there are multiples of the same type of data, follow the name with a unique identifier, e.g.: (a) Beatrice 1, Beatrice 2; (b) John_self, John_mother, and John_teacher (where John is the case).
Individually identified speakers in a focus group or Interviews with more than one interviewee or Notes from a committee meeting.	Portions of one or more sources.	Speakers need to be uniquely identified, with their name on a separate line and formatted using a heading style, e.g.: **Dagmar** (in Heading 2 style) This and that, that and this (Normal style) **Daniella** (in Heading 2 style) Chatter, chatter (Normal style) **Ricardo** (in Heading 2 style) I think that ...... (Normal style)

Structure of data sources	What qualitative data will be included in each case node? (in addition to demographic and/or numeric attribute data)	Formatting requirements when preparing data, for most efficient handling of cases (other methods applied later will be much slower)
Any other files that include data relating to multiple cases, e.g., field notes.	Portions of a source, unless data have been extracted for each case separately.	If data relating to each case can be separated within the file, include headings (as above) in the field notes. The alternative will be to use interactive coding for relevant text – much slower!
Responses to a survey or questionnaire, recorded as a dataset in Excel (see Chapter 9).	One or more codable fields in a dataset, one row per case.	Standard row and column identifiers for a dataset.
Combinations of any of the above, e.g., where you have survey responses as well as individual interviews.	Portions of sources in addition to whole sources.	Format individual files as above. Ensure that each data item or part-item relating to the same case uses the same unique name to identify the case.

✓ Record attribute data (e.g., demographic details) as you gather your qualitative data. Try to think of all the kinds of comparisons you are likely to want to make, and, when you are gathering your data, record the details needed to make those possible. For example, if you want to compare what is said by people from different locations, then you will need to record information about where each person lives.

✓ It is much more helpful to have attribute data recorded in checklists or, even better, in a spreadsheet, than to extract them from within the text of interview documents (where it is also a waste of a transcriptionist's time!).

Preparing data sources

It is possible to start working on your data really fast if you want to – just type up, save, and import as a source and you're ready to go. But you gain significant advantages from careful preparation, especially if your data contain any regularities or structure that can be exploited to facilitate management or coding.

What often works best, especially if you have mixed types of data and/or data that require special formatting or organization, is that you devise a plan and start by preparing only a small subset of your data. Play with that subset through all of the primary tools you plan to use such as coding, classifying and querying (this could take several weeks) and by the time you are done with this pilot set of data, you may realize things about preparing the data that you'd like to change.[4] Of course, it may not be possible or practical to conduct this pilot with a small portion of the data, but if you are able to do so it could save you significant time and frustration as the project gets bigger.

✓ Sources may be added to a project throughout the life of the project. Coding and classification systems remain flexible throughout a project.

Preparing text-based data

Text in an NVivo document can include most of the familiar richness of appearance that word processors provide, such as changes in font type, size and style, colour, spacing, justification, indents and tabs. So when you're making notes or transcribing your interview, focus group or field observations, make use of this to help shape your data, express emphasis, convey the subtleties of what is

---

[4] For many qualitative researchers, analysing some initial data before collecting more is an important principle in any case – often leading to changes being made in questions asked and/or theoretical sampling. This initial data should be retained within the project, however.

happening, clarify how your respondents were expressing themselves, or draw attention to critical statements.[5]

What can be imported as part of a text-based document?

- Any formatting that helps enrich or clarify presentation of text, including headings, bold, different font types, and coloured fonts (but not highlighting).
- Text in different languages can be included within the one document.
- Embedded items such as images, text boxes, and illustrations (although you can code the entire embedded image, text box, or illustration only, not portions of these items).
- Tables (the text coded into a node from a cell will appear in the context of its entire row when you open a node).
- *Ignored* items include: headers, footers, page numbers, line numbering, shapes, highlighting, and comments.

- ✓ Preparing data records is one of those areas where 'fools rush in'. Careful editing and thoughtful structuring each reap rewards. As an analyst, you are dependent on the representation of reality that is contained within those records.
- ✓ If you have any unusual formatting features, check out how well they import, and check how the coded text and other items look in a node, by importing and coding one or two prepared sources before you spend time preparing all the others.

Making transcriptions ...

What appears at first sight as a purely mechanical task is, in fact, plagued with interpretive difficulties.

> Transcribing involves translating from an oral language, with its own set of rules, to a written language with another set of rules. Transcripts are not copies or representation of some original reality, they are interpretative constructions that are useful tools for given purposes. (Kvale, 1996: 165)

When you transcribe, you discover the value of using a high-quality recorder for your interviews and, even more so, for group discussions (using two recorders is recommended for the latter). It is also valuable to do your own transcribing, if at all possible – building familiarity with your data. At the very least, if another person typed the transcripts, it is absolutely essential for the person who did the interview to review and edit the transcript while listening carefully to the recording. A typist who unintentionally reorders or omits words can reverse the intended meaning in some sentences – typists routinely miss *n't* on the end of verbs, for example.

---

[5] Although these features can be added to the text once it is imported into NVivo, in most instances it is easier to add them while working in Word and it is often best done while checking the transcript, that is, with the recording playing.

The flat form of the written words loses the emotional overtones and nuances of the spoken text, and so it is beneficial for the interviewer to format or annotate the text to assist in communicating what actually occurred with a view to the purpose and the intended audience for the transcription. 'Transcription from tape to text involves a series of technical and interpretational issues for which, again, there are few standard rules but rather a series of choices to be made' (Kvale, 1996: 169). The goal in transcribing is to be as true to the conversation as possible, yet pragmatic in dealing with the data.

Kvale (1996) and Mishler (1991) provide useful discussions and examples of issues involved in transcription, and Bazeley (2013) lists general guidelines to follow when transcribing. Whatever procedural decisions are made, they should be recorded as clear decisions and formatting guidelines for the typist(s) to ensure consistency in the transcription process, in your project journal to aid interpretation from the data, and (if you are a student) in the methods chapter of your thesis.

... or not transcribing

Interviews and other sources for sociolinguistic, phenomenological or psychological analysis generally should be fully transcribed. When nuances of expression are not needed for the analytic purpose of the research, verbatim transcriptions may not be needed; notes may be adequate for the task. Using a computer program to assist analysis does not automatically mean you are required to use full transcripts. As with transcripts, however, keep the comments in their spoken order and context rather than rearranging them into topic areas.

When Pat had assistants interviewing researchers about the impact of receiving a small financial grant on their development as researchers, the conversations were recorded. Much of the recorded conversation was not directly relevant to the topic of her research (researchers have an irrepressible urge always to tell what their research is about), and so the interviewers made notes from the recordings, supplemented by occasional verbatim quotes.

Again, in a different setting, when Australia's corporate watchdog set out to investigate 'boiler room' share-selling scams, the researchers worked entirely from notes of their telephone conversations with those who had been approached by the scammers. These were sufficient to trace the chain of events and the interviewees' responses to them (Australian Securities and Investments Commission, 2002) – deep emotional responses or phenomenological essences were not the concern of the sponsoring body!

Then there are always times when you discover the audio recorder wasn't working. And times when your participant opens up just as you have your hand on the door to leave ...

Formatting text-based documents with heading styles

Where different sections of a source identify contributions from different people or responses to different questions or notes from different days, the use of headings formatted with heading styles will be critical to your being able to easily differentiate and create separate cases or coding categories from those sections of your documents.

Headings are usually less than one line, for example 'Q01 History' or 'Danny', but in Word they are treated as being a whole paragraph. The heading describes what is contained in the (normal text) paragraph(s) immediately following it.

Heading styles in Word are always applied to whole paragraphs. Thus the use of styles for headings means that a built-in style in Word has been selected and applied to the paragraph that comprises the heading. NVivo will not see text as a heading just because it is bold or in a different font. Figure 3.1 shows part of one of the interviews in the *Environmental Change* project with a map of the heading styles and levels used in that document.

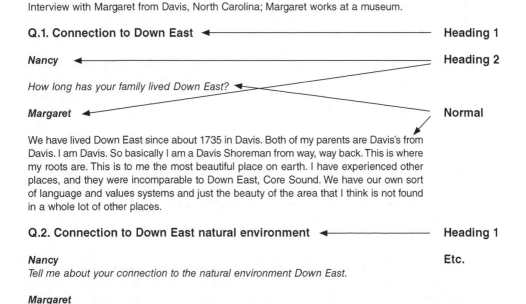

Interview with Margaret from Davis, North Carolina; Margaret works at a museum.

Q.1. Connection to Down East ◄——————————————————— **Heading 1**

Nancy ◄——————————————————————————————— **Heading 2**

How long has your family lived Down East? ◄——————

Margaret ◄————————————————— **Normal**

We have lived Down East since about 1735 in Davis. Both of my parents are Davis's from Davis. I am Davis. So basically I am a Davis Shoreman from way, way back. This is where my roots are. This is to me the most beautiful place on earth. I have experienced other places, and they were incomparable to Down East, Core Sound. We have our own sort of language and values systems and just the beauty of the area that I think is not found in a whole lot of other places.

Q.2. Connection to Down East natural environment ◄————————— **Heading 1**

Nancy   **Etc.**
Tell me about your connection to the natural environment Down East.

Margaret
I do love to go clamming and stuff but I never have the chance anymore I am sorry to say. The last time I went fishing was with NCCAT–the North Carolina Center for the Advancement of Teaching.

Figure 3.1   Sample of interview text showing headings

As in Word, heading styles in NVivo are hierarchical, breaking a document into parts, with subparts. A heading level allows NVivo to select all of the text between it and the next point where there is another heading of the same level.[6] NVivo recognizes three features within the heading:

1   the heading level that has been applied;
2   the exact string of characters where the heading level has been applied; and
3   the associated text that follows the heading.

These features allow NVivo to differentiate between Nancy's and Margaret's texts, since they are separated by and identified with headings with a style of Heading 2. (The questions are given a Heading 1, which we will talk about later, but for now let's focus on being able to sort the data by person.)

Using headings to separate and identify cases

When speaker names are set out as headings so that turns in conversation are separated in the document, this presents several opportunities.

- If you are analysing a *focus group* or a source with multiple speakers, you can apply auto coding to efficiently separate out all of the contributions from each individual and store them as part of the case information for each of those individuals (see Chapters 5 and 6).
- In *field notes*, the heading might be used to identify the case being observed, or perhaps the date or site or circumstances of the events being described. This might be simply to clarify the structure of the notes, or so you can auto code sections of them.
- If the document is an *interview* with two speakers (the interviewer and the participant), you will be able to auto code for who is speaking, and then run a text query to look for the word *sustainability*, for example, and limit finds to occurrences within the participant's text (see Chapter 5).

✓ We usually recommend using Heading 2 for speaker names, so Heading 1 is available should you choose to insert topic headings (the assumption is that the topic covers more than one speaking turn). Consistency in the level of heading chosen for a particular kind of item (such as speakers, or questions, or anything else you are using headings for) across *all* your documents is important, as this will facilitate use of auto coding and query tools in NVivo.

---

[6] In this regard, NVivo is slightly different from the way heading levels work in Word. In Word, selecting text on the basis of a heading style will select all text to the next heading of that level *or higher*; that is, Word recognizes the hierarchy of levels, so that if you select on the basis of a Heading 2, it will select down to the next *Heading 1 or 2*. Because NVivo has to work with names of the styles from across all languages, it works on the basis of finding the next example of the same style only, without considering the hierarchy of levels (hence the reference to paragraph styles rather than heading styles in its dialogue boxes).

✓ Have an observer at your focus group to record a speaker identifier and the first word or two said for each speaking turn. If the typist is having trouble identifying different voices from the recording, this can be used to verify who was speaking.

✓ Add heading styles as you transcribe using a keyboard shortcut,[7] or after you have typed the transcript by using Replace (click on the **More** button in the Replace dialogue).

Using headings for separating questions or other sections

Heading levels in NVivo can be useful also to efficiently separate data in a file based on question asked or topic covered, again using auto coding. This strategy is often applied when researchers want to collect all the answers for Question 1 and separate these out from all the answers to Questions 2, 3, 4, etc., or when several topics are covered in a focus group discussion or in a set of field notes. By using a heading level for each question or section (usually Heading 1), you will be able to use auto coding to create nodes, each of which will contain all the answers to a particular question or comments or notes on a particular topic.

Storing qualitative data in NVivo

Qualitative data in NVivo are held in internals which, along with memos and externals, comprise the sources for your project.

- Internals are your primary sources for your project. These might include text sources, pictures, audio or video files, pdf sources, datasets, or web-based material. They are usually imported, but text sources can be recorded within NVivo, for example if you are keeping running field notes.
- Memos are records of your reflective thinking about the project as a whole, particular sources or cases, or about particular concepts (as coded in nodes). These are usually recorded within NVivo, as shown in Chapter 2.
- Externals are proxy documents for items that cannot be imported (see below).

Naming and importing internal sources

Files should be saved with a name that you want to use as the name for the source in NVivo. NVivo will sort sources alphabetically in its folder system (treating numbers as text),[8] and will display coding in that order as well.

---

[7] Word has built-in shortcuts for the first three levels of headings (Alt+Ctrl+1, Alt+Ctrl+2, and Alt+Ctrl+3) or you can set up your own by formatting a shortcut key for any style, in that style's Modify Style dialogue.

[8] Instead of ordering numbers as 1, 2, 3, 9, 10, 11, they will order as 1, 10, 11, 2, 3, 9, so (if it matters) add zeros as required in front of the first digit (e.g., 01) to ensure that all are written with the same number of digits so they list in the correct sequence.

It is best to keep the source name reasonably brief and straightforward. Don't include unnecessary words in the title, such as 'Transcript of interview with ...' or dates or demographic details or even details of the context of the interview, as the name is likely to be truncated in the display and all sources will end up looking the same! For text sources, file information such as location, interviewer and date of interview is more appropriately recorded (briefly!) all in the first paragraph of the text, as this will be stored by the software as a description for the source, providing useful reference information.

Sources prepared for importing into NVivo can be stored anywhere in your computer system, though you will find it useful to have them all together in a clearly identified folder. Basic instructions for importing sources (**Right-click** in *List View* > **Import** > **Import Documents**) were provided in Chapter 2. Clicking on the **More** button at the base of the import dialogue will convert the first paragraph of your source to a description that is recorded in the properties box for the source (Figure 3.2).

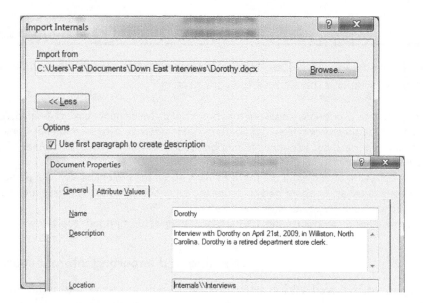

Figure 3.2   Importing the description for an internal source

Creating records for external sources

You might choose to include sources in the project as externals when:

- documents such as diaries or early research journals are not available electronically;
- sources are too large or are otherwise unsuitable for importing (such as a reference work, thesis, artwork, music, videotape, photographs, maps, company reports); or
- having access to the detail of the whole is not needed (perhaps for minutes of meetings or a set of guidelines).

For these kinds of materials, creating an external will create a record within the program that indicates the existence of the source, and that allows you to code, annotate or link numbered references (e.g., pages) for that source.

✓ For reference works and similar sources, our generally preferred alternative to creating an external of this type is to simply create (or import) a regular document in NVivo that contains a summary or description of the original source, adding reference details (such as page numbers, grid references) where appropriate to identify the material being described. Relevant information is then more accessible for coding, reviewing or searching.

? Access Help for further guidance about creating and using sources, including externals. Start from *Sources > About sources* and follow the links through to the kinds of sources for which you want more information.

Managing data sources in NVivo

It was the realization that computers could assist with managing data, rather than a belief that they were appropriate for analysis, that prompted early work in qualitative computing (Kelle, 2004). Over the decades since their early development, computer programs for assisting with qualitative data became sophisticated toolboxes providing multiple ways to approach the management of data – with choices about how these tools are used depending on both data type and the methodological orientation of the user.

Overview of available tools

Your use of NVivo's data management tools will vary throughout your project, with some being appropriate from the start, and others coming into play more as the project develops. Available tools for managing data include case nodes, folders and sets. While these topics will be reviewed in more detail in Chapter 6, it is helpful for you to have some basic understanding of what they do now.

✓ Any coding you apply is preserved and links you create are updated automatically if you rearrange your sources into folders or sets or subsequently code them to cases.

Managing sources in folders

Just as you group books on your bookshelf, file papers in folders or put nails in a different set of tins from screws, if you have sources which differ in some way you have the option to store them in different folders to reflect that. Additionally, by placing sources in folders, you make it easy to query just those sources that are within a particular folder.

NVivo's Sources area has built-in folders for your major types of sources (Figure 3.3):

- Internals (for the data you make);
- Memos (for your reflections on the data); and
- Externals (for those sources you can't import).

There is a fourth folder, for storing framework matrices. These are created within NVivo to summarize data by case; they cannot be imported. They are not so much a source as a tool for analysis, and will be explained in that context in Chapter 11.

In the *Environmental Change* project, the researchers have created additional folders for separate storage of different types of data and memos.

It is up to you whether you decide to create further subfolders within those primary folders. Doing so is a simple matter of right-clicking where you want the subfolder to be, choosing to make a new folder, and naming it. You can then drag sources from the *List View* into the folder of your choice.

You can place each source in one folder only. Typically the main basis for sorting data sources is according to their type, that is, by whether they are records of interviews, focus groups, literature, observations, photographs, or other kinds of source. This is partly to help you keep track of what you have,

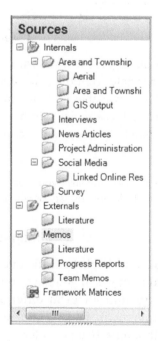

Figure 3.3 Folders for sources

and also because it allows you to easily select an appropriate subset of sources for particular analyses (e.g., some types of queries that work for interviews do not work effectively with focus groups). Sources from different phases of the project or sites for data collection could be sorted in subfolders within those, although, as will be seen below and in Chapter 6, these are probably more usefully identified using sets rather than folders.

Some of your memos will be of a general type (a general journal, a methods journal), while others will be associated with sources, or with nodes, or just see ideas at large. (see Bringer et al., 2006, which is based on Joy Bringer's doctoral thesis, provides a useful table summarizing her extensive use of memos in an earlier version of NVivo.) If you have multiple memos of several different types, you could find it useful to sort those into subfolders under Memos, to make it easier to see what memos you have or to find a particular memo.[9]

✓ Folders and sources can be rearranged easily as your knowledge of your sources and your ideas about organizing them develop.

! Beware of making layers of folders within folders. Remember you will have to click your way through them every time you want to select a source to code or enter in a query! The use of many layers also suggests you are using folders for things better handled with sets or attributes.

Managing sources in sets

In Chapter 6, you will learn that sets provide an additional way of organizing your data sources. A set simply holds aliases, or shortcuts, for the items within it, so identifying a source as part of a set does not alter that source or the structure of your data sources. In many ways, it is like an alternative folder structure, but you can organize things with a variety of lenses in mind for grouping items because an item can be in more than one set. Sets are particularly valuable in situations where you have more than one source of data for each case, where each person has been interviewed on more than one occasion, or where you have interviewed a number of people related to the case. A set can be viewed as a single entity, or as a group of members, giving it some additional flexibility when used in queries and models. You can arrange (or rearrange) your sources in sets at any time during your project.

---

[9] If you create a linked memo from a source or node, the program will default to placing it at the top level of the Memos folder. You can safely move it afterwards if you wish, without breaking the link – or alternatively, add a colour marker, as suggested in Chapter 2.

Reviewing and arranging your sources

By now you might have several sources in your project. To check, look at **Sources** in the *Navigation View*, and at the folders you have already created and populated.

▶ If you have several types of sources and they are not arranged in folders, you might like to set those up now, and drag your sources into them. If all your sources are of the one type, then of course there is no need for additional folders.
▶ Click on each folder, in turn, to review the contents of that folder. Information for each source in the folder will show in the *List View*. Sources with a memo will have an additional icon showing in the column next to their name.
✓ Data types are not normally differentiated on the basis of your method of recording. Thus, video interviews generally would be stored in the same folder as transcribed audio-recorded interviews. Video records of children's play would, however, be regarded as different from interviews with children, and would thus warrant being placed in a separate folder under Internals.
✓ Sources can be sorted by clicking on the top of a column in the *List View*. For example, if you want to find your most recently added sources, or all the sources with no coding (a single text reference probably indicates coding to a case node only), then click on the header for the relevant column in the display. NVivo will apply this sort order to all folders (in Sources *and* Nodes), and will remember the order next time the *List View* is opened. Mostly you will leave them sorted alphabetically by Name.

Review – options for data management

Let's imagine you have two projects, one in which you have interviewed the same people more than once, and another in which you have asked people, within a single interview, about three different time periods. Table 3.2 outlines the most useful way of managing those different types of data.

Table 3.2 Arranging data sources in NVivo

Data sources	Management in NVivo
Interviews done in waves.	Use cases for people, with a set for each wave of interviewing.
Multiple sources with multiple people in each case.	Use: a case node for primary person, with all sources relevant to that case coded to it; folders for different types of data; sets for each category of person connected to the case. Sources can be in more than one set, e.g., if data are also collected on multiple occasions.
Time data embedded within each document, e.g., when an interviewee refers to times before, during, and after changes.	Use cases for people, coding for times. If you also have some whole sources relating to specific times, you can continue to just use codes (code whole source), or you can make sets that combine sources and codes.

Questions to help you work through these early phases

1 Data preparation:

   a How important is it to have verbatim text for this project?
   b Do I need to identify non-verbal aspects?
   c Is it better to import my sources from other programs, or write them within NVivo?
   d What is a good naming strategy for my files?

2 If I have cases in this project:

   a What are they (people, teams, policies, theories, phases, etc.)?
   b Do I want to work with more than one case type? (e.g., organizations *and* individuals *and* policies)?
   c Do I have more than one case within any of my files?
   d How does this inform my document preparation (e.g., use of heading styles)?

3 What file features might be useful to me, whether I have to separate cases or not?

   a Formatting features (e.g., bold, italics, underline)
   b Headings to indicate sections within the data
   c Embedded objects (e.g., tables, illustrations).

4 Will I use folders to organize files?

   Do I have different types of data (e.g., interviews, focus groups, photographs)?

4

Coding basics

Qualitative analysis is about working intensively with rich data. The tools provided by NVivo support the analyst in making use of multiple strategies concurrently – reading, reflecting, coding, annotating, memoing, discussing, linking, visualizing – with the results of those activities recorded in nodes, memos, journals and models. Each of these strategies is integrated in a process of learning from the data, and indeed, they work best when they are carried out as integrated activities. The process of thinking about a code prompts a memo, and similarly, the process of writing an annotation or a memo assists in clarifying what a code is about, or which codes are most appropriate.

At first your progress in working with the data will be slow; gradually your project will grow into a web of data, categories and thinking, illuminating your research question. As your ideas and categories develop, working with the data will become faster.

In this chapter:

- Understand how coding supports analysis.
- Discover strategies for seeing and naming relevant concepts and categories in your data.
- Develop practical strategies to manage the coding process.

Goals for early work with data

It helps to have a sense of what you are trying to achieve at any stage. Here is a general picture of what you might seek in this early work with your sources:

- You need both distance from and closeness to your data to secure a rounded perspective. After working through a document, be surprised and excited and informed by nuances in the text, but also stand back and see the whole, and where that whole fits in a larger whole.
- Strive, even from this early stage, to develop the concepts you will be working with, to go beyond descriptive labelling and to think about them independently of the

source. Why is this information important? Where will these ideas take me? This will be reflected in the way you name nodes and in the memos you write.

- Early work with text and concepts is about laying the foundation for identification of key themes in the data. Beware of jumping to conclusions too early, however. Constantly challenge your first ideas by drawing comparisons, by purposively sampling diverse cases, or by reviewing what the literature says on the topic. The project journal is probably the best place to record these ideas.
- Right from the start, it is helpful to identify patterns in the data: you will notice them as you are coding, for example, when you consistently find you are applying particular codes at the same time. These should also be noted in the project journal (colour them so they stand out when you review later); you will then be off the starting block early, en route to your final analyses.

Be prepared to experiment as you work; you are not trapped by your early work with data. The tools in NVivo are flexible, allowing for changes in conceptualization and organization as the project develops. Moving, splitting or merging nodes does not mean they lose their coding links. Editing the text of documents does not invalidate earlier coding on that text. As your knowledge about your data and your confidence in using NVivo each gain in sophistication, it is likely you will reconsider and reconfigure what you have been doing. What you already accomplished will not be lost, and the effort already applied will not be wasted.

If you lay a sound foundation with your first document(s), then you will confidently move on to adopt further strategies for advancing your thinking about data, as outlined in following chapters. Whatever path you take, it is important to see this early work with documents and coding as beginning analysis, and not simply as preparation for analysis or a mechanical task to be passed over to others.

Selecting documents for beginning analysis

If you are just beginning to gather data, selecting a first document to work on is probably easy: you will have only one or two to choose from. If, however, you have already completed a number of interviews or have a variety of data items, then you might:

- choose one which you remember as being 'typical' in some way, or which was contributed by someone who was representative in some way of a group or subgroup in the sample; or
- choose one which seemed to be particularly interesting, or 'rich' in its detail.

The first source you code can have a significant influence in determining the categories you create and the ideas you carry through the analysis as it will sensitize you to watch for certain types of detail. When choosing a second data item, therefore, you will benefit from selecting one that contrasts in some important way with the first. In addition, you are likely to generate the majority of your categories while coding your first few sources, so it is useful to maximize the potential for variety in concepts (or in their forms of expression) early in the process.

> In the Researchers project, Pat chose Frank and Elizabeth as the first two documents to work through in detail, because, as academic researchers, they provided an absolute contrast in terms of career development. Elizabeth's path into a research career was characterized by digressions and serendipitous events, while Frank's path was direct and purposeful.
>
> When Pat first worked through Elizabeth's document, the impact of her changing image of research was striking, and so she coded that and further documents for the way in which the speaker viewed research – only to find in later analyses that it had no particular significance for anyone else. It became more useful to see (and code) Elizabeth's re-visioning of research as a turning point, rather than focusing on her image of research. The nodes that dealt with images of research could then be 'retired'.

Building knowledge of the data through coding

Coding is one of several methods of working with and building knowledge about data; use it in conjunction with annotating, memoing, linking and modelling (see Chapter 2). 'Any researcher who wishes to become proficient at doing qualitative analysis must learn to code well and easily. The excellence of the research rests in large part on the excellence of coding' (Strauss, 1987: 27). Guidelines outlining the process of coding follow, but exactly how and what you code will vary significantly, depending on your choice of methodology.

Codes and coding

A code is an abstract representation of an object or phenomenon (Corbin & Strauss, 2008: 66), or, more prosaically, a way of identifying themes in a text (Bernard & Ryan, 2010). Codes range from being purely descriptive ('this event occurred in the *playground*') through labels for topics or themes (this is about *violence between children*) to more interpretive or analytical concepts (this is a reflection of *cultural stereotyping*') (Richards, 2009).

Raw field notes and verbatim transcripts reflect 'the undigested complexity of reality' (Patton, 2002: 463), needing coding to make sense of them, and to bring order out of chaos. Coding in qualitative research, in its simplest sense, is a way of 'tagging' text with codes, of indexing it, in order to facilitate later retrieval. Naming a concept or topic aids organization of data and so assists analytic thinking (Corbin & Strauss, 2008). As data are seen afresh through the coding category rather than the source, coding allows you to 'recontextualize' your data (Tesch, 1990), assisting you to move from document analysis to theorizing. Access to the data sources is always retained, however.

Approaches to coding

When it comes to the actual task of coding, there are 'splitters' – those who maximize differences between text passages, looking for fine-grained themes – and 'lumpers' – those who minimize them, looking for overarching themes (Bernard & Ryan, 2010), and then there are those who 'have a bet each way' and do a little of each. A common approach is to start with some general categories, then code in more detail (e.g., Coffey & Atkinson, 1996), while those who employ grounded theory, phenomenology or discourse analysis more often start with detailed analysis and work up to broader categories. If you are feeling a bit uncertain about how to tackle the coding task (most of us do when first faced with a complex paragraph of rich data!), then a rough sorting of data into major categories could be a useful way of getting started – but you will then need to take a second look. Most end up working with some combination of the two approaches, and the software, happily, supports either or both.

Lynn Kemp, of the Centre for Health Equity Training Research and Evaluation at the University of New South Wales, tells students that choices about coding are like choices in sorting the wash. Some hang the clothes just as they come out of the basket, and, when dry, throw them into piles for each person in the family, ready for further sorting and putting away – preferably by their owner! Others hang the clothes in clusters according to their owner, so they are already person-sorted as they come off the line, although pants and shirts might be mixed up and socks still need pairing. And yet others hang socks in pairs and all like things together, so they can be folded together as they come off the line. Ultimately, the wash is sorted, people get their clothes and (hopefully) all the socks have pairs. Similarly, whether you start big, then attend to detail, or start small and then combine or group, your coding will eventually reach the level required.

Broad-brush or 'bucket' coding

This one is for lumpers! Because you can recode text at a node in the same way as you code a document, there is no need ever to treat coding as unchangeable – you can code on from already coded data. Your initial coding task, then, would simply be to 'chunk' the text into broad topic areas, as a first step to seeing what is there, or to identify just those passages that will be relevant to your investigation – or indeed, those that aren't immediately relevant but which could become so later.

Lynn Kemp's doctoral study of the community service needs of people with spinal injuries employed broad-brush coding as an initial sorting strategy. In response to her question, 'You came home from hospital and ...?' her interviewees talked extensively across all areas of their lives. In order to manage this large pool of data, Lynn coded her interviews first into very broad categories (e.g., community services, employment, education, recreation). She then coded on from the community services text (which was her immediate focus), capturing the detail of what people with spinal injury were seeking from life, what services were being offered, and how these supported or impeded their clients' capacity to fulfil their 'plan of life'. After recovering from the doctoral process, Lynn (or indeed, her students) could then focus attention on topics that were set aside, to engage in further analysis and reporting.

In the Researchers project, broad nodes were used to code when the researchers were talking about becoming a researcher, and when they were being a researcher. Later, these nodes were used to see how stage of development was associated with different strategies or experiences for researchers.

Coding detail

And this one is for the splitters! While broad-brush coding relies on the capacity of the software to facilitate recoding, or coding on from text at a node, coding in detail makes use of the capacity in the software to cluster like things together in a hierarchical (tree-structured) system, to gather related concepts in a set, or perhaps to merge nodes.

For some methods, most notably grounded theory, your initial analysis will involve detailed, slow, reflective exploration of early texts – doing line-by-line coding, reading between the lines, identifying concepts and thinking about all of each concept's possible meanings as a way of 'breaking open' the text, recording what is learned in both codes and memos. At the beginning of the analysis process, you will explore each word or phrase for meaning, perhaps considering theoretically the difference it might have made if an alternative word had been used or a contrasting situation described, or how this chosen word or phrase is similar to or different from others used (Strauss, 1987). Micro-analysis of this type generates an awareness of the richness of the data, of how many ideas can be sparked by it and of how much can be learned from it; and a coding process that involves detailed attention to the text helps you to focus attention on the text rather than on your preconceptions. You will not continue to code at this level of intensity beyond the first few sources, however, unless you come upon new ideas to explore or contradictions to resolve.

In practical terms, capturing the detail of the text does not mean you should segment it into tiny, meaningless chunks. Rather, the goal is to capture the finer nuances of meaning lying within the text, coding a long enough passage in each instance to provide sufficient context without clouding the integrity of the coded passage by inclusion of text with a different meaning (unless, of course, the whole passage contains contradictory messages).

In the Researchers *project, Frank begins his response to an open question about his research journey as follows:*

My PhD was both a theoretical and empirical piece of work; I was using techniques which were novel at the time. (Interruption by secretary.) I was using novel mathematical dynamic techniques and theory and also I was testing these models out econometrically on cross-country data. I think it was a strong PhD, I had a strong supervisor, he was regarded as – it is fair to say he would have been in the top 5 in his area, say, in the world.

In the first place, it is interesting that Frank begins his response by focusing on his PhD experience. In broad terms, one could simply code this passage descriptively as being about the PhD or learning phase of becoming a researcher, and indeed, that is relevant as contextual (or structural) coding even if one is looking to capture detail in the text. But this passage is also saying considerably more than just that Frank's research career included a PhD student phase. He implies that the PhD provided a strong foundation for his later career. Linked with that strong foundation are the kinds of work he did in his PhD and the role of his supervisor.

This text tells us also a great deal about Frank and his approach to research. His PhD was both theoretical and empirical (characteristics which are repeated in the next sentence). Not only does he have credibility in both these aspects of his discipline, but his work was novel. Here, he is both validating and emphasizing the strength of his foundational work. He is also suggesting, in describing his work as using novel mathematical techniques, that he is making a mark on the development of the discipline – presaging a later, critical theme.

That his PhD was a 'piece of work' also suggests wholeness or completeness, so research work can have the dimension of being partial, incomplete and ongoing, or of being finished and completed with loose ends tidied up. This, along with the dimension of research discoveries as being novel (developed at a point in time) versus occurring in incremental developments, could be interesting in relation to the nature of research activity (and being a researcher), but they are not necessarily relevant to the current question of how one becomes a researcher – and so they are noted but not coded.

Frank's emphasis on his PhD being strong and (noting repeat use of 'strong') on the strength of his supervisor brings into more focus the idea also evident in the first sentence – the status of his work matters. It is important to him that his supervisor was at the top, and he was moving up there too (with leading-edge work). This theme of ambition (incorporating status) is evident also in several further passages, for example:

I then teamed up quite soon with another 'Young Turk' ... we hit it off and both of us were interested in making some sort of an impact, so basically we were young and single and just really went for it. ... our two names became synonymous with this certain approach, and we went around Britain and into Europe giving research papers and getting ourselves published. ... it was us carving out a niche for ourselves in the research part of the profession and that was our key to success so we kept at it.

(Continued)

(Continued)

How important is this level of ambition, both from the point of view of the research question, and for detailed coding? At this early stage, the safe move is to create a node for ambition: if no one else talks in these terms, then later it can be combined within a broader category of, say, drive or commitment.

Coding for the opening passages might therefore look as shown in Figure 4.1. Other ideas and reflections prompted by the passages were recorded in annotations and in the memo attached to Frank's document.

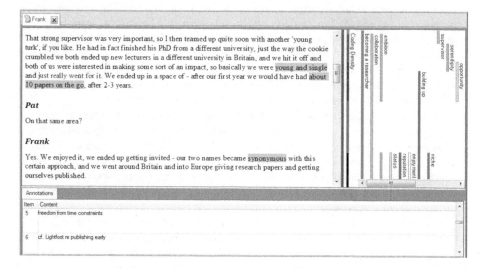

Figure 4.1   Frank's document showing application of multiple codes to each passage of text, and annotations

✓ You might use annotations as a 'quick note' area while you are engaged in coding, and then, when you have finished going through the document, review them as a basis for more reflective memoing.[1]

Fracturing or slicing data

The coding on Frank's document clearly illustrates how multiple nodes can be and are used in coding a passage. Coding is a way of 'fracturing' or 'slicing' the text, of resolving data into its constituent components. The term most commonly used in the literature is 'fracturing' but, in the context of computerized coding, 'slicing' seems to be more appropriate as a way to describe the process of applying multiple codes to a single passage of text.

---

[1] Annotations, like see also links, can be reported as endnotes on the source if you print or export the text of the source (in *List View*, **Right-click** > **Export** or **Print**).

- Slicing suggests taking a layered view, where all codes are present across the entire passage of text that comprises a meaning unit.
- Fracturing suggests breaking apart each element of that meaning unit, making separate pieces.

Each passage is read carefully to identify who and/or what is present, and when, where and how they are present, with each of these components potentially recorded as a separate code. Thus, *multiple codes are used simultaneously to capture what is happening in a single passage of text.*

At a first level of interpretation, this type of coding allows you to review each component code independently, giving a recontextualized perspective on each concept or topic as all text relating to it is brought together. Seeing your data in terms of the category rather than the document gives a stronger sense of what the category is about (Richards, 2009). If the category is potentially significant in your project, or sparked further ideas, create a linked node memo (see below) to record the new insights gained through this recontextualized view.

At a second level of interpretation, slicing data into their component parts opens up analytical possibilities through the recombination of coded passages. You can ask NVivo to show you, for example, how often people had a positive attitude to real estate development (because the same passage was coded for both attitude and what the attitude was to), or to what extent real estate development was associated with community change (by locating passages coded with both those nodes). You can see this by turning on the coding stripe for one node while looking at the other (see below for how), or you can use a coding query (see Chapter 11) to locate the exact text coded by both nodes. The critical point, here, is that this manner of coding gives you incredible *flexibility* when it comes to asking questions of your data, because you are not limited to the combination inherent in a single comprehensive code.

Storing coding in nodes

Coding in NVivo is stored in nodes. In information systems the term 'node' is used to indicate either a terminal point or a point of connection in a branching network. Sociologists might be familiar with the idea of nodes in a social or a semantic network. Horticulturalists know the node as the point at which branching might occur in a plant. Similarly, in a fully developed NVivo coding system, nodes become points at which concepts potentially branch out into a network of subconcepts or dimensions.

In NVivo, you make a node for each topic or concept to be stored, much like designating a hanging file for the cut-up photocopies in a manual system. What NVivo keeps there, however, are not actual segments of data, but *references* to the exact location of the text you coded in the source document. Using those text references, the software is able to locate and retrieve all the coded passages from the document records. The passages themselves are never copied, cut or physically moved into the nodes. Unlike cut-up photocopies on the sitting-room floor or in hanging files:

- the source always remains intact;
- information about the source and location of a quote is always preserved;
- it is always possible to view the coded passage in its original context;
- changes to the source are immediately reflected in the text viewed through nodes;
- annotations and links applied to passages of text in nodes are recorded in and visible from the source; and
- passages can be coded at multiple nodes, with queries able to find passages coded by co-occurring nodes.

At first, you will probably use nodes that do not presume any relationships or connections to store your coding. They serve simply as 'dropping-off' points for data about ideas you want to hang on to. Later these are likely to be organized and moved into a branching structure (a 'tree') – a hierarchy in which nodes representing subcategories are placed under higher-level or 'parent' nodes. The topic of establishing a coding hierarchy will be covered fully in the next chapter. At this stage we recommend you focus on creating nodes without worrying about structuring them – it is easy to reorganize them into trees when you have a better understanding of the data.

Beginning coding

Detailed coding will be quite slow at first. Not only are you orienting your thinking to the issues raised by the data – which is likely to mean spending time in reflection and in adding to memos and annotations – but you have the practical task of creating new nodes as you work, and making decisions about them. You might be new to the qualitative research process altogether, too. So, while new ideas are exciting, you might additionally feel anxious about how much time this is taking. The number of new nodes you are creating will decrease markedly after the first two or three documents. Once you create a node, you can access it easily for further coding. As the text referenced by your nodes builds up, your coding will start to develop a clearer structure, you will gain more confidence in working with your data, and you will find your pace increasing.[2]

---

[2] People often ask, but it is very difficult to say how much time is needed for coding. Our best estimate is that, *once you have an established coding system*, you should allow at least 3 hours per hour of transcript – the actual amount will very much depend, however, on your methodological approach. This should be read in the context of understanding that experienced researchers (including Miles & Huberman, 1994) routinely recommend allowing a working period for analysis of data that is two to five times as long as the period taken to make arrangements and gather the data.

There are multiple ways of making nodes, either as you are working through the text or when you are just thinking about the categories you might need. We will describe the most common methods of working to start with, and then point to other alternatives.

✓ Remember each node should hold one category or concept only. If you need to capture two or more elements of what is happening, use two or more nodes to do so, applied to the same text.

Beginning coding

Preparing to code

▶ In *Navigation View,* select **Sources > Internals.**

▶ In *List View,* double-click an internal to open it.

▶ **From** the *View* ribbon, select **Detail View > Right.** Adjust the pane divider on the screen by moving it to the left so you can see the full width of your source (Figure 4.2).

▶ Select **Nodes** in *Navigation View,* while keeping an internal source open in the *Detail View.*

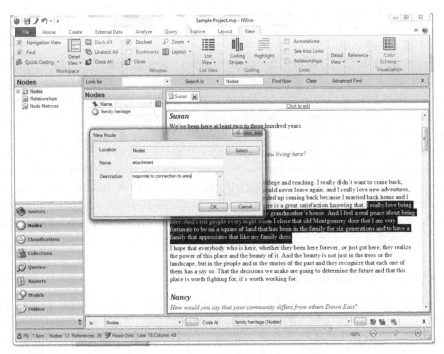

Figure 4.2 Screen arrangement for coding

(Continued)

(Continued)

Making nodes and coding at the same time

▸ Select text, then **Right-click > Code Selection > Code Selection At New Node**. Or select text and press **Ctrl+F3** on your keyboard.

▸ Type a **Name** for your new node (Figure 4.2). Add a **Description** if you wish. Press Enter (**OK**).

✓ To avoid losing control of the text selection when the mouse pointer is moved below the base of an open window, click where you want the text selection to start, use the scroll bar or your mouse wheel to move further down in the text, then Shift+click where you want the selection to finish. All text between the two clicks will be selected.

Making a node without coding

Sometimes you have an idea for a node but don't have data for it yet. You can create it ready to receive coding when some data appear:

▸ In *List View* (in the white space below any existing nodes): **Right-click > New Node**.

▸ Provide a name for the new node (and a description if you want).

Adding a description to your node

As you create a node, get into the habit of documenting what it is. Name it carefully with a meaningful title, and add a description (from *List View* of your nodes, **Right-click** on a node > **Node Properties**; or **Ctrl+Shift+P**). Descriptions serve as accessible reminders of what this node is about – and they are *very* useful when there are multiple people working on the same project, when other responsibilities have taken you away from this project for a time, or for seeing when you have created separate nodes for too many versions of the same concept. These descriptions essentially serve as your codebook, and can be exported later as a reference or appendix. Node names are not fixed, so if you find the name you have given a node no longer fits well, change it by selecting it, click on it again and then edit, or change its name in the properties dialogue.

Adding further coding

There are several ways to add coding to existing nodes. One of the 'problems' with NVivo is there is more than one way of achieving most tasks, and it takes experience to know which most suits your purpose at a particular time. For now, you need to find a method of coding you are comfortable with, because you're going to be doing quite a lot of it! We recommend using drag-and-drop coding for most purposes.

Adding further coding to an existing node

▶ Arrange your screen for drag-and-drop coding – as above.

✓ To prevent text from being inadvertently moved, make sure you are in read-only mode (**Click to edit** will be showing at the top of the *Detail View*) and **Read-Only** will be showing in the status bar at the base of the NVivo window.

▶ With nodes showing in *List View*, and the text you are coding in the *Detail View*, drag selected text to a node.

Alternative ways of adding coding

You might find one or other of these useful in some situations, such as when it is not convenient to have the nodes displayed in *List View*.

▶ Highlight a passage (in *Detail View*), then choose one of the following:

1 Right-click to see and select a recently used node; or
2 Select a recently used node from the coding bar at the base of the *Detail View*, and click on the green tick; or
3 **Right-click > Code Selection > Code Selection At Existing Nodes**. Choose one or more nodes as are required (Figure 4.3).

Figure 4.3 Alternative ways to add coding to text

(Continued)

(Continued)

Oops!

✓ Coding can be 'undone' on a *selected* passage either by choosing to **Uncode** at the node showing in the coding bar at the base of the *Detail View* (click on the red cross), or by immediately clicking **Edit > Undo** (see below for more information on revising coding).

✓ Nodes can be deleted: select a node, **Right-click > Delete** or click Delete on your keyboard. This also deletes all coding done at that node.

✓ Nodes can be merged: if you accidentally make two nodes about the same thing, select one > **Right-click > Cut**, then select the other > **Right-click > Merge into Selected Node > OK**.

Identifying and naming codes

The idea of coding a portion of text (or audio, video, images, etc.) to index its content sounds simple enough, and observing someone else's coding can make the task look deceptively easy. When you meet your own data, however, you find many things are going on at once: something is happening in a particular setting or at a particular time, particular people or groups are involved, perhaps their responses are based on their belief systems or cultural background, and there are consequences to be considered. Perhaps there is a twist to the way this experience, belief or feeling is being reported that makes it just a bit different from other reports, or difficult 'to get a handle on'. Narrative is inherently complex: a group can argue about the content and meaning of just one paragraph for a very long time.[3] It helps when you code each component in the data separately, using multiple codes to pick up the various threads within each passage of text. Later you can check whether this combination of codes forms a pattern, or was a 'one-off' occurrence.

What follows is a collection of ways in which codes might be identified and named, particularly those requiring more than a simple descriptive label. Further suggestions and extended examples of coding strategies can be found in Bazeley (2013, Chapter 6) and in Saldaña (2013).

- **Repetitions and regularities**: People repeat ideas that are of significance for them (see the use of *strong* by Frank in the example above). Repetitions therefore suggest useful concepts to use as a basis for nodes.

---

[3] This is a very useful activity to engage in when you are struggling with conceptualization. If you aren't part of a team project, then link up with a group of other researchers undertaking qualitative work – the discipline area is irrelevant – and meet with them on an occasional basis. Each takes a turn to bring a short sample of data (maximum one page, de-identified) as the basis for discussion in that session.

- **Use questions of the text to generate codes** – who, what, when, why, how, how much, what for, what if, or with what results? Asking these kinds of questions will help to ensure thoroughness of coding and also to develop relational statements (do the actions or strategies change under different conditions and, if so, what are the implications?) and so will hugely benefit development of a theoretical model.
- **Compare and contrast** passages of text; think about the ways in which they are both similar and different. This will help you go beyond simply deciding which chunks might go together: it will help you discern the dimensions within concepts, or perhaps to discern previously unobserved variables running through the text.

In a study of parental and peer attachment among Malaysian adolescents, Noriah Mohd Ishak, in the Faculty of Education at the University of Kebangsaan, Malaysia, found boys and girls spoke in contrasting ways about their parents' role in their relationship choices, for example:

Boy: I trust my parents with their choice; I might have a girlfriend here in America, but the girl I finally marry will depend on my parents' choice. I think theirs is always the right choice.

Girl: I choose whom I will marry. My parents might have their own choice, but how can I trust their choice, because they live in a different generation than I do!

In relation to young people's acceptance of parental leadership, then, trust is a significant dimension. Other possibly relevant concepts arising from these comparative passages are parental adaptability, parental authority, cultural expectations, and cultural change. Also of interest in the boy's comment about having an American girlfriend is what it says about attitudes to women and commitment in relationships.

- **Compare with hypothetical or extreme examples** – again, to identify dimensions within concepts.

As his career was unfolding, Frank's total focus was on research: 'When you go out in the pub you are talking research, when you go to bed at night you are thinking it'.
Seeing this as being a form of addiction *prompted Pat to talk with a colleague who was studying youth gambling behaviour. Researchers and gamblers alike follow a passion, often (but not essentially) to the detriment of their health and/or family relationships; both provide financially insecure career paths that benefit from careful strategic planning but which are also subject to luck or whim; both can be characterized by emotional highs and lows; both can experience problems with self-regulation. There were differences of opinion over whether addiction was necessarily 'bad'. As the project developed further, Pat saw addiction as one expression of a larger category of* obsession, *which she came to define as* driven passion *to capture the dimensions of emotional engagement and the potentially blind (unregulated) commitment of the obsessed researcher.*

- ***A priori*, or theoretically derived, codes** come from your prior reading and theoretical understanding to give you a start list of concepts to work with. Use, also, the categories embedded in your research questions. Don't let your *a priori* codes confine your thinking, however. Strauss (1987) and Patton (2002) each referred to these as sensitizing concepts, rather than as fixed categories.
- ***In vivo*, or indigenous, codes**, in direct contrast to *a priori* codes, are derived directly from the data (Strauss, 1987). They capture an actual expression of an interviewee or label used by participants as the title for the node, but they can sometimes have the unfortunate problem of not being useful in exactly that form for expressing what is learned from other participants. Change the term to a more general construct as the project develops, but keep a record (in the description, or a memo) about how the code arose in the first place.

When a member of a corporation which underwent a radical change programme talked about the hard labour *of working through that change process, this expression was appreciated for its valuable imagery – of what goes on in a birthing process, of the slogging work of someone held in a prison – and hence became an* in vivo *code available for use in coding other text.*

- **Narrative structure and mechanisms** take account of how things were said as well as what was said. You might note, for example:

  o transitions and turning points in the narrative, signifying a change of theme or a subject to be avoided;
  o inconsistencies, endings, omissions, repetitions and silences (Poirier & Ayres, 1997);
  o indications of time, or tenses in verbs, indicating identification with the events described or attempts to distance an event or bring it closer;
  o the use of metaphors and analogies;
  o the sequenced, structural elements of a narrative (Elliott, 2005; Riessman, 2008); and
  o use of articles or pronouns pointing to particularized or generalized referents, for example, the staff, my staff or our staff; indicating level and type of ownership or involvement (Morse, 1999).

- Explore **discourse** that reflects a particular construction of the topic, or of society (Willig, 2003; Wodak, 2004). What has led to these constructions? What are the implications of seeing the world in this way?

Among some more experienced researchers one can detect a discourse of performance (being successful, competing, building a reputation), and alternatively, of play (following curious leads, puzzling, playing with new ways of doing things) in the way they talk about their engagement in research activity. Coding these varying constructions of 'doing research' would facilitate assessment of what they mean for their work and career.

'Seeing as': generating conceptual codes

> If sensing a pattern or 'occurrence' can be called seeing, then the encoding of it can be called seeing as. That is, you first make the observation that something important or notable is occurring, and then you classify or describe it. ... [T]he seeing as provides us with a link between a new or emergent pattern and any and all patterns that we have observed and considered previously. It also provides a link to any and all patterns that others have observed and considered previously through reading. (Boyatzis, 1998: 4)

At first, you are not quite sure what is relevant, or how it will be relevant. It is very easy, when coding, to be beguiled by fascinating things your participants have said and so to become sidetracked. To 'break in' to the text and make a start, try the following three steps Lyn Richards (2009) developed for undergraduate teaching. They will help you move from 'seeing' to 'seeing as':

- Identify: What's interesting? Highlight the passage.
- Ask: *Why* is it interesting? This can generate a useful descriptive code or perhaps an interpretive code – if so, make a node for it. It could also warrant a comment in an annotation or memo.
- Then ask: Why am I interested in *that*? This will 'lift you off the page' to generate a more abstract and generally applicable concept, which, if relevant to your project, will be very worthy of a node (and perhaps a memo).

That critical third question is giving you a way of generating concepts for nodes that will be useful *across* documents rather than nodes which code only one or two passages in a single document. These more general or abstract concepts are essential for moving from description to analysis. They link also to the broader field of knowledge, and so you might record node memos for them. In a strategic sense, that third question also helps keep you 'on target', to keep the focus on issues relevant to your research questions.

In a doctoral project on the role of support groups in assisting young people with a mental health problem, a participant reported moving from sheltered to independent accommodation. The student deemed this to be of interest, and created the node accommodation to code it. Only one participant, however, had anything to say about accommodation, and accommodation was not an issue of concern for this project. (Had the project been about issues faced by young people with mental health problems, then of course accommodation could well have been a relevant node to make.) When the student was challenged about why the text at that node was interesting, she said it was the evidence of improvement in mental health status indicated by the young person's change in accommodation that had attracted her attention. She then changed the node name to reflect this more pertinent (and more interpretive) concept. She could then use this node across other documents to code other indicators spoken of in the same way, such as gaining employment or repairing a relationship. If she wished to examine the nature of the evidence given to indicate improvement in mental health status, she could simply review of the text coded at the node.

Further coding in NVivo

New nodes proliferate early in the project, but as you work through further documents, you are more likely to add coding to existing nodes. If you keep making a new node for each passage, then it might be time to rethink. Very specific categories tend to be of little value for analysis. Check after a few documents to identify those nodes that code only one passage (number of references is shown in *List View*), then challenge each of these with Lyn Richards' question 'Why am I interested in that?' to identify a broader concept or purpose for this node. The discipline of writing a description for each node (in the Node Properties dialogue) can also help sort out what they are about, and which you need and which you don't.

Seeing what you coded

You might want to check what coding you already added to a passage:

- You're still getting used to the software and want some reassurance your coding is really happening.
- You've been interrupted in your work and want to check where you are up to.
- You want to check if you picked up all important aspects for this passage. *Or*
- You need to review what you have, to know whether a new passage will fit.

You can achieve these various goals in several ways.

Viewing coding

Using coding stripes to see nodes used alongside the text they code

▶ With the source open in *Detail View*, select **View** ribbon > **Coding Stripes** > **Nodes Most Coding**.

▶ Hover with your mouse pointer over the coding density bar to see the nodes associated with the adjacent text, and where coding ceased.

▶ With coding stripes displayed, right-click on a stripe for further (sometimes useful!) options.

✓ To see more than seven nodes at a time, change: **File > Options > Display > Maximum number of stripes** (e.g., to 50 or 100 or 200).[4]

✓ Many people find it helpful to have coding stripes in view while they are coding – displaying either **Coding Density Only**, or if they have enough screen width, then **Nodes Recently Coding**. This allows you to confirm you have

---

[4] You can change this temporarily from the *View* > **Coding Stripes** options. Changing it in the Application Options dialogue means it remains changed.

indeed coded the text, or to review what codes you have used on a particular passage.

? See NVivo Help on *Use coding stripes to explore coding* for additional options.

Viewing text coded at a node

▶ Check the text coded at a node by double-clicking the node in *List View*. Passages coded will be displayed in *Detail View*.

✓ Nodes can be reviewed while you are thinking about which to use for coding. (Use the tabs at the top of the *Detail View* to move between open nodes and sources, but avoid having more than a few open at the same time!)

✓ Open a node's **Properties** (**Ctrl+Shift+P**) to check (or add to) its description.

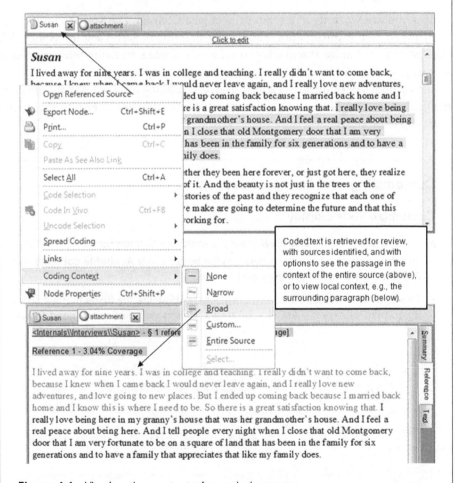

Figure 4.4 Viewing the context of a coded passage

(Continued)

(Continued)

Viewing the context of a text passage

▸ **Right-click** in the passage of interest > **Coding Context** > **Broad** to see the rest of the surrounding paragraph for the passage; or

▸ **Right-click** > **Open Referenced Source** to see the passage in its original context (Figure 4.4).

✓ We will cover ways of *reviewing* your coding in Chapter 5.

Customizing your display and listing nodes

Unless you are working in a team project (see Chapter 12), you are unlikely to need much of the information shown, by default, in *List View* for Nodes. We suggest you customize the display to remove columns showing who created or modified nodes and to add descriptions into the display.

Listing nodes periodically is a useful way of making a record of your developing project, as part of an audit trail for your work. It is useful also to share with a colleague or adviser.

Customizing and listing nodes

Customize your display

▸ Go to **View** ribbon > **List View** (near the middle) > **Customize**.

▸ Use the arrows to move items between the boxes under **Available columns** and **Selected columns** to suit your preferences.

✓ The items you select here to show in your *List View* are the items that will show if you print or export a list of your nodes. Unless you particularly need to see

		A	B	C	D	E
	1	Name		Sources	References	Description
	2	Attitude		17	992	A person's general feeling of favorableness or unfavorableness. Synonym: affect (Ajzen and
	7	Balance	6		16	
	8	Community		18	101	Text coded to topics around the concept of community (not around specific named Down Ea
	9	Community change		18	62	Change to the people, culture, or built structures of the communities Down East
	10	Connection to Down Ea		13	35	
	11	Local identity	14		43	A non-local resident or tourist. Someone who is from "off" the islands, or who does not have
	12	Local knowledge		5	7	Local or indigenous knowledge about the coastal environment and fisheries.
	13	Economy		25	303	Text coded around issues of economy, jobs, livelihood, cost of living, etc.
	14	Agriculture		8	20	
	15	Fishing or aquaculture		19	184	Harvesting of wild seafood is termed commercial fishing. Aquaculture is growing and harvesti
	16	Fishing industry declir		14	184	

Figure 4.5 Exported node list with descriptions

who created and last modified nodes, we would recommend removing those from selected columns and replacing them with the **Description** field.

List your nodes

▶ Right-click in *List View* and choose to **Print List** or **Export List**.

✓ The list will include whatever information is showing on the screen at the time. If you want to create a codebook with descriptions (Figure 4.5), customize your *List View* to include Descriptions.

Write a memo about a node

As you think about a particular node – either while you are creating it, or as you view the text coded there – it can be useful to record those thoughts in a linked node memo. These work in much the same way as memos linked to sources, except they are designed to focus on a concept rather than a source.

Record a linked node memo

▶ With a node selected in *List View*, **Right-click > Memo Link > Link to New Memo** (or press **Ctrl+Shift+K**).

▶ Record your ideas about that node in the memo. It can be useful to add a date (**Ctrl+Shift+T**), and it is *very useful* to note which source prompted the idea.

▶ Copy text to support your ideas (from the source as you are coding it or the node when you are reviewing it) and **Paste As See Also Link** into the linked memo for the node.

▶ Retrieve the memo at any time using **Ctrl+Shift+M**. Next time you open it to write in it, you will need to **Click to Edit**.

Making changes to coding using Uncode

Uncoding removes a text reference from a node. The way you approach this task will depend on the context within which you are doing it, whether that is simply to 'clean up' in a node or to move the passage from one node to another. In general, the options parallel those for coding.

✓ If you want to move text to another node, involving uncoding and recoding, make sure you do the recoding first – if you uncode first, you have lost immediate access to the passage for recoding!

? Search Help for *Remove coding* to find all the ways of uncoding in NVivo.

Using colour when you code

As you create nodes you can add a colour marker to them, or you can add a colour later by selecting a node and modifying its Properties. NVivo provides seven colours designed to serve as a way to group nodes that are similar in some way (at this stage, you might use colour to identify nodes that you might end up grouping into the same tree).

▶ To sort your nodes by colour in *List View*, click on the colour icon in the header bar.
▶ To see your customized colours in the coding stripes, go to the **View** ribbon, *Visualization* group (far right) > **Color Scheme > Item colors**.

Coding a second document

When it's time to open a second document, the nodes remain in place, ready to use with the new document. You will select from the same (expanding) list of nodes to code all your documents – there is no need to create a new version of existing nodes each time you start on a new document.

There is also no need to create a new version of the same node for documents that come from a different subgroup of your sample – those differences will be handled by attributes, and it makes really good sense to have *everything* you know about a particular concept or category stored in the *same* node, regardless of context or subgroup. The query tools will allow you to see how that concept looks for different subgroups.

Practical issues in coding

Knowing about how to code in theory, and making it work effectively and efficiently for your project, can be two quite different things! What follows is a series of pointers to things you might need to consider, practical issues to be aware of, and additional hints to help you along the way. Many of these issues have come up regularly as questions or concerns of participants in workshops, or they are lessons from our experience in dealing with client projects.

What is happening as I code?

As you code, NVivo is indexing (tagging or adding flags to) the text (or other type of data) by storing references to the source document at the node. NVivo is *not* making a copy of the text at the node. In the process, you are connecting your ideas about the concepts in your study to the data about those concepts. All the text (or other content) you have been coding will be accessible from the nodes. The source file name will be shown for each fragment of data that appears in the node. In addition, any annotations, memos or other files linked to the content will be accessible along with the text. Reviewing the text stored at a node, therefore, will allow you to review the context of a passage as well as *all* the associated ideas linked to that text.

NVivo stores the same text reference once only at any node, so if you code the same passage twice at the same node, the text at the node is *not* doubled. Similarly, if you merge the contents of two or more nodes (or use the query tool to combine nodes) and the same passage was coded at more than one, it will appear once only in the merged node. If you edit coded text in the source document, those edits will also be reflected in the text retrieved through the node.

Do I code the question?

When a conversation is being held about a particular topic, there is often an exchange between the participant and the interviewer while on the same topic area, such that you will want to code more than one paragraph or speaking turn. When you do so, include the interviewer's intervening text as well as the participant's text, for methodological and practical reasons:

- It is helpful to know how the interviewer was prompting or responding to what the participant was saying. *And*
- Every time the coded passage is broken by a non-coded interviewer's turn, then the parts will be displayed as separate retrievals and will consequently break up the text when the node is being reviewed.[5]

Where the passage you are coding is not interrupted by the interviewer you might not need to include the question – unless it is needed to understand the participant's response (e.g., when interviewing someone who can't say more than 'yeah' or 'nah').

✓ Any time you are reviewing text for a node, you can return to the original source to see what prompted the coded passage.

Coding with analysis in view

Coding can be applied to a word, phrase, sentence, paragraph, long passage, or a whole document. The length of the passage to be coded is totally dependent on context and analytic purpose. You need to include a sufficient length of passage for the coded segment to 'make sense' when you retrieve it, but at the same time, avoid coding long, drawn-out, vaguely relevant passages that are going to clutter your reading when you review the text at the node. This is about balancing specificity and context. It helps, too, to have a basic understanding of how the

---

[5] It will also be counted as more than one passage.

reporting and query functions of the software work (see Chapter 11 for an overview of these). This is rather a 'big ask' at this stage, so here are guidelines to help with those areas most likely to create problems:

- Very precise coding of multiple small segments within the same broad passage at the *same* node will result in multiple retrievals rather than the single one that would result from coding the whole passage at the node. Not only does this make the retrievals hard to read, but it slows processing, because retrieving 200 passages is much more demanding on your computer processor than retrieving 50, even if there is less actual text retrieved.
- Sometimes, rather than coding all of a meaningful passage for all relevant nodes (slicing the data), researchers code each tiny component of the text at separate nodes (fracturing the data), and so connections between nodes become less clearly defined. Rather than being able to use AND (intersection) queries to find associations, the researcher has to rely on NEAR (proximity) queries. For NEAR queries, it is much more difficult to specify exactly what text should be retrieved, and it is more difficult to interpret the results as there is less guarantee the association is meaningful.
- If you find you want to add further coding immediately following the passage you just coded, select the text to ensure the passages overlap so the two are counted together as one when NVivo gives counts of coded passages for that node (unless, of course, you really do want it to be counted as two). Also, it will then show in *Detail View* for the node as a single retrieval.
- If you want to find whether experiences or emotions (or whatever) are related to particular contexts (e.g., where or when things are happening, or who is present), then be sure to code the passage with a node or nodes to identify that, as well as for whatever is happening there, *even if the context is not specifically mentioned in that part of the passage* (as long as it is clearly relevant). For example, coding the context as well as a strategy on the same passage will allow you to use a matrix coding query to discover patterns of association between strategies and contexts.
- Similarly, if you want to examine something like the ways people responded to issues, events, decisions, behaviours or other stimuli, ensure passages are coded for both the situation being described and their response to that. For example, if you are asking about the strategies counsellors adopt to deal with adolescent behavioural problems, then the description of a particular strategy, if used for a particular problem, is best coded for both problem and strategy, even if the text referring to the problem is in an earlier part of the passage. Doing so will ensure that strategies can be associated with the problems that prompted them (again, using a matrix coding query).

Flexibility and stability

Codes are organizing principles that are not set in stone. They are our own creations, in that we identify and select them ourselves. They are tools to think with. They can be expanded, changed, or scrapped altogether as our ideas develop through repeated interactions with the data. (Coffey & Atkinson, 1996: 32)

Expect your ideas about what is relevant or important to code to develop and possibly change. It is very easy to become beguiled by a thread of thinking you later realize is not important or relevant to the current project. At the same time, to set the parameters of what might be relevant early in the project and limit change thereafter is deadening. Beware 'shoving' data into a node – think about whether they actually fit. Check what's already coded there, and if you're not sure, create a new node; it can always be dropped or merged later if further data for it aren't forthcoming.

Your task is to balance flexibility in coding with purposefulness and consistency. Developing and keeping a sense of direction in what you are doing is also important, if you are ever going to finish!

✓ Use the description field in the node properties dialogue to record what a node is about, including perhaps a record of how the concept was developed. Alternatively, if the history is significant, record its development in a linked memo.

Coding also involves balancing between completeness and clutter, between coding the text exhaustively and coding just enough to ensure that each idea canvassed is adequately represented for analysis purposes. This balance will change as the project develops, with coding becoming more strategic. Unless there's a particular reason for picking up every possible mention of something, code only those texts which clearly illustrate what the node is about. Ask before coding: 'Why am I doing this?' Not everything in your data will be equally relevant (though it is hard to know what is or is not at the beginning).

You might also expect to engage in periodic rereading of earlier material, when the salience of particular texts becomes more obvious. In any case, it remains likely that you will create codes which you later drop, and you will occasionally miss relevant passages, but that should not be a major concern. Firstly, important ideas will be repeated throughout the data; secondly, it is likely you will pick up on missed instances of something as you review other nodes, or later as you are querying your data.

✓ Your coding system will stabilize after your first half-dozen or so sources, but it should nevertheless remain open and flexible, and coding should be interspersed with other activities (memo-writing, querying, modelling) in order to keep your thinking focused and fresh.

Managing the coding process

When coding was referred to as a 'head-wrecking' activity on the *qual-software* forum, Helen Marshall (2002) analysed the discussion to identify three ways in which coding could wreck your head. These were:

- through the miserable feelings (frustration, confusion, self-doubt) which can be generated during coding;
- because of the possibility of it going on interminably – there is always something else to be found – a sense that coding needs to continue until the task is completed, even if it appears that saturation has been reached; and
- because it might impact negatively on analysis – that researchers would focus too much on coding to the exclusion of imaginative, reflective thinking. The problem here was seen as coding rather than computing, however. Marshall quotes the initiator of the discussion as responding to suggestions of computers creating 'coding fetishism' with:

> ... I am a poor veteran of both methods and they both WRECK MY HEAD ... When I used paper and scissors I was constantly chasing scraps of paper – now I am a zombie in front of a confuser. (Marshall, 2002: 62)

From the responses given on the list, she then distilled a number of 'ground rules' for managing qualitative coding (2002: 69):

- Expect that your emotions will be involved, and that some of the emotions will be unpleasant.
- Respect this emotional involvement. Give yourself room to be reflexive, and plan your processes so that you can periodically step back and view your methods. Ask yourself how you will know when it is time to stop coding.
- Give yourself time and time out so that your imagination and unconscious can be involved in coding. ... Include the time for 'the scholarly walk' in your calculations of expense and progress rates in the planning stage.
- Set routines for coding that will minimise alienation and confusion. These routines should usually involve moving between putting chunks of data in conceptual boxes and thinking about what this means.
- Consider seriously the issue of limiting time spent coding.

Lyn Richards often commented that: 'If you've been coding for more than two hours without stopping to write a memo, you've lost the plot.' She recommended regularly stepping out of coding, not only to write memos, but also to monitor and review the nodes you have been making. Be free about making new nodes (rather than sweat over each one as you create it), but also periodically do a check to ensure the categories you are making are relevant, and occasionally review one or two in depth for a useful change of perspective on your data.

When do you stop?

If coding is becoming routine, with no new categories being developed and no new ideas being generated, it could be time to stop, or at least to review your sampling strategy. Of course, if your project is one in which it is essential to code all texts in order to thoroughly test hunches/hypotheses or because counting the frequency of occurrence of nodes (e.g., issues raised for a strati- fied sample) is part of the research strategy, you might need to persist until the task is completed. You will need to have worked with enough texts, suffi- ciently thoroughly, to be able to generate convincing answers to your ques- tions or to develop your explanatory theory. If you have additional data you want to just scan through, then scan or listen carefully to those to check if any include comments or images which extend or contradict the model or theory or explanation you have generated from the transcripts you have already ana- lysed. Alternatively, if you have additional data transcribed, then import them into a separate folder for uncoded documents, and use word frequency or text search queries to identify text that contains especially relevant terms from within those sources (see *Automating coding* in Chapter 5).

Checking reliability

Sometimes, researchers (especially students) are expected to have a second person code some of their data as a check on the 'reliability' of their coding, or to code some data a second time, as a check on consistency. These kinds of checks are sometimes seen as an indicator of the trustworthiness of the coding process, and as contributing to the validity of the conclusions drawn from the codes.

While we support the need to check for reasonable consistency across coders in team research, driven by their need to work towards a common goal (see Chapter 12), we question the value of doing so in a project with a solo investi- gator. Each person approaching the data will do so with their own goals and perspective, and so each will see and code differently. Coding is designed to support analysis – it is not an end in itself. What becomes important, then, is that the coder records the way he or she is thinking about the data, keeps track of decisions made, and builds a case supported by the data for the conclusions reached. The alternative is to train someone, like a machine, to apply the same codes to the same data – but all this proves is you can train someone, not that your codes are 'valid' or useful. What can be of value is to have someone else review your data and some of your coding for the purpose of having a discus- sion about what you are finding there, especially if you are new to the task of qualitative coding. As noted earlier, discussing a passage of text or other source in a group can open your mind to new possibilities and enrich your interpreta- tion of your sources.

Moving on

After working your way through a few sources, you will have built up quite a list of nodes. In the next chapter, we start by thinking about how these might be organized to better reflect the structure of your data, and to make your coding system and the coding process more manageable.

In the meantime, you might consider using the nodes you created in coding a source to visualize what you have learned from that source, as demonstrated in Chapter 10. If you haven't already, you might also find it helpful to write a brief case vignette (in the linked memo) or make a summary of what you learned from the source or case about the main issues of interest in your study.

5

Going on with coding

You've built up a list of nodes from coding your initial data sources, perhaps so many that they are becoming a bit 'unruly' and difficult to work with. It will have become obvious that some of the concepts you are working with are the same 'sort of thing': anger, frustration, satisfaction and enjoyment are all emotional responses, for example. Alternatively, some are clearly subcategories or dimensions of broader concepts – for example, timing, cost and location are all dimensions of the issue of accessibility of services. Organizing concepts into coding hierarchies (like branching trees) – creating a catalogue or taxonomy of your concepts – helps to clarify what your project is about and, later, to point to the patterns of association between them.

In this chapter:

- Learn how to best organize your nodes into a structure with categories and subcategories.
- Discover how to use auto coding tools for routine coding tasks.
- Decide if and when word- and text-searching features might assist coding.
- Take time out to review your coding system and text coded at your nodes.

Creating a structured coding system

Some nodes are easy to see as one of a larger group (*in the park* is one of several possible *locations*), and some you see as an instance of a more general concept (*conflict* is one of several *interpersonal issues*). It is natural to categorize and organize objects so that the category at the top of a hierarchy describes the contents, in general terms, of the items below. In NVivo, nodes can be structured in a branching tree system with categories, subcategories and subsubcategories. So, just as folders and subfolders in your computer filing system help you to organize your files, nodes in 'trees' will allow you to organize your categories into conceptual groups and subgroups.

Think about how a department store organizes its mail-order catalogue. There will be major sections dealing with clothing, kitchen, linen, entertainment, and so on. Within the clothing section, there will be subsections for shirts, dresses, pants, underclothes, shoes. This doesn't mean that the different shirts bear any particular relation to each other, or that this dress is worn with that dress – only that those in the same section are the same kind of thing, and it is useful for clarity and comparison to have them all located in the same place. A coding system that reflects this arrangement might look as shown in Figure 5.1. The shopper, after scanning the various sections, could then put together a coordinated outfit that comprises shirt, pants, jacket and shoes. Putting together the outfit is more like making theoretical connections between the nodes: these things go together to build a larger concept, they occur together, or they impact on each other in some way – these kinds of connections will be shown in another way.

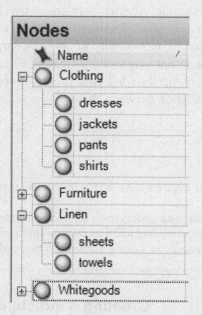

Figure 5.1   The shopping catalogue 'tree'

Hierarchical, branching systems are often the subject of debate, are open to revision, and may be more or less helpful, but the principles on which they are built remain consistent. Things in one group are more similar to each other, with respect to critical variables, than they are to things not in that group. In the world of Australian plants, *Eucalypts* will be classified separately from *Banksias* – not much argument there, but as botanists gained further knowledge and understanding of the development of *Casuarinas*, differences were perceived, and the categorization of some species was changed from *Casuarina* to *Allocasuarina*. If there is a change in the critical variables around which the system is built, the final categories might look different, *but the system, or taxonomy will have been constructed using the same principles.*

The coding system in NVivo works as a filing system or catalogue for nodes. And like other cataloguing or filing systems, the organization of nodes in trees can be the subject of debate, open to revision based on new understandings, and more or less helpful for particular purposes. Those coming to the same data from different perspectives or with different questions will be almost certain to create differently labelled and organized coding systems. The structure for your nodes will evolve over time, particularly when you engage in a period of review to check the consistency and salience of each one. Nevertheless, each will find a place with other concepts of that sort; there will be a logical fit.

✓ Later you will use sets, queries, relationship nodes and models to identify and record connections between concepts of different types, such as a combination of place, event and response. While these tools (described in later chapters) are independent of the coding system, having your nodes effectively organized as branches in a tree greatly facilitates their use.

Why bother sorting nodes into trees?

If the trees don't show the relationships (theoretical connections) between nodes, then why bother with them? What is the point of just listing things in groups? Using trees to create a structured organizing system for concepts brings a number of benefits:

- *Organization:* The hierarchies help to create order out of randomness or chaos. The logic of the system means you can find nodes and you can see where to put new nodes.
- *Conceptual clarity:* Organizing nodes helps to give meaning to them; sorting them into hierarchies prompts you to clarify your ideas, to identify common properties, see missing categories, and sort out categories that overlap. And you clearly see what kinds of things your project is dealing with – the structure of your data. The coding system, when established, will 'tell' your project (Richards, 2009). Indeed, when someone approaches Pat for assistance with a project, there are just two things she asks them to send ahead: their research question(s) and a list of nodes.
- *Prompt to code richly:* Well-organized trees provide a useful tool for ensuring the thoroughness of your coding, as you progress. You stop to code a passage because an interesting issue is raised in the data. Capture that, but before you leave the passage, run an eye over your coding structure as a quick visual prompt to see if there are other nodes that are relevant. Should you also note (code) who the key players are, what the context is, how people felt or otherwise responded? Do you need reminding to always code the outcome? Making sure that the text is coded at nodes across all relevant trees allows for more effective and more complete answers to queries.
- *Identifying patterns:* Identifying patterns of association between groups of nodes can make a significant contribution to an emergent analysis. If all events are sorted

together and all responses are in another tree, for example, it becomes a simple matter to set up a query to identify the overall pattern of which events give rise to what responses. Additionally, it will be possible to see what each of those responses might look like in relation to particular events, and so, for example, although it occurs for both, enjoyment is expressed differently depending on whether it is in response to working on a task or playing sport.

Building your coding structure

To create some conceptual order in your coding system ('point-and-click' instructions for moving nodes around follow):

- Start with a thinking-sorting process, to decide how the nodes might be arranged. When you ask yourself why you are interested in a particular category or concept (abstracting), ask yourself also what sort of thing this concept is about – what group it belongs to. Work through each of your nodes in this way, making organized lists of things (if you're struggling to do this, look for ideas in the section on *Kinds of trees*, below).

- ✓ Create a model which holds each of your nodes, so that you can push each around the screen to help sort them into groups of like things – see *Sorting concepts to build a hierarchical code system* in Chapter 10.
- ✓ 'Tell' your project to someone. Both the telling and the discussion will help you work out the main kinds of things you are dealing with.

- Decide on what might be top-level nodes in your *Nodes* area, as needed. You may already have some nodes which represent broad categories (e.g., emotions, attitudes, environmental issues) that will be suitable to keep in position as top-level nodes. Others will need to be created especially for the purpose of providing a structure, rather like coat-hangers for others to hang from – the way *Clothing, Furniture, Linen* and *Whitegoods* are in Figure 5.1.
- Rearrange your nodes by placing some under others, so that their arrangement makes sense for you. Not all nodes will immediately find a place in the system – that's OK. Some nodes may need to be copied into two trees because they embrace two ideas. In that case, they will also need renaming once they are in their new locations, to reflect each of the two aspects.
- Once you have a structure, check that it serves the main ideas you set out with, and the research questions you want to answer. If part of the structure doesn't fit, ask whether you need to modify the structure, or your original purpose and questions.

- ✓ When you create a new node now, you should be able to see where it will go.
- ✓ Experience teaches that projects typically don't have more than about ten trees, and that tree structures usually don't go more than two or three layers deep; it just isn't possible to subcategorize much more than that without starting to confuse what class of thing you are dealing with. There may be a large variation in the number of nodes within a tree, although if you get too many (say, 30+) at a single level in a tree, it could be time to group them into further branches, or to see if some of them could be merged.

Regard your coding structure as a work in progress. Some nodes may take longer to group (and may never be grouped), and others will move from one tree to another until you crystallize just what it is they are 'a kind of'. Some start out as a fairly random collection within a tree that you return to later, to sort into branches. We often have an *Issues* group (for things about which there might be debate for this topic) which later turns into issues of various types as we gradually realize that we are dealing, say, with structural issues, political issues, interpersonal issues, and so on; these are then set up as subgroups under the top-level node of issues, with the specific issues at a third level (or each main type of issue becomes a new tree).

Organizing and coding with nodes in trees in NVivo

Having decided on how your trees are going to be arranged, it is now time to start moving nodes around. Nodes can be moved, appended, merged and split as needed to create your structured coding system.

Rearranging nodes

! *Before* making drastic changes to your project, be sure to save it. Also, if you haven't done so recently, it would be a good idea to make a backup copy of it (**File > Manage > Copy Project**).[1]

✓ Use the strategies outlined above to help you think about how to rearrange and organize your nodes. Print a list of nodes to help (see Chapter 4), or play with arranging nodes in a model.

? The most common strategies we use are listed below. Go to **Help > Nodes > Reorder and refine nodes** for additional guidance.

Create a parent tree node (without coding)

▶ In *Navigation View*, select **Nodes**, then in *List View* (in the white space below any existing nodes): **Right-click > New Node**.

▶ Provide a name for the new node (and a description if you want).

(Continued)

---

[1] You can't decide to make a copy after you make changes without saving the changes first.

(Continued)

! If you have an existing node selected when you choose to create a New Node, the new node will be placed as a subnode (child) of the selected node.

Moving nodes into trees

▶ Nodes can be dragged into a tree, or from one tree to another. Click to select, then click and drag to the parent node.

▶ Alternatively, **Cut** (or **Copy**) and **Paste**.

Dragging or pasting a node places it as a subcategory of the node you drag to or paste to (so you are moving it to a new parent).

✓ To place an existing node at the top level, drag to or paste to **Nodes**.

✓ If dragging just seems to select everything in between, make sure you *first* select the node, *then* click on it to drag it.

Merging nodes

▶ If you have two nodes which are about the same thing, then **Cut** the first node (or **Copy** if you are anxious), select the second, **Right-click > Merge Into Selected Node**. Confirm whether you want all the ticked options to apply, then click on **OK**. This will place all coded passages from the first (source) node into the second (target) node (without creating duplicates).

✓ Open the Node Properties dialogue for the target node (**Ctrl+Shift+P**) to amend its description to indicate that another node has been merged with it, for example by adding 'includes [source node]'.

✓ You can select more than one source node at one time, to merge with a target node.

! Check the options carefully if the node you are merging has subnodes.

Coding when nodes are in trees

▶ To expand your list of nodes: Right-click in *List View* and select **Expand/ Collapse > Expand All Nodes**.

▶ To use drag-and-drop coding, remember to change the display to **Detail View > Right** (*View* ribbon), and ensure the text of your source cannot be edited. (If you are uncertain, right-click in the *Detail View* and see if Edit is illuminated. If it is, select it to turn it off.)

▶ To create a new node *within a tree* while you are working, right-click on the node you want it under, then select **New Node** (Figure 5.2). You will then have to drag selected text to the node (creating the node in this way does not code text at the same time).

✓ If you 'lose' a node because you can't remember which tree it is in, you can locate it using **Find** in the bar across the top of *List View*.

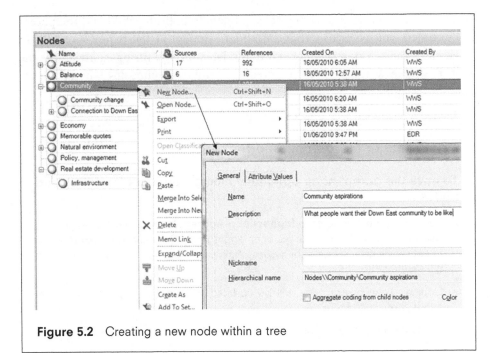

Figure 5.2 Creating a new node within a tree

Code text at the parent node also?

When you code at a child tree node (subcategory), the coding references are stored at that node only; the data are *not* automatically coded at the parent tree node (larger category) – nor, in general, would you want it to be. The parent node might be used to store general references to that concept, or as a temporary dumping spot for data still to be coded to more detailed child nodes. It may also serve as the location for a linked memo dealing with the general category of things that the tree (or branch) is about.

Occasionally there are situations, however, where you *do* want text to be coded at both broad and specific levels (parent and child) for the same concept. For example, in a project analysing injury types related to motor vehicle accidents, the team needed to consider injuries at both general and specific levels; thus *orthopaedic* was parent to various types of *fractures* and *dislocation*; *psychological* was parent to *anxiety* and *depression*, and so on. Most analyses in the injury study were conducted at the broader injury level, but the detail remained available if needed.

If you do want the text of the child nodes at a parent node also, you have two choices in NVivo, depending on whether you want the parent to constantly update for you, or whether you want to do it at a single point in time. Both solutions free you from dragging selected data to both the child and the parent node (unless you want *only* that particular segment at the parent as well). In most cases the solution that constantly updates for you (using aggregate) is the most desirable, as it also gives you greater flexibility in choosing when to aggregate or disaggregate.

Aggregate or merge child nodes?

To have the parent node optionally incorporate data from the child nodes

▶ Select the parent node, then **Right-click > Aggregate**. A tick next to Aggregate will indicate that the nodes have been aggregated. Selecting **Aggregate** again to untick will disaggregate the nodes, that is, will remove the copied data from the parent node.

✓ Coding at the parent node will be updated to reflect changes to coding at aggregated child nodes.

! Moving either the parent or the child nodes will alter what is aggregated.

To add current (but not future) data from the child node(s) into the parent

▶ Select the child nodes to be copied: drag across them, or use click–Shift+click from first to last, or use Ctrl+click to selectively choose from them.

▶ Copy them as a group: **Right-click > Copy**.

▶ Select the parent node, and merge: **Right-click > Merge Into Selected Node**.

! Consider very carefully whether you want to copy all the associated items (memos, see also links, relationships) when merging nodes with a parent node (e.g., if you repeat the copy and merge, you will duplicate the memos).

! Coding at the parent node will *not* be updated to reflect changes to coding at merged child nodes (including if you delete, remove coding from, or move a child node).

✓ If you repeat the merging process later in the project, because you have done further coding at the child nodes, that will not be a problem – data will continue to appear once only at the parent node, and meanwhile they will remain also at the child nodes.

Kinds of trees

It is perhaps surprising to new researchers that it is possible, ahead of time, to predict some of the trees you will use in your study. For research projects that deal with the lives and interactions of people, this is broadly possible because the kinds of labels that most appropriately become top-level nodes are typically quite general terms. This is not to say that you can't have more specific types of trees, nor to suggest that these are mandatory. It might be helpful to those struggling with the idea of trees, however, for us to indicate what kinds of things might become trees.

The kinds of trees we find turning up again and again in projects involving interviews or observations with people include (but are far from being limited to) selections from the following list. The list is far from exhaustive – it is provided simply as a stimulus for thinking. *Your* list will be influenced by both methodological approach and discipline, as well as by the substantive topic you are investigating. Remember, not all of these suggestions are going to turn up in one project.

- *People* or *actors* or *players referred to* – people, groups or organizations *to whom reference is made*. These are rarely, if ever, coded without coding also (on the same text) the reason for the reference to that person, organization or group. Depending on the project, these nodes might be very specific (*Dr Smith*), or simply role-based (*doctor, nurse, manager, partner, friend*).
- *Events* – things that happen at a point in time.
- *Actions* – things that are done at a point in time. These would often be coded also by an actor node (unless it is an action of the speaker).
- *Activities* – ongoing actions.
- *Context* – the settings in which actions, events, etc. occur. This may include branches to identify phases, stages, timing, location. (Note that if contextual factors apply to whole cases, attributes should be used rather than nodes.)
- *Strategies* – purposeful activity to achieve a goal or deal with an issue. In some projects this might be more specific, such as *coping strategies*.
- *Issues* – matters raised about which there might be some debate. Typically both 'sides' of the debate are included under a single node. If the number of these proliferates they might later be grouped into branches or separate top-level trees, as noted above.
- *Attitudes* – listing the nature of the attitude, rather than what the attitude is about or to (this gets coded separately).
- *Beliefs, ideological positions, frameworks* – intellectual positions (or discourses) which are evident in thinking and action.
- *Culture* – likely to have a number of branches, depending on the type of culture (organizational, societal, etc.) being considered.
- *Emotional responses* – feelings.
- *Personal characteristics* – descriptors applied to people.
- *Impact, outcomes* (e.g., facilitator/barrier, or help/hinder). In general there should not be further nodes under these, specifying particular facilitators or barriers; rather the same passage should also be coded with whatever is acting as the facilitator or barrier.[2]

---

[2] A matrix coding query will then quickly identify when something acted as either a facilitator or barrier.

As well as the types of nodes suggested above, which are all directed towards capturing the content of what people are talking about, there is at least one other area worth considering:

- *Narrative* – to pick up on the narrative features discussed in Chapter 4, such as turning points, omissions, contradictions, high (or low) emotion, climax, objectification, subjectivity, and types of speech.
- *Suggestions,* or *good quotes* – these nodes do not have nodes under them, but text coded at either of these nodes would always also be coded with another node; a coding query will then find suggestions (or good quotes) about topic X.

You might also keep an area for 'retired' nodes, in case you're too scared to throw them out. What all this points to is that you should experiment with and revise the coding system to suit your own purposes.

'Viral' coding systems

New researchers are often tempted to create more or less duplicate sets of nodes under some key comparative attributes of their sample, such as when they are dealing with two (or more) sites or subgroups of people. Other common mistakes are to include *Yes* and *No* as nodes under each of a long list of alternatives, or to code for various people repetitively under different actions. The consequence of doing so can be to create what has come to be known as a 'viral' coding system where subtrees keep repeating themselves throughout the system, to generate an ever-expanding set of nodes that rapidly becomes unmanageable. Such a system also inhibits your ability to look for interrelationships between nodes in your data and so to discover anything new, because you have predetermined exactly how you will see each component of your data (e.g., you will see encouragement only in terms of who provides it).

There are two rules that help keep you from creating a viral coding system:

1 *Each category or concept or theme (i.e., each node) should appear in one place only in the coding system.* If nodes are repeated throughout, it not only makes for many more nodes, but also for difficulty in putting together everything you know about any particular event or feeling or issue. When all you know about something is in one place, you can easily review it, and you can ask whatever question you like about it by using coding queries to look at it in relation to any other nodes or attributes.

2 *Keep attribute data that apply to whole cases (such as role or location) separate from the coding system* (see Chapter 3, and more detail in Chapter 6). Comparing data on the basis of different roles or locations or on the values of any other attribute is achieved with a straightforward matrix coding query or a framework matrix, whereas, if you use those values to divide up your coding system, you will not be able to see the comparisons as easily. Furthermore, if you build an attribute into the coding system, to compare that data in any other way becomes much more complicated.

In the *Environmental Change* data, for example, one could argue there is unnecessary duplication between the nodes *Real estate development* and *Economy\Fishing or aquaculture\Fishing industry decline\Due to tourism and development*. With all the data about real estate development in one node, and all the data about tourism in another, using a coding query to find co-occurrences of each of these (separately) with *Fishing or aquaculture* would show where and how real estate and tourism developments were impacting on the fishing industry. Similarly, the other sources of fishing decline could be dealt with at a higher level (combined with, or as new aspects of *Economy* or *Natural environment* where both their positive and their negative aspects could be included – perhaps not all aspects were in decline), and the whole *Fishing industry decline* subtree removed (after first 'permanently' merging all the data at the aggregated node for *Fishing industry decline* with *Decline*, and permanently coding the aggregated data already at *Fishing and aquaculture* before removing the subnodes). Figure 5.3 shows one possible alternative arrangement,[3] with the possibility remaining that the *Attitude* and *Viewed as* trees could also be rationalized, given the likely degree of overlap (this would need to be explored first).

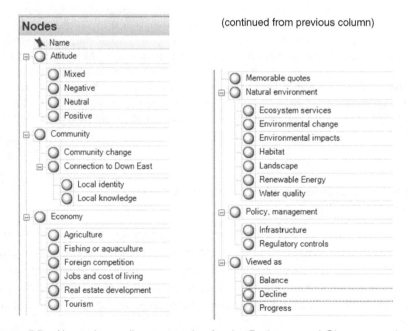

Figure 5.3 Alternative coding suggestion for the *Environmental Change* sample project

---

[3] Recognizing that there is no absolute right or wrong about coding structures!

✓ You will find some sample coding systems (from real projects) in a resource file on this book's companion website – these might provide you with further clarification or ideas. Additionally, if you already have a coding system which is in a tangle, with a repeating (viral) node system, you will find suggestions there for ways to sort out the mess.

Pat writes: When I started using software and working with some data about researchers' experiences, I created a node called motivation *and then created a series of nodes under that of things that had the effect of motivating academics to do research. That was fine until I began wondering what to do with these things if they were talked about in a different way – perhaps as part of the researcher's developmental experience, or simply as an outcome of their work, or even as a limitation. And so many of them reappeared in trees for development, and/or experience, and so on – and unfortunately not in neat repetitions. After some period of struggling with this cumbersome system, application of a flash of insight saw what had become a four-page list reduced to one: have one tree for* impact *(with subcategories of* stimulate, develop, maintain, reinforce, limit*), with separate trees for each of the kinds of things that had an impact, such as people, events, activities, and other trees for the contexts that moderated those things, and for the way people felt or otherwise responded. For any interesting segment of text, code at as many of these as were relevant, and always think about applying a code for* impact. *This would allow me to rapidly determine the impact of any person, event or activity, using a query, to see when it is that something stimulates research, and when it becomes a limitation, or to find all those things that might act as stimulants to motivate engagement in research. The difficulty I had then was that reorganization of the existing nodes was complicated by their varied usage. Coupled with a sense that a lot of what was in the data had been missed because of the way I had been coding it, I scrapped my first coding (and its attempted reorganization) and started again. Early intervention is a much better option!*

Using a set to create a metaconcept or to cluster nodes theoretically

It is likely that you can see associations or connections between nodes that belong in different trees. Sets are a great way of showing these nodes 'hang together' because they focus around a larger concept, or because they have a theoretical (e.g., causal) association. A set is simple to create or modify using the right-click menu (see *Using sets to manage data* in Chapter 6 if you are unsure).

In the *Researchers* project, Pat used a set to draw together selected nodes from the *personal qualities* tree and the *strategies* tree, to create a metaconcept of *purposeful commitment* (Figure 5.4). The set holds aliases for (or shortcuts to) the nodes, rather than the nodes themselves. This means that putting nodes into a set will not change the member nodes; nodes can be in more than one set; and when you add further coding to any member nodes in a set, the set will be updated as well. The practical advantages are: (a) an ability to choose to treat the set as a single item in a matrix coding query, or alternatively add its members separately; and (b) you can add a set (with or without its members) to a model. The principal advantage, however, is conceptual – the set acts as a reminder of the linkage between these nodes.

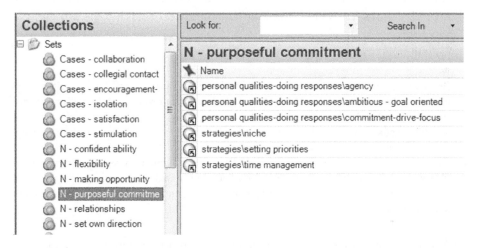

Figure 5.4   Using a set for a metaconcept

Keeping a record of changes in your journal

When you are making significant changes to your coding system, keeping a record of the changes you are making, and why you are making them, is particularly important. In the process of making decisions about your tree structure, you will be thinking seriously about the goals of your project, and the concerns it embraces. Keep a record of these thoughts in your project journal (located in the Memos folder) as they will assist when you come to writing up your project.

Additionally, you will find it valuable to export and store (dated) lists of nodes at various points during your project. These provide a historical archive which helps to chart the shifts in and progress of your thinking.

Automating routine coding

A significant amount of what any researcher does is routine work – the 'dogs-body' tasks which are boring but essential to the overall project. Licking stamps and sealing envelopes is one Pat remembers from her (pre-web) days of running surveys, along with the tedious but essential task of entering numeric codes into a spreadsheet. Fortunately for researchers and for the progress of research, technology has come to our aid and machines have taken over some of the drudgery.

Even in qualitative analysis, the researcher can automate some routine coding-related tasks, giving more time to concentrate on less mechanical, more interpretive work. In NVivo, the auto code and text search tools are ways to achieve this.

For example, use auto coding to:

- Delineate the contributions of each speaker in a focus group, meeting or multi-person interview, where speakers are identified by headings, in order to code each speaker's text to a case node.
- Identify cases, where each person's responses to one question have been saved, under their participant code, in one document.
- Code responses for topic or the question asked, when these are standardized throughout sources and identified by headings in the text.
- Delineate the components of regularly structured documents, such as submissions or annual reports.

The resulting nodes will give immediate access to, for example, all the answers to Question 3, all submissions about Eligibility Criteria, or everything that Jim said in the focus group. Critically, being able to do this depends on your having used consistently applied headings to identify the relevant sections in your sources (see Chapter 3). All passages of normal text to be coded at the same level should be preceded by the same heading style.

- ✓ Most features that support auto coding, particularly use of heading styles, are less cumbersome to add when you are preparing your documents, rather than after they are imported. Once the document has been imported and coded (so that you can't simply delete, fix and reimport), the option to use the Edit > Replace function within NVivo to modify the text and apply styles is available, but is less user-friendly than that in Word.
- ✓ If your project doesn't have particular features which readily support auto coding (e.g., there aren't regularly occurring topics or questions which can be identified by headings), don't force the issue by attempting to apply auto coding strategies. It will be more efficient and effective to code the text interactively.

Auto coding sources

▶ In *List View*, select the source or sources you wish to auto code (these should all be of the same general type). If you are auto coding surveys or question- naires, then select the whole set at once. If you are auto coding focus group transcripts, it will be safer to do them one at a time, and essential if your method of identifying different people is repeated in different groups.

▶ Hovering over the selected sources, **Right-click > Auto Code**.

▶ Select the **Paragraph Style** (i.e., the heading level)[4] identifying the text you wish to code, and indicate where you want the resulting nodes to be located. Note that you will need to create a parent node or folder to 'foster' or house the new nodes (Figure 5.5).

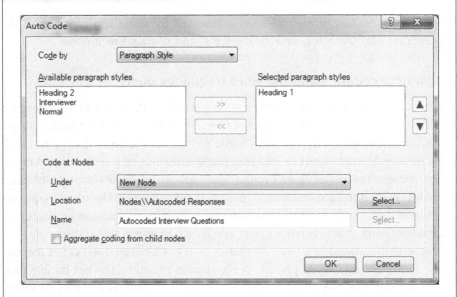

Figure 5.5 Setting up for auto coding

✓ For sources that have headings at different levels (e.g., Heading 1 for topics and Heading 2 for speakers), code for each heading level in separate passes.

(Continued)

---

[4] NVivo uses the term 'paragraph style' rather than 'heading level' to ensure recogni- tion of style names in other languages.

(Continued)

✓ If you code for multiple levels of headings at the same time, this will produce a node structure which replicates the structure of the sources. This is generally used only for structured survey responses.

✓ If you mess up, simply undo, or delete the nodes you have created and start again!

? Search Help for *Automatic coding in document sources* for additional information and examples.

Automating coding with word frequency and text search queries

Other coding tasks can also be semi-automated by using the capacity of the program for searching text and saving the found passages as a node.

Exploratory coding using the word frequency query

When hopeful students ask whether NVivo will find themes and analyse their data for them, it is a text-mining kind of function they are usually thinking about. The word frequency query will search selected text and identify the (up to 1,000) most frequently used words in that text, displaying finds as a summary list or tag cloud. Review the list of words found, then follow up by reviewing particular keywords in their immediate context, or save them as a node. The word frequency query will find words used in sometimes surprising ways and can be useful for exploratory work, but it is not a magic alternative to interactive coding.

You were introduced to a word frequency query in Chapter 1 as part of the tour of the *Environmental Change* project. While caution regarding the text-mining tools is well advised, this may be an appropriate strategy for generating ideas for follow up with other tools in the software (or other interpretive moves by the researcher). In some forms of conversation or discourse analysis, text-mining is used to identify passages suitable for detailed coding and analysis from within the larger body of text.

A word frequency query

▶ In *Navigation View* select **Queries**.

▶ In *List View*, **Right-click > New Query > Word Frequency**.

▶ For **Finding matches**, use **Exact** match, or **Including stemmed words**. The latter combines different forms of the same word into the same 'find', as shown in Figure 5.6.

▶ Set the options you want for where to search in the Word Frequency Query dialogue. Usually you will **Search in: Text**, but you might want to restrict where NVivo searches (**Of > Selected items** or **Items in Selected Folders**).

▶ Indicate how many finds you want displayed, and whether you want to set a minimum size for found words (usually 3 or 4 characters is a good minimum).

▶ NVivo will display the found words in order of frequency (Figure 5.6); you can change the sort order to alphabetical by clicking on **Word** in the header row.

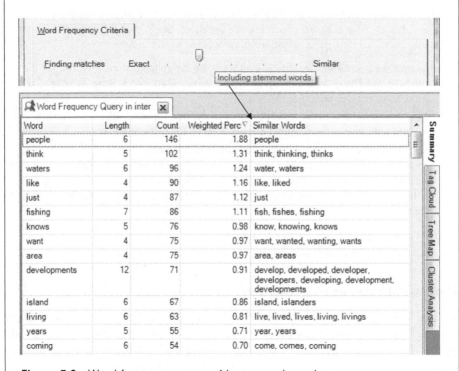

Figure 5.6 Word frequency query with stemmed words

You now have a number of options for viewing and working with the results from the word frequency query:

▶ Double-click a word of interest and view it in context. NVivo will provide 5 words either side as default; to see paragraphs, select one or more finds, then **Right-click > Coding Context > Broad**. Code relevant content to a node in your coding system as desired (not every find will be relevant). *Or*

▶ Save all the finds for a word as a node. Select the word from the list, **Right-click > Create As Node**, then **Select Location** (i.e., a folder or parent node for it), and

(Continued)

(Continued)

provide a **Name** for the new node.

✓ Incorporate something in the name or the description for the node to indicate it was created as a result of an automated search, rather than through interactive coding – at least until you have 'cleaned up' the finds recorded there.

Viewing and adjusting stop words

Stop words are not found as results when you run either a word frequency query or text search. These include such English words as 'any', 'the' and 'yours'. In most cases, these words would be regarded as 'clutter' in the results.

▶ Select the text search language and view the default list of stop words for that language in **File > Info > Project Properties > General > Stop Words**. Stop words are project-specific.

▶ Words can be added by typing them in to the list. Alternatively, in the results of a word frequency query, **Right-click > Add to Stop Words List**.

▶ To remove a word from the default list, select and **Delete**. We recommend that you remove conditional words like 'because' and 'if' as these can be useful to follow up and view in context. Also, to compare use, say, of 'the baby' with 'my baby' (in a text query), you will need to have removed 'the' and 'my' from the list, at least temporarily.

? Search Help for *Run a word frequency query*.

Coding with text search queries

The capacity to search through sources and identify passages where a particular word, phrase or a set of alternative words is used as a pointer to what is said about a topic unquestionably offers the hint of a 'quick fix' to coding, at least where an appropriate keyword can be identified. The conundrum is that searching text offers much more than that, but also much less.

Searching for 'sleeping' and 'feeding' quickly identified passages (paragraphs) relevant to those tasks in infant care, in the first stage of Katey De Gioia's (2003) study of the continuity of microcultural care behaviours between home and child care for culturally diverse families. Analysis of those passages then revealed that this was not so much an issue for the parents, but that what was more important was the quality of communication between the child-care centre staff and the families. This new direction then became the focus of further interviewing and analysis.

A text search query will find, in selected sources or in text coded at selected nodes, all instances of a specified word or phrase or set of alternative words, and save them as a node. As a strategy for locating, viewing and coding text, a text search can:

- Code passages based on repetitive features, such as speaker initials appearing at the beginning of a paragraph. It can, thereby, provide you with an alternative to auto coding based on headings, although it is much less convenient to run, so if you can auto code using headings, take that option in preference.
- Code topics, people, places or groups identified by a keyword, for example, in a tourism project, identifying passages (paragraphs) about regularly mentioned locations or environmental features.

✓ If you are using NVivo to analyse field notes, whether written in Word or NVivo, facilitate rapid coding of those notes by strategically placing routine keywords within the notes you write (or dictate). This would be particularly useful if you are in a situation where you are unable to code as you go.

As a tool for coding unstructured text, a text search can be less adequate, generating what we typically call 'quick and dirty' coding suitable primarily for exploration, or for use in an emergency. Attempting to use it for more than that, and particularly as a primary tool for interpretive coding, is bound to disappoint. As Lyn Richards (2009) noted, searching for words in the text is a mechanical process, so why should one expect it to help in interpretive research?

> Some years ago Pat led a team under pressure to complete a report for a large time-limited project in which some of the interview data had not been coded (Bazeley et al., 1996). They needed to write about mentoring of early career researchers, and they knew it had been specifically asked about in the later interviews. A search for the word 'mentor' pointed to all those passages where the question was asked or that otherwise dealt with this topic, and so it was easy then to review the original sources, to find what was said, and to confirm and elaborate what they already sensed were the issues around mentoring. However they found it was impossible to do the same thing with respect to the importance of building a niche area in research – there were no keywords to unlock that aspect of the texts. Similarly, if you try to run a search for time management, or even just 'time', in data from researchers (and probably from most people), you will find everything you didn't want to know about next time, first time, full time, at the time, whole time – and virtually nothing at all relevant to managing time.

The primary difference between a word frequency query and text search is that text search allows you to look for any word, even if it is not in the top 1,000, and it allows you to look for alternative words and for phrases instead of just solitary words. As with the word frequency query, you can also look for stemmed words and synonyms. Like most other queries in NVivo, text search allows you to choose between viewing a Preview Only of your results or placing them in a Results node in the database (see Chapter 11). You can specify how much context from the original document is returned along with the search term, or you can view the context of your finds after the search is complete (Figure 5.7). It is then up to you to review the passages found, and to determine which are actually useful and which are not. Those that you want to retain are best coded on into a new or existing node. You can then delete the original (temporary) results node.

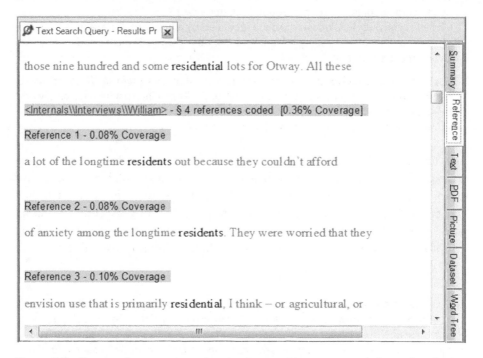

Figure 5.7 Results of a text query, showing keyword in context and alternative display options. Additional context is available from the right-click menu

---

Running a text search query

Setting up the query

▶ In *Navigation View* select **Queries**. In *List View*, **Right-click > New Query > Text Search**.

▶ ☑ **Add to project** and enter a **Name** for your query in the **General** tab. Note that this window does not determine your search criteria; it is simply a way of storing the query with a name you will recognize so you can run it again later if you wish.

▶ Move to the **Text Search Criteria** tab. Type the word or phrase you wish to search for into the dialogue.

o If you want an exact phrase, enclose it in double quotation marks.

o If you are using the stem of a word rather than a whole word (so as to find variations on it), add an asterisk (*) to the end of what you type; e.g., fish* will find fish, fished, fishing, fishermen, etc.[5] NVivo will not find partial words.

o To specify alternative words or phrases, type OR between them.

o The **Special** button to the right of the search window provides additional criteria (search Help for *Special characters and operators* for more information).

▶ Choose whether you wish to search in **Text**, or in **Text and Annotations**.

▶ Choose whether to search **All Sources**, or to limit your search to **Selected Items** (e.g., responses to a single question), or **Items in Selected Folders** (e.g., to exclude Memos).

▶ Move to the **Query Options** tab.

o In the Option drop-down menu, choose to Preview Only or to Create Results as New Node.

o If you choose to save as a node, the default location is the **Results** folder, and this is quite appropriate. The Results folder is a subfolder in *Navigation View* under **Queries**.

o **Name** the result node and provide a **Description** if you wish.

o Indicate whether you want to **Spread** the finds from the search: for now leave it as **None**. (Then, in true research mode, try it with **Broad Context** selected, and compare the difference!)

▶ Click **Run**. This will both save the query (if you selected Add to Project) and run it. The results of the query will open in *Detail View*. (Clicking **OK** will close the query without running it.)

✓ Whether you choose to spread the finds to broad context (usually paragraph) before you run the search or choose to see additional context afterwards will usually depend on how long your paragraphs are, and how repetitively the search term(s) are used within a paragraph. Experiment to see which works best for your data.

✓ To review or change the query, select it in *List View*, **Right-click > Query Properties**. To run it again, simply double-click it.

(Continued)

---

[5] This is a safer alternative than using the stemmed search options, if you want to ensure finding all variations on the word – it is based on character recognition whereas stemming is based on a dictionary. If you want to do more than find variations in the end of the word, then experiment with the various options provided on the **Finding matches** slider bar. Search Help for *Understand text match settings* for more information.

(Continued)

Viewing the results of your text search query

▶ By default, the results appear with a narrow coding context (5 words on either side).[6] Select the **Word Tree** tab for a more visual way of seeing your finds.

▶ To see more context in the Reference view, go to *Home* ribbon > **Select** > **Select All** (or **Ctrl+A**), then, hovering over the *Detail View*, **Right-click** > **Coding Context** > **Broad**. If you want to save any of the found text (and context), then select and code it in the normal way to a new or existing node in the Nodes area (you cannot add to or uncode the output in a results node).

✓ Text search will not find part words, symbols or punctuation, or stop words (as for word frequency query).

! Never send the results of a text search into an existing node unless you know exactly what the search is going to find, and you are sure you want all of those finds in that node.

What else can you do with word frequency and text searches?

Now you have seen what happens when you ask NVivo to search through your text for a word or phrase, let's look at some additional ways you might use this versatile tool. Here are some of them:

▶ You may have a node for *Community* and you want to know what concerns people have in this area. You can do a word frequency query in the node for *Community* (instead of on the original sources), and do additional coding based on the results.

▶ Use word frequency counts to compare the major concerns in published articles, or changes of emphasis in annual reports.

▶ If you become aware of a new issue or topic or your thinking about the project takes a new direction, quickly explore across your data to see if this is a viable area for deeper investigation.

▶ Similarly, in the course of working through a later document you might come upon a new concept or category that is 'nodeworthy', and then wonder whether it was there before, but you just hadn't seen it. Use text search to rapidly check whether such things were indeed mentioned earlier (such a search might be scoped to just the already coded documents).

▶ For routine or repetitive coding where there are clear pointers to what needs to be coded (such as initials at the start of a paragraph, or known keywords in the text, text search can provide a viable method of locating relevant passages. Results should be checked, however.

---

[6] If you wish to change the definition of *narrow* or *broad* context, you can do this by going to **File** > **Options** > **General** and clicking on the **Narrow** and **Broad** buttons.

Text searches depend, of course, on whether you can identify suitable keywords to 'get a handle' on the concepts or categories you are looking for – an issue which becomes even more pointed when you want to use text search as a tool for coding. That people don't necessarily use those keywords when talking or writing complicates the issue. For these reasons, while recognizing its usefulness in a range of situations, we strongly recommend that you do not rely on text search as a primary coding strategy for interpretive analysis.

Closeness and distance with coded data

At various stages throughout your project you will benefit from stepping back from the frenetic pace of working with your data to take stock of your progress, reflectively reviewing what you have already found, and exploring alternative and further possibilities in preparation for moving forward again. By now you have worked through a number of documents, you have started organizing your nodes into trees, and you are starting to see relationships between different data or coding items. Perhaps this is a good time for review and revival.

You see your data differently through nodes; as noted in Chapter 4, data in nodes are recontextualized in terms of the concept rather than the case (Richards, 2009). As you move more deeply into your data, don't be surprised if you find yourself spending as much time in your nodes and thinking about nodes as you spend in documents. Indeed, one of the signs of a maturing project is that the ideas being generated from your sources become more important than the sources themselves. In viewing your data through nodes, you will become aware of repeated ideas that are central to the experiences, events, and stories people tell (Coffey & Atkinson, 1996). You will see data linked by concepts and associations – and you will note discrepancies and misfits. You will find you want to reshape some nodes, to look at others in combination, and to explore responses that don't quite fit.

In NVivo, there are several strategies you might adopt as you review your nodes.

Seeing the whole (nodes in overview)

As suggested earlier, nodes 'tell' a project.

▶ Export or print a list of your nodes, as described in Chapter 4 (**Right-click** in *List View* then **Export > Export List** or **Print > Print List**). It helps to see, all at once, the range of concepts and categories you are working with, with their descriptions.

▶ List your nodes with a summary of how much content is at each for each type of source in your project: go to Reports, select Node Summary Report, and filter to include just your thematic nodes (click in the check box to access your choices).[7]

Does the range of nodes you created from your documents so far reflect the focus and range of questions your project is designed to answer? Are the categories and concepts embedded in your questions represented by nodes, and which nodes are being used more or less extensively for coding? Answering these questions from your list of nodes will assist you in determining whether you need to adjust your sampling strategies, the questions you are asking of your participants (or other data you are generating), or perhaps your strategies for handling the text. Or do you need to modify your research questions?

Node lists provide a historical archive of the development of your project. When you make a list of nodes, therefore, store the output (with its date) for review when you are writing your methodology, and to remind you of the development of your ideas as you worked towards your conclusions.

Seeing the parts (nodes in detail)

Viewing all the text stored at a node changes your perspective on the text. It is an exciting process to see your concepts come alive with data! Sometimes you simply want to check what is there to ensure coding consistency, but it is really beneficial to take time out occasionally from coding and working with documents to walk through some nodes, clarifying what they are about and reflecting on what they mean. You may find yourself surprised by what you find! This exercise also lays a necessary foundation for using nodes in queries, to answer your research questions.

▶ Open up and read the text stored at particular nodes, so you see the data in the context of the category, rather than the original source. Of course, wherever necessary, you can gain immediate access to the original source to see the data in its original context, perhaps to explore why this segment seems to be a little different from others.
▶ Refine the content of a node: recode what would fit better elsewhere; code on to new nodes as you see new possibilities; uncode what is irrelevant.
▶ When you complete your review, record or add to your description for the node in the Properties dialogue for the node, defining or summarizing it, noting its boundaries – what it includes, what is excluded.
▶ Where too many detailed or descriptive nodes were created, the exercise of writing a description for each helps you see repetitions and commonalities among them. Seek to justify each node, as a way of targeting nodes for merging, deleting or 'putting into storage'.

---

[7] See Chapter 11 for additional guidance on viewing and designing reports.

▶ Examine what other nodes were applied to data coded at the node you are reviewing (use the coding stripes to do so) – and record what that suggests about relationships between nodes in the node memo or project journal.

If your review of the node gives rise to interesting ideas, or is at all interpretive or abstract, make a linked node memo to record what made you see this as a category (see Chapter 4 for how), and write also about what other categories are linked to this one. Whereas a document memo stores background information and the ideas and thoughts generated by the particular document or case, a node memo is likely to contain a record of more conceptual thinking, insights from the way a concept appears in the text. The node memo holds the 'story' of the category, and will become invaluable in the analysis and writing-up phases of your project (Richards, 2009). For less important nodes, you might just record those thoughts in the project journal, but remember to reference them (with the source prompting the thought), and code them!

Don't print out the text of all your nodes! Although you are taking time out to go through each of your nodes, it is with a view to refining them, recording ideas, and thinking about how to use them in combination. Printed text is 'dead' data that allows you to do nothing more than descriptively summarize. Your purpose at this time is to analyse, involving you perhaps in returning to rethink what someone has said, perhaps in moving forward to develop the concept theoretically as you code into finer dimensions, and most certainly to ask questions about who thought this, when it was evidenced, what conditions encouraged it, and so on. For this you need interactive access to data at the node.

In a study of children's self-management of asthma for her PhD at the University of New South Wales, Jacqueline Tudball had a node for physical activity. In reviewing this node, she found that children might use physical activity in order to stay fit and healthy and so to prevent asthma attacks, or they might reduce physical activity as a way of managing asthma attacks when they occurred. This led her to develop two new nodes (under Focus) into which she then coded whether strategies adopted by children (physical activity, and also text coded for a range of other strategies) had a preventative or a management focus.

Printing the content of a node

If you really do need to export and/or print the content of a node, perhaps for another team member or a supervisor, or to review as you travel to work, there are two ways to do so.

Exporting or printing node content

From *List View*

▶ In *List View,* select the node(s) to be exported or printed. Right-click then **Export > Export Node** or **Print > Print Node**.

▶ Choose from the **Options** in the Export or Print dialogue. Unless you are choosing to export a node with video or audio content, you are most likely to export the Reference view.

▶ NVivo will print or save a separate file for each node.

Using a Report

▶ In *Navigation View*, select **Reports > List View > Coding Summary by Node Report**.

▶ Filter to select just the node(s) you need to print (first filter check box – you can probably ignore the rest).

▶ NVivo will report the text content of all nodes selected, in a single file.

▶ **Right-click** on the report to **Export Report Results** or **Print**.

Checking thoroughness of coding

By using a compound query to combine a text search with a simple coding query, you can check for instances where a word in the text might indicate a potentially relevant passage that has not already been coded to the appropriate node(s); for example, you can find all the times the word *enjoy* appears, where it has not already been coded at the node *enjoyment*. It is then up to you whether or not you code the additional material found.

Using compound query to check coding

▶ In *Navigation View*, select **Queries**. Right-click in *List View* > **New Query > Compound**.

▶ ☑ **Add to project** and enter a **Name** for your query in the **General** tab.

▶ Under **Compound Criteria**, for **Subquery 1**, click on **Criteria** to set up a text search for any keywords that might point to passages you have missed coding.

▶ Change the options for combining the queries to **AND NOT**.

▶ For **Subquery 2**, use the drop-down options to select **Coding Query**, then click on **Criteria** to bring up the Subquery Properties dialogue (Figure 5.8).

▶ To set up a **Simple** coding query, click on **Select** and then select the node you have been using to code those data. (If there is more than one node it might have been coded at, then click on the Advanced tab, and select for data **Coded at <u>Any</u> Selected Node**.)

▶ If you don't change the Query Options, NVivo will just show you the keywords found and you will then need to explore their context. Alternatively, choose to return finds with Narrow or Broad Context included.

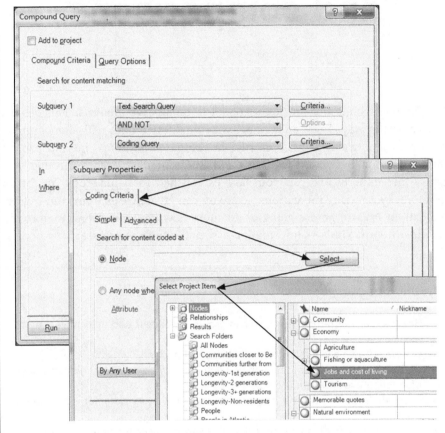

Figure 5.8   Checking coding with a compound query

Moving on

Once you have an established coding system, your focus can shift to different ways in which you might use that coding system to interrogate your data. For that to happen, however, we need to consider how setting up and using attributes will help – so that is the task we turn to now.

6

Cases, classifications, and comparisons

Comparative techniques are foundational to qualitative analysis. This chapter focuses on the ways you can connect your qualitative data with demographic, categorical and scaled values in order to compare subgroups in your project. The connection between these different kinds of data occurs through your cases – the units of analysis you have established for your study. We begin, therefore, by covering the various ways you can create cases from your qualitative data in NVivo, before going on to show how you can connect, store and use the different kinds of information associated with your cases.

In this chapter:

- See the many different ways you can create cases and add qualitative data to them.
- Consider how cases differ from other kinds of nodes.
- Discover what kind of information you can store with cases, and different ways of entering this into your project.
- Find out how to combine quantitative and qualitative data for comparative analyses.
- Consider the use of sets as an alternative way of grouping items.

Understanding case types and case nodes

Cases serve in NVivo as the units of analysis you will create from your data sources. We provided a range of examples of what cases in qualitative data might look like in Chapter 3, with the goal of helping you think through cases in your study. If you are still unsure about what a case is in your project, it would be a good idea to review that part of Chapter 3 before moving ahead with this chapter. We also explained there the many ways you can prepare data to make it easier to create cases in your database when you are ready to do so.

Cases in NVivo are stored as nodes. This allows for a lot of flexibility in the kinds of data that can be associated with the case. Because they are nodes, they can reference (i.e., code) one or more whole documents (or audio, video, photographs, etc.), parts of documents, or combinations of partial and entire documents. Data can be coded at them, or uncoded (removed) from them. Case nodes function in much the same way as any other nodes in that they are containers for qualitative data, but they differ from other nodes in two primary ways:

1 A case relates to a bounded, definable unit of analysis (e.g., a person, a place, a policy), rather than a concept (such as honour, access, anxiety).
2 Instead of just having qualitative data in them, case nodes differ from your other nodes because they also have demographic, categorical or scaled data – referred to as attributes – associated with them. The case node is a tool for holding together *everything* you know about a particular case.

In the majority of projects, you will have only one case type (e.g., individual participants), and any particular segment of data will be coded to only one case node. It is possible, however, to have more than one case type, reflecting either:

• different types/sources of data (e.g., *participants* for interviewees, and *authors* for literature), where any segment of data will still be coded to just one case node; or
• multiple levels of analysis, such as organizations and members, or schools, classes and individual students, so that the same text might be coded to more than one case node.

Each case type that you have will be associated with a unique classification involving different attributes and values from classifications associated with other case types. Because most projects have only one case type, they will also have only one classification system.

While we encouraged you to *think* about cases and attribute values early on (because it has implications for project design and data preparation), you might *create* them at any stage of the analysis. Some researchers prefer to create this system as part of the preliminary construction of the database; others want to wait until they better understand what they are doing or they are ready to start carrying out comparisons of subgroups. Depending on the research design, we sometimes recommend one over the other, but your personal preference or style is probably a good guide.

Making case nodes

To begin, if you haven't done so already:

▶ In *Navigation View*, right-click to make a new folder under **Nodes** for *Cases*. (Alternatively, call it *Participants* or *Units of Analysis* or whatever suits you. You can always change this name later.)

This will keep the case nodes out of the way of the nodes you have been using to code the thematic content of your sources.

Essentially, after that, case nodes representing cases can be created as you import sources. Alternatively, if you didn't create cases when you imported the sources (indeed, most people don't), they can be created:

- as cases, converted directly from your list of sources in *List View*;
- by coding groups of sources (selected in *List View*) to named nodes;
- by coding sections of a source, using auto coding, text search, or interactive coding.

We will use text-based sources in our examples to help you understand case creation. For additional instructions on creating cases from multimedia data, turn to Chapter 7, or if you have a dataset (mixed qualitative and quantitative data recorded in a spreadsheet), turn to Chapter 9 to see how you can use an auto coding wizard to make cases from each row of that data.

Making cases where each case comprises a single, whole source

Where participants are separately interviewed on one occasion only, single documents will be coded to separate cases. Similarly, if you have a single report only from each of several companies, then each company's case node will refer to just one, whole source. There are two simple methods for creating cases in these circumstances. You can either create them as you import the sources, or you can select from the list of already imported sources and have the program create a case node from each listed source with a couple of clicks of the mouse.

Creating case nodes from single sources

There are two alternative ways you can do this.

1. Create cases as you import sources

If you set up a folder for case nodes, then *as you import your sources* you can automatically create a case node for each and code the source to that case node at the same time (Figure 6.1).

▶ When you are importing using the Import Internals dialogue, click on the **More** button at the base of the dialogue to access additional options.

▶ Select the node folder where you want the case node to go (or a particular parent node within that if you have more than one case type, as in Figure 6.1; the new node will be placed *under* the selected node).

✓ When you create case nodes as you import, the nodes will be given the same name as the source, and each source will be assigned to its own node (you can do more than one at a time).

✓ If the case nodes already exist, your sources will be coded to those nodes *as long as the source files have exactly the same name as the node*.

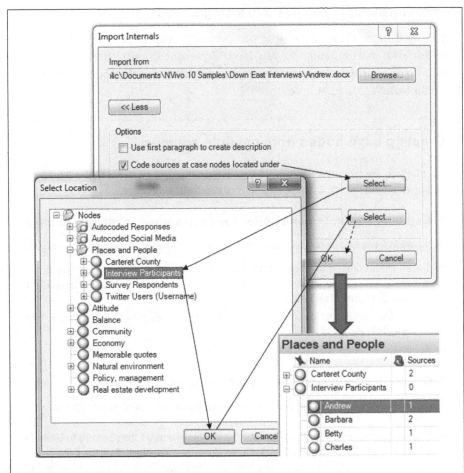

Figure 6.1 Automatically assigning a source to a case node when importing

! You will be asked to also assign a classification (explained later in this chapter) to the case nodes at the same time.

2. Create cases from imported sources

If you have just one source for each case:

▶ In *List View of* **Sources**, select all of the sources that you want to turn into cases. If you have multiple folders with sources in them, you'll need to work through each one separately, repeating the steps for the data in each folder.

▶ **Right-click** (on the sources you've selected) > **Create As > Create As Case Nodes**. Select your **Cases** folder (or a parent node or subfolder within it) as the location for them.

▶ Go to your case folder to see the cases you created. Double-click on a case to open it, and you will see that 100% of the content in the source has been coded to the case node.

Combining multiple sources into a single case

If you have more than one source per case (e.g., you have data collected over time for your participants, so you have three documents that represent one person), you will want to create a single case node for that person containing the data from all three sources.

Creating case nodes from multiple sources

Again, there are two alternative ways you can do this, depending on whether or not you have already made case nodes for the separate sources.

1. Combine separate case nodes for each source to make one case

If you made a case node for each source using either of the methods described above:

▶ Select all but one of the case nodes you want to combine into a single case. For instance, if you have *Barbara 1*, *Barbara 2*, and *Barbara 3,* select *Barbara 2* and *Barbara 3*. **Right-click > Cut**.

▶ Select the remaining case node (i.e., *Barbara 1*), **Right-click > Merge into Selected Node > OK**.

▶ Rename *Barbara 1* as *Barbara*.

2. Code multiple sources to a case node, from *List View*

If you imported your sources, but you have not made case nodes from them yet:

▶ Use Shift+click or Ctrl+click to select the various sources that belong to a single case, in *List View*. **Right-click > Code Sources At New/Existing Nodes >** select a location (folder or parent node) for the new (or existing) nodes and (if necessary) name the new node.

✓ If the sources are in separate folders, you will need to code from within each folder in separate steps.

▶ Double-click to open a case node, scroll down (or go to the Summary tab on the right-hand margin of the text), and you'll see all of the sources combined into the one case node.

Making cases from sections of a source

If your project contains a source that has more than one case in it, such as a focus group transcript or a multi-person interview, you have three options: to auto code based on the headings for each section (e.g., each speaking turn); to use text search on names or initials at the beginning of each paragraph; or to return to the strategy for coding you've been using all along such as dragging and dropping text into a case node.

Using headings to auto code

Headings are often used to differentiate speakers in a focus group. If each person's name in the transcript is assigned a heading level (we recommend Heading 2 for all speakers), and if the talk they contribute is transcribed underneath in normal text, you can use the auto code tool.

Preparing your document with heading styles to identify separate sections (for questions and/or speakers) was explained in Chapter 3. Use of the auto coding tool for coding based on heading styles was described in Chapter 5.

✓ When you use the auto code tool to make case nodes from speaker names, select the heading level you used for the speaker names, and make sure the resulting nodes are located in your Cases folder, a subfolder within it, or under a parent node in your Cases folder.

✓ If you do not have heading levels *and* your data have been imported and coded already, it probably isn't worth the trouble to type them in and format them at this stage, because it would take less time to code the data to case nodes using one of the other two methods. Alternatively, if you have speakers identified at the beginning of paragraphs, you might try using a complex Replace to create headings after you have imported and coded your sources (save a copy of your project first).

Using a text search to create case nodes

This strategy is appropriate to use if the documents you already imported (and coded) have speaker identifiers *entered in standardized ways* at the beginning of each paragraph of text. How to use a text search for coding also was described in Chapter 5. When using it to make cases, you will search for the exact name (or initials) used, spread the finds to broad context (so as to include what was said in the remainder of the paragraph), and create each result as a new node, in the Cases folder.

✓ When you use a text search for coding to case nodes, it is worth checking that passages were correctly assigned (a problem might occur, for example, if someone used a person's name in their conversation). The easiest way to do this is to run a matrix coding query (see later in this chapter for how), where the case nodes are cross-tabulated with themselves, that is, you select the same case nodes for both the rows and columns of the query set-up dialogue. The only finds from running the query should be in the diagonal. If you have finds in any other cells, check them out with coding stripes selected for Cases, and uncode as needed.

Interactive coding

To create case nodes step by step, simply create a node in the Cases folder for each person (just as you created thematic nodes in Chapter 4; or create as you import attribute values for the cases – described later in this chapter), and then use drag and drop (or any other coding strategy you learned in Chapter 4) to code the qualitative data into the node.

Understanding attributes, values, and classifications

Now that you have created case nodes and added the qualitative data to them, it's time to move on to the next phase in understanding NVivo's system for adding demographic, categorical or scaled values to the cases. Usually you will know all the values you need ahead of time, but some of them might become evident to you only after you start to code the data. Sometimes, too, you will create a new attribute as you are working through your data, to categorize your cases on a variable that has become important to your analysis.

Understanding attributes and values

Whether we like it or not, our position in society and our membership in groups influence the way we think and act, and the kinds of experiences we have. An interviewee's sex, class, nationality and religion may singly, or in combination, colour what he or she says in response to an interviewer's questions. Within an organization, it matters what role or position one has, and perhaps how much education or training, or how many years of experience. And at a personal level, attitudes, behaviours or experiences may relate to one's work history, education, family responsibilities or health. To record these kinds of demographic variables in a project becomes important, therefore, so that their impact can be assessed.

In NVivo, the particular values one has on each of these (e.g., Education = secondary) are referred to as the attribute values of a case (see Figure 6.2).

- If you are accustomed to working with statistics, you would think of *Sex* (or *Gender*) as a variable, and *male* and *female* as the possible values for this variable.

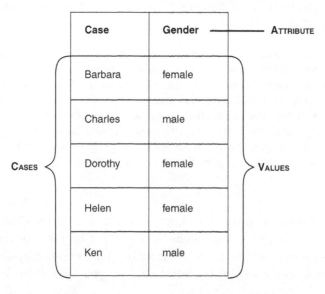

Figure 6.2   Cases, attributes and values

- In NVivo, we refer to attributes and values instead of variables and values.
- An attribute is the same thing as a variable.

Attributes record information known about a case, whether it is specifically mentioned in the course of conversation; collected purposefully with a check list or through a survey; 'given' by virtue of their location; or perhaps contained within archival records. While attributes are routinely used to record demographic data, you can use them also to record any of the following types of data:

- categorized responses to fixed-alternative questions such as those found in surveys – for example, 'often', 'sometimes' or 'never', in response to a structured question about experience of harassment;
- categorical data you might generate in the course of analysing your data – for example, whether the interviewee who is caring for her mother did or did not mention getting help from other family;
- scaled responses on instruments designed to measure attitudes or experience – for example, a visual analogue scale measuring level of pain experienced, level of attachment to community, or a score from a standardized inventory;
- characteristics of a site or organization, where sites or organizations (rather than people) are cases.

Having attributes attached to cases makes them especially useful in an NVivo project as a tool for comparing subgroups and for filtering data. For example, you might want to compare the opinions or the experience of males and females, of leaders and followers, of locals and new residents, and so on. If you recorded these kinds of attributes with the cases, then the comparison becomes a straightforward task using NVivo's query processes or visualization tools. Similarly, you can use the values of an attribute to filter cases. This would allow you to (a) run a query only on data from females; or (b) to find out whether opinions on real estate development are associated with attitudes to the natural environment, filtered for locals; and (c) then compare the result with a similar query, filtered for new residents.

When you attach an attribute to a case, as we indicated earlier in Chapter 3, you flag the entire swath of data within the case with the characteristic of being *female* or *male* (or the values of the attribute you're attaching). This is what allows you to compare what females say about *tourism*, or *trust*, or *loyalty* with what males say about those things.

Creating case nodes and adding attribute values to the cases has several consequences:

- Attributes apply to *all* of the data in a case – they cannot be added to part of a case.[1]
- Any further data added to the case node will automatically acquire the attributes of the case.

---

[1] This means if you want to add values to only one of three documents within a case – such as whether it was the first, second or third interview – this will need to be done by creating a set of documents with that characteristic (explained later in this chapter). Another alternative (which we are less inclined to recommend) is to add source attributes to your system and assign these values directly to your sources.

- Any coding you apply to passages within a source (e.g., *trust, love, honour*) intersects with any case-level coding (e.g., *Barbara, Charles, Dorothy*) and thereby with the attribute values on that case.

For now, the point is that once you create cases, you'll be able to add attribute values to these cases with the long-term goal of sorting the cases, and the data stored at them, by attribute values. In the discussion above, we were using the example of people as cases (and comparing attribute values such as male and female), but keep in mind that your cases might be policies, groups, sites, or critical incidents; the types of cases you study and the kinds of attributes you associate with them are entirely up to you.

Understanding classifications

We suggested, above, that you might have more than one *type* of case within a particular project (e.g., schools, classes and pupils as three case types in one project; sites and individuals as two in another; or people and artefacts in yet another). Each of these case types will usually require different attributes. NVivo's classification system is what makes it possible to attach unique attributes to different types of cases.

Thus, a *Person* might have attributes of *gender* and *age*; *Organization* might have an attribute of *funding source* and *Policy* might have an attribute of *ratification date*. *Gender* will never apply to *Organization* or *Policy*, nor ratification date to *Persons*. *Person, Organization* and *Policy* are examples of classifications that you might have in NVivo. Figure 6.3 presents a structural summary of how this would work for these example classifications.

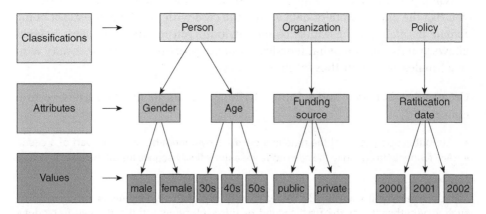

Figure 6.3   The structure of classifications, attributes and values

Values are always associated with attributes. Attributes are associated with classifications. So, to be able to create a location in the database where you can store the possible value of *female*, you create a classification first, and then an attribute, with values. If you have more than one case type in your project, you might find it helpful to plan out what your classification and attribute system might look like by creating a diagram like the one in Figure 6.3 on paper, or in the NVivo modeller.

Creating classifications, attributes, and values

Now that your case nodes are set up, we'll walk you through the steps for creating a classification system with attributes and values, so you will then be able to compare subgroups in your sample. You have three alternative ways to create the system:

- Step by step inside the software – probably the best way to start if you are new to the software. Also, you will use this method if you need to infer attribute values from within your sources while you are coding their thematic content.
- Import an Excel file with all of the data – a useful and efficient way to do it if: (a) you already have the data in Excel; (b) you have a large number of cases and/or attributes (e.g., more than 20 cases and more than five attributes); or (c) you are bringing in data from a statistical program.
- Using a dataset comprising responses to a combination of categorical and open-ended questions – to be covered in Chapter 9.

✓ Even if you intend to use Excel, it might be helpful for you to follow the step-by-step process for a few sources first, so you understand the various components of the database.

Create a new classification

▶ In *Navigation View* for Classifications, select Node Classifications.[2]
▶ In *List View* > **Right-click** (in the empty space) > **New Classification**.
▶ Name your new classification, and select **OK**.

✓ There are default options to create *Organization* and/or *Person* as classifications. These could get you started, but are unlikely to contain just the attributes you need, so you might as well do it yourself!

---

[2] Source classifications are used to store general information about your sources, such as interview date, interviewer, and location of interview. They are not used to hold case information.

Planning for attributes and values

When you are planning what attributes and values to create, remember the whole point of creating attributes is to group cases for comparison, so if everyone, or nearly everyone, has a different value on a particular attribute, then that attribute is not going to be useful for analysis and there's not much point in recording it. This is often an issue, for example, with attributes like age, especially if you've collected precise birthdates, or with years of service. You'll need to categorize these into a few groups to make them useful. Make decisions like these on the basis of what is likely to be most relevant to your research questions and based on what you know about developmental (or other) stages in your topic area. If you have the original data, you can always change these ranges or add another attribute later with different ranges or groupings. Similarly, there is not much point in recording an attribute for which almost everyone has the same value – again, it will not be useful as a basis for comparison and you will probably be well aware of the one or two cases that are different in this regard, should they also turn out to differ in some more qualitative way as well.

The other major planning issue is that, as for any data of this type, only one value per attribute can be applied to a particular case. If a case fits two categories (e.g., Fred has two different jobs) then you have three options:

1 Record the most relevant or important value for that person and ignore the secondary one.
2 Create all possible combinations of values under the attribute (e.g., *counsellor, coach, teacher, counsellor/coach, teacher/coach, counsellor/teacher and counsellor/coach/teacher*). However, you should only do this if you are likely to have more than one case with the same combination because your goal is to compare subgroups.
3 Abandon your attribute for *occupation* (with values of *counsellor, coach, teacher,* etc.) and create new attributes based on each value, e.g., have an attribute called *counsellor* and then use *yes* and *no* as possible values. This creates many more attributes and becomes extremely cumbersome if you have more than a few options.

Create attributes and values

▶ In *List View* of **Node Classifications > Right-click** on the classification you created earlier > **New Attribute**.

▶ Provide a **Name** for your new attribute and determine the attribute **Type** (Figure 6.4).

✓ Most attributes will be **Text**, as that is any combination of letters and numbers. If the attribute comprises numeric values only, then choose **Integer** (whole numbers) or **Decimal** to ensure that they can be correctly sorted. **Date** values can be entered in local format with day, month and year, so if you want to record years only, then use **Integer**, and if you want just month/year use the date format with the same day (e.g., 01) for each month. A **Boolean** attribute can assume two values only (e.g., Yes, No; True, False). If you are uncertain which type to select, choose Text because this type will accommodate any combination of alphanumeric characters.

✓ While age might be recorded as integers (numbers), age expressed in ranges (e.g., 0–4, 5–9, 10–14; or 20s, 30s, 40s) is a text attribute. The same applies to years of service or any similar variable.

! The most common error we see when people are creating attributes is that they use what should be a value label to name the attribute as a whole, e.g., they call the attribute Male, instead of Gender (or Sex). Then they are limited to using yes/no values, and their use of the attribute for comparisons becomes more cumbersome.

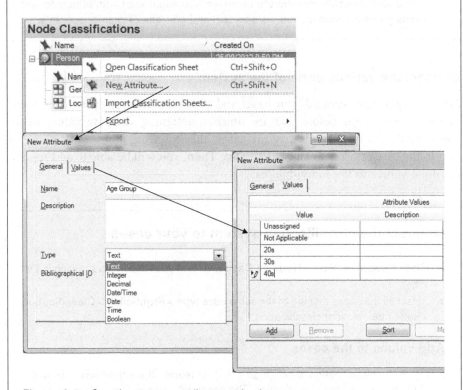

Figure 6.4 Creating a new attribute and values

▶ Select the tab for **Values**.

▶ Use the **Add** button on the bottom left to create new rows so you can type in the values for your attribute (Figure 6.4). When you are finished, click on **OK**.

(Continued)

(Continued)

✓ You will see two values already listed. These are assumed to be valid options for any attribute and they cannot be removed. The default value is set at *Unassigned*, and in general you should leave this as the default.

✓ You cannot have an empty row in this table, so if you accidentally create one, select the empty row > Remove.

✓ If you find you want to add another value later, or change the order in which the values have been entered, it will not be a problem – you can come back to this screen at any time.

✓ Regardless of the timing of your management of classifications, attributes and values, or the number of times you may import a classification sheet, NVivo creates a single aggregated table for each classification, with the columns initially sorted alphabetically by attribute name, so you might start with attributes and values you are confident you want to use, and add others later if necessary.

Connect the various parts of the system

Now that you have created your cases and your classification system, there are just two more steps before you are finished assigning attribute values to the cases. First, you need to classify the cases; this connects the classification system to the cases stored in your case nodes. Then, you will be able to add specific attribute values to the individual cases.

Connect the classification system to your cases

▶ Go to *Navigation View* > **Nodes** > **Cases**, so that your cases are showing in *List View*.

▶ Select all the cases that are of the same case type > **Right-click** > **Classification** > select the relevant classification.

Add values to the cases

▶ Open the classification sheet (Figure 6.5): in **Node Classifications** > **Double-click** on the relevant classification. The sheet will open in *Detail View*, with your case nodes in the rows, and the attributes you have created as the columns. Currently all the values will be listed as *Unassigned*.

▶ Click in a cell, and select an appropriate value from the drop-down list for that cell.

▶ If you wish to create a new value 'on the run', double-click in the cell and over-type *Unassigned* with your new value. The new value will be added to your list and made available for other cases with the same classification.

✓ Rows and columns in the classification sheet cannot be deleted. You need to go to the actual node in the *List View* of Nodes (for rows) or the actual attribute in the *List View* of Classifications (for columns) to delete them. Alternatively, you can simply 'declassify' a node by selecting it, **Right-click > Classification > No Classification**. (Neither of these steps removes the source or other coding you might have applied to it.)

	C : Community ▽	D : Gender ▽	E : Generation... ▽	F : Education ... ▽	G : Income Ti... ▽	H
1 : Barbara	Bettie	Female	2	Completed under	yes	a
2 : Betty	Straits	Female	3 or more	Unassigned ▼	Unassigned	U
3 : Charles	Atlantic	Male	Unassigned ▲		Unassigned	U
4 : Daniel	Davis	Male	Not Applicable / Completed high school		Unassigned	U
5 : Dorothy	Williston	Female	Some trade school/community college ≡		Unassigned	U
6 : Helen	Otway	Female	Some undergraduate college		Unassigned	U
7 : James	Marshallberg	Male	Completed trade school/community college / Completed undergraduate college		no, but was	tc
8 : Ken	Cedar Island	Male	Some graduate school ▼		Unassigned	U
9 : Margaret	Davis	Female	3 or more	Unassigned	Unassigned	U
10 : Maria	Davis	Female	1	Unassigned	Unassigned	U
11 : Mary	Marshallberg	Female	3 or more	Unassigned	no, but was	a
12 : Patricia	Cedar Island	Female	3 or more	Unassigned	Unassigned	U
13 : Paul	Straits	Male	3 or more	Unassigned	Unassigned	U
14 : Richard	Cedar Island	Male	3 or more	Unassigned	Unassigned	U
15 : Robert	Harkers Island	Male	1	Completed under	no, never	a
16 : Susan	Harkers Island	Female	3 or more	Unassigned	Unassigned	U
17 : Thomas	Harkers Island	Male	1	Unassigned	Unassigned	U

🔵 Person ☒

Figure 6.5 Classification sheet with attribute values for interview participants

When you are done, check one or two of your cases to see that the values are added:

▶ Go to your **Cases** folder in **Nodes**. In *List View*, **Right-click** (on any case node) **> Node Properties > Attribute Values**.

✓ If you add or change values in this dialogue, the changes will be reflected in the classification sheet.

Create and apply classifications, attributes, and values using Excel

You can achieve all the steps outlined above by setting up a spreadsheet in Excel, and importing the information from the spreadsheet.[3]

---

[3] A classification sheet can also be imported from a text file (.txt) exported from another program. Search Help for *Import classification sheets*.

✓ You might want to do a pilot with a small number of columns and rows as a test before importing a large classification sheet.

Importing classifications, attributes, and values

Prepare the spreadsheet

▶ In the first cell (cell A1 – highlighted in Figure 6.6) enter the name for the classification.

▶ Enter attribute names in the first row of the table (do *not* use more than one row).

▶ List case names in the first column, *exactly as they appear in NVivo*.

▶ Enter values for each case in the cells below each attribute. Leave empty cells blank.

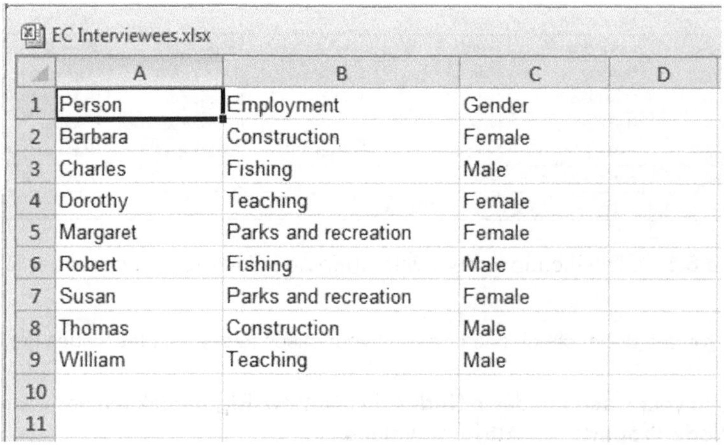

EC Interviewees.xlsx

	A	B	C	D
1	Person	Employment	Gender	
2	Barbara	Construction	Female	
3	Charles	Fishing	Male	
4	Dorothy	Teaching	Female	
5	Margaret	Parks and recreation	Female	
6	Robert	Fishing	Male	
7	Susan	Parks and recreation	Female	
8	Thomas	Construction	Male	
9	William	Teaching	Male	
10				
11				

Figure 6.6 Setting up a classification sheet in Excel

✓ Case information in the table can be in a different order from the case names in NVivo.

✓ Use either **names** or **hierarchical names**. When you import the Excel sheet into NVivo, you can choose between names and hierarchical names to match the format you use.

- ○ A **name** is simply the name of the case, such as *Barbara, Dorothy, Charles.*
- ○ A **hierarchical name** contains the name of the case in its specific location in NVivo, such as *Nodes\\Places and People\\Interview Participants\ Barbara.*

✓ If you have hierarchically structured cases under the same parent node and with the same classification in NVivo, and you want to import data for all subgroups at the same time, your spreadsheet will need to contain full hierarchical names. Alternatively (and probably more simply), use names only and import data for each subgroup separately.

✓ While SPSS and other statistical packages prefer you to use numeric codes for values (e.g., 1 for male), in NVivo it is better to use text labels, as these make more sense when you are reading output from the data. To export data from SPSS (or similar) for use in NVivo, **Save as** Excel 97 or later, choosing to save the **variable names** and **value labels**. Be selective about which variables you keep!

✓ Dates should be entered in accordance with your local settings.

✓ Close the sheet in Excel before you try to import it, and remember where you saved it.

! Excel has a habit of converting low number ranges (e.g., *1–3*) into dates, so it is safer to write them as *1 to 3*. Alternatively, re-format those cells as Text.

! Make sure you have something entered in the last (bottom-right) cell of your table (rearrange rows or columns if necessary), so that NVivo can figure where the datasheet ends.

! Make sure there are no whole blank rows or columns within your table.

! Also ensure there is no stray information below your table in the Excel sheet.

Importing the Excel sheet into NVivo

▶ In *List View* of **Node Classifications > Right-click > Import Classification Sheets**.

▶ **Step 1**: Use **Browse** to find the Excel file > **Open > Next**.

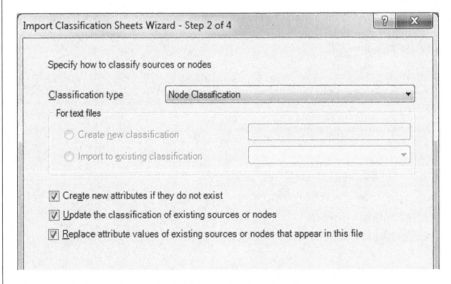

Figure 6.7 Importing a classification sheet – Step 2

(Continued)

(Continued)

▶ **Step 2** (Figure 6.7): Choose the correct **Classification type (Node Classification)**, and check against all three boxes.

○ **Create new attributes if they do not exist**. This tells NVivo that you want to create the attributes listed in the first row of your table.

○ **Update the classification of existing sources or nodes**. This will connect the case nodes listed in the table with the classification identified in cell A1 (if you haven't already).

○ **Replace attribute values of existing sources or nodes that appear in this file**. If you are adding to or correcting any existing attribute values, even if all values are Unassigned, this is required to overwrite the existing cells. Checking this box will never remove entire attributes from the system: it simply changes values in existing cells.

▶ Click **Next**.

▶ **Step 3** (Figure 6.8): Choose between the first two radio buttons to match the case name structure in your classification sheet (**As names** or **As hierarchical names**). If you choose **As names** then you also need to use the **Select** button to choose the exact location of these names in your node structure, e.g., **Nodes > Cases > Interviews**.

▶ Uncheck ☑ **Create as nodes if they do not exist** unless you are deliberately trying to create case nodes that don't already exist in the database. The danger is that you will accidentally create case nodes you do not want, especially if you are importing data from a large statistical file.

▶ Click **Next**.

▶ **Step 4**: Change the default options for dates, times and numbers if necessary to match your data.

▶ Click **Finish**.

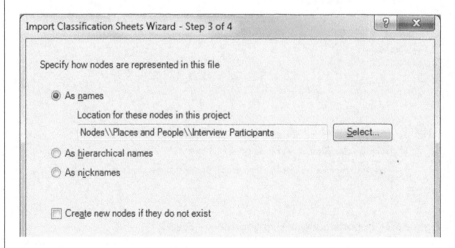

Figure 6.8　Importing a classification sheet – Step 3

✓ If you get a message saying NVivo couldn't parse your data, it is because you've missed one of the steps or tips or warnings outlined above regarding the placement of information in your data table (e.g., wrong name for classification in cell A1; no data in last cell, etc.).

✓ If your table only partially imports, check where it stopped importing for a clue about what caused the problem, e.g., an illegal character in a name, a blank column or row.

✓ Check for any rows (cases) in your classification sheet where all values are Unassigned. Is this because they were not entered in your Excel spreadsheet, or because you didn't write the name exactly as it is in NVivo, and so the values for that case did not import?

✓ If you make corrections inside NVivo (e.g., on reading the transcript for a case), be sure to make the same correction in your Excel sheet in case you have need to import it again.

Obtain a report of your attribute data

For later analyses, particularly for subgroup comparisons, it is useful to have a report that tells you how many cases there were with each of the values for your attributes (as in Figure 6.9). This will allow you to better assess the results you obtain when you run comparisons of subgroups. It makes a difference, for example, when 6 males and 6 females have talked about *trust*, to know that actually you had 12 males in your sample, but only 8 females.

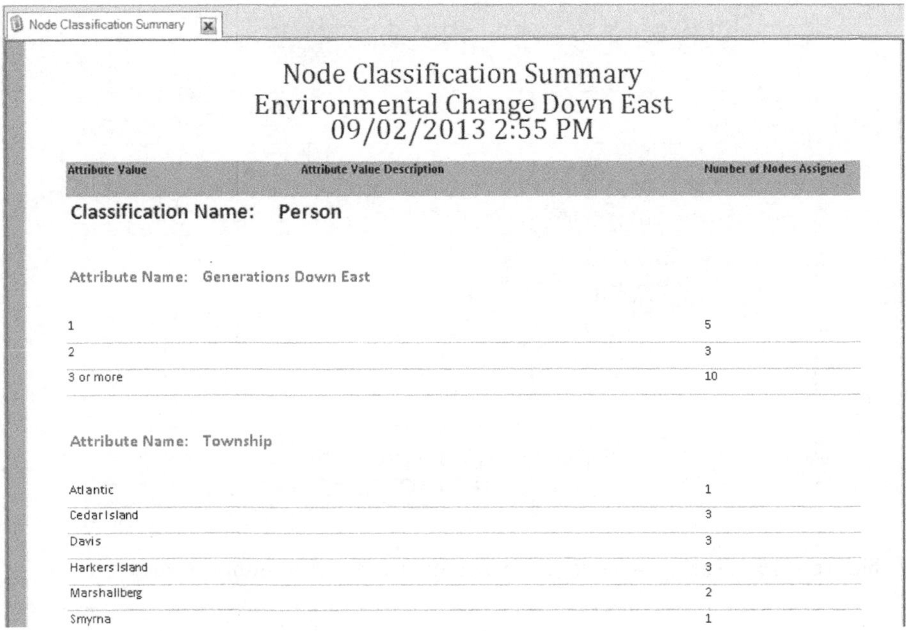

Figure 6.9 Report of cases with attribute values

Reporting attribute data for your cases

▶ In *Navigation View*, select **Reports** > *List View* > **Node Classification Summary Report**.
▶ **Filter Options**:

   ○ *If you have just one classification*, and you want a report of all attributes for all cases, then you do *not* need to filter the results. Do not check against any of the fields. Click on **OK**.
   ○ *If you have more than one classification*, or you want to limit your report in some other way, you *will* need to filter the results. Check the box for the field you want to modify, and click on **Select** to make your specific selections. Figure 6.10 shows selections made to get a report of some attributes only for interviewees with the classification of *Person* in the *Environmental Change* project. If you wanted all attributes for the selected cases, you would leave the third field unchecked (greyed out).

✓ If you're not sure what the field labels refer to (the second one in particular is a bit obscure), click on the **Select** button to see what you're offered as a choice.
✓ See Chapter 11 for additional view and design options for reports.

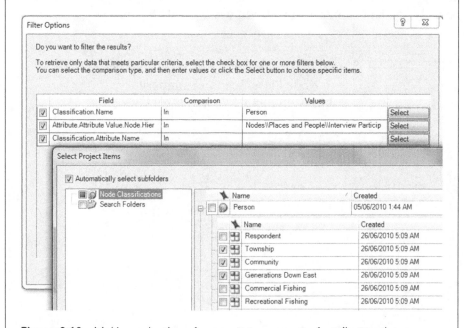

Figure 6.10   Making selections for a summary report of attribute values

Using attributes for comparison

In Chapter 4 you were introduced to the idea that you can use a coding query to find when the same data were coded at both of two nodes, such as when an emotion or experience was associated with a particular person or setting or time. Thus, you could find all the passages where any participant talked positively about real estate development, or, by changing the query, how much and in what ways real estate development was a feature of community change.

Attributes can be used similarly in a coding query, but to answer a somewhat different question. By using a combination of an attribute value and a node in a coding query, you can find just what was said *by* females rather than *about* females, or *by* newcomers to Down East, or *by* those over 40, about their experience of real estate development, or of community change.

But attribute values invite comparisons! When you're thinking about this kind of data, you want to directly *compare* what different demographic groups have said about an experience, an attitude, or an issue (or multiples thereof). Is it gendered? Influenced by length of residence? Impacted by level or type of experience? How do verbal reports of an experience match up with participants' numeric ratings of that experience? And for convenience, you want to make these comparisons in a single operation. So, although you can incorporate attribute information into a regular coding query, you will almost always use a matrix coding query when your query involves attributes. This produces a table in which project items (usually a node or multiple nodes) define the rows of the table, and the values of an attribute define the columns. Each cell then shows text that results from the combination of a particular node (or other item) with the value of an attribute – effectively, the table comprises a whole series of coding queries put together. These data are initially presented in tabular form with counts of passages in each cell, but with each cell able to be opened with a double-click to show the text resulting from the particular combination of node and attribute (Figure 6.11).

On the one hand, the numeric output from a matrix coding query provides a basis for comparative pattern analysis where it can be seen *how often* different groups report particular experiences or attitudes. Is one's gender associated with a different pattern of responses to a crisis situation? Do those with a different history of association with Down East have different ideas about some of the contentious issues in the area? On the other hand, comparison of the text for a particular node for those in different groups allows you to see *in what way* different groups report particular experiences, and so has the potential to reveal new (or previously unobserved) dimensions in those data, and potentially raise further questions about why this group was different from that. This strengthening of the comparative process is one of the more exciting outcomes of using these techniques.

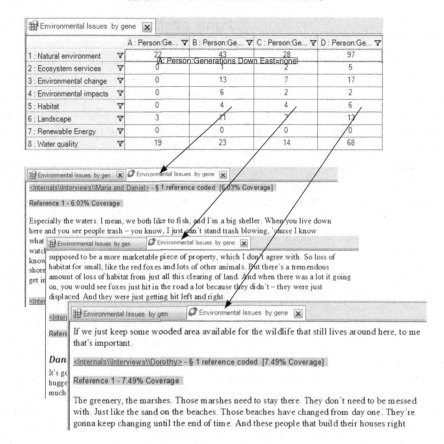

Figure 6.11   Using a matrix coding query to view data sorted by attribute values

We'll suggest using matrix coding queries for other kinds of analyses later. For now we'll just show you the bare bones of how to use it for comparative purposes with attributes.

Run a matrix coding query with attribute values

▶ Go to *Navigation View* > **Queries**. In *List View*, **Right-click > New Query > Matrix Coding**.

▶ Check ☑ **Add to Project** and provide a **Name** for the query. This will ensure that it is saved for repeated use or modification (it will be listed in **Queries** > *List View*).

▶ Go to **Matrix Coding Criteria > Rows** tab (Figure 6.12).

▶ Under **Define More Rows > Selected Items [1] > Select > Nodes [2]**.

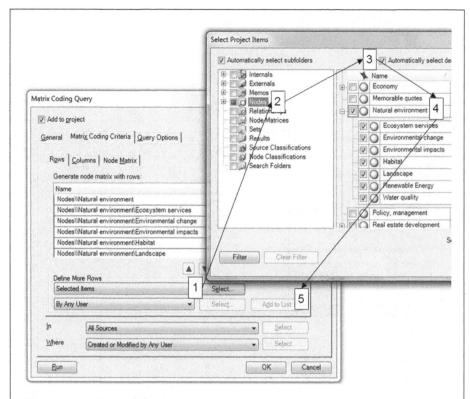

Figure 6.12 Selecting nodes for rows in a matrix query

▶ Check the boxes next to the nodes you want in your query **[4]** or **[3] > [4]**. **OK**.

▶ Click on **Add to List [5]** in the Matrix Coding Query dialogue.

▶ Go to **Matrix Coding Criteria** > **Columns tab** (Figure 6.13).

▶ Under **Define More Columns > Selected Items [1] > Select > Node Classifications [2]**.

▶ Expand **+** the desired classification **[3]**, and then expand **+** the desired attribute **[4]**. We recommend you do not select values from more than one attribute for any one matrix.

▶ Check the boxes next to the attribute values you want to include in your query **[5]**. **OK**.

▶ Click on **Add to List [6]** in the Matrix Coding Query dialogue.

▶ Optionally: alter the order in which the attributes are listed by selecting those you want to move, and clicking the up or down arrow below the list.

(Continued)

(Continued)

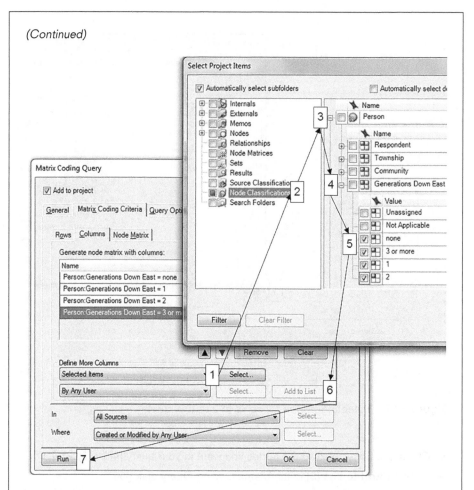

Figure 6.13 Selecting attributes for columns in a matrix query

▶ You can then safely click on **Run [7]** at this point, *for a basic query involving attributes*.

✓ The **Node Matrix** tab default is to **Search for content of rows AND of columns**, which is what you always want when attributes are involved. This means that for any particular cell, NVivo will find text that matches both the node for that row AND the attribute value for that column.

Your query results will open as a matrix in *Detail View* (appearing as was shown in Figure 6.11).

▶ Open any cell to see the associated text by double-clicking in the cell (you now have a tab open in *Detail View* for the cell content as well as for the matrix table).

▶ In *Detail View* > return to the tab for the **matrix table**.

You can change the way NVivo is counting the data. The numbers in the cells currently represent **Coding References** – the number of times a passage of text (or a clip of audio/video or a portion of a picture) was coded to this node from the identified subgroup in the column.

To obtain a raw count (not a rate) of the number of cases represented in each cell:

▶ **Right-click** anywhere in *Detail View* > **Cell Content** > **Nodes Coded** > **[Classification]**.

? For more information on the various counts and options that are available, search Help for *Work with the content of a node matrix*.

If you want to save the results of your matrix:

▶ **Right-click** anywhere in *Detail View* > **Store Query Results**, and work your way through the options for saving to the **Results** folder (this is located under **Queries** in *Navigation View*).

Reporting the results of a matrix coding query

Often you will do nothing more with a set of matrix results than review them on screen, and maybe make a few notes or jot some ideas for follow up. If the results warrant it, however, a table with the numeric results can be exported either to Excel or as a text file (**Right-click** > **Export Node Matrix**), or you can simply click in the top-left corner to select the table, copy, and paste into Word.

The process of obtaining a report of all text coded at all cells in the table that results from a matrix coding query is more complex and is not a strategy we recommend, although there are situations when you might need to show the text to a supervisor or colleague who is not using NVivo. Reporting text from a matrix query involves (1) pasting the resulting node matrix into the general Nodes area so that it becomes a branching, tree-style node, and (2) reporting the 'third level' nodes (each of which represents one cell of the table) from there, using a filtered Coding Summary by Node Report (see Chapter 11).

A more useful approach to working with the text from a matrix table is to copy and paste the NVivo results table you have produced into Word (or export to Excel if it is large), and then add a summary of cell contents into each cell of the table, to supplement the numbers already there (see Bazeley 2013, Chapter 9, for examples of summary tables and more on comparative analyses). Not only will a summary table further your analysis, but also a version of it can become a useful inclusion in a report. Making summaries in this way 'forces' you to deal with the results as they are generated, when they will mean most to you. It also saves a lot of time and paper, and avoids the risk of your being daunted by large volumes of results texts at a later stage.

In an earlier version of the Researchers project, an assessment of how females compared with males with regard to experiencing satisfaction through research did not reveal any noticeable differences in either the proportion talking about it (about half of each group) or in the way they talked about it. When scientists were compared with social scientists, however, a difference became apparent, although with some exceptions. When scientists expressed satisfaction, they were talking about having agency in what they did, whereas most social scientists referred to achieving a goal or task. Two social scientists went against the trend, as did one scientist, in their expression of agency – the former were both experimental psychologists, and the scientist's current writing was primarily about the history and biography of scientists. These exceptions, then, refined the notion of discipline to reflect the nature of the research undertaken, rather than a formal attribution. At the time, agency was contrasted with achievement as two potential sources of motivation for researchers (Bazeley, 2007). Further contemplation has led Pat to thinking that, in fact, both groups were talking about agency, but about different dimensions of agency: agency as taking (or having) control over a process, and agency as achieving a result (for self or others) through the process of research. The disciplinary trend was less clear when data from more scientists were added to the project, although the ideas prompted by this exercise remain of some value in the context of the project as a whole.

Using sets to manage data

Sources can be in more than one set. Apart from providing a visual reminder of some common feature, sets of sources are used primarily when setting up queries – but why bother with sets when you already have your sources in folders and coded as cases?

- Sets are more flexible than folders. Whereas a source can be in one folder only, a source can be included in multiple sets because the set comprises only shortcuts to the items in it (its members). As a result, sets containing some sources in common might be created for different purposes.
- Attributes on case nodes apply to all sources within a case. Sets can be used to differentiate sources within a case.[4]
- You have the option of treating sets as a single item when selected for rows or columns of a matrix coding query (the default, and the option you will almost always use) or you can choose to display the members of the set as multiple rows or columns (select this option in the Node Matrix tab when you are setting up your query). Selecting a folder of sources always results in a separate row or column being created for each of the sources from that folder.

---

[4] Source attributes can also be used for this purpose, although we find sets to be more flexible and useful than source attributes for setting up queries.

- Sets can be used to scope a query, that is, to limit the range of sources considered when running the query; for example, you might limit your query to your literature sources, or to your memos, or to a set of cases that have an attribute value in common (e.g., all males over 40).

Sets are particularly useful, therefore, as a basis for comparing groups of sources or groups of cases, especially where you have multiple sources for each case that differ in some consistent way, for example, to compare data from Time 1 interviews with data from Time 2 interviews. Similarly, if you want to compare what your literature says with what you have found in your own data (or interview data with focus group data), you simply create sets for the various groups of interest.

Creating sets of sources or nodes

Sets of sources or nodes (e.g., case nodes) can be created directly from both *Navigation* and *List Views*, or through using Advanced Find or Group Query.

Create a set of sources or cases

✓ Any kind of sources or nodes can be added to any set as members.

Create from *Navigation View*

▶ Select the folder of items to be created as a set. **Right-click > Create As Set**, and name the set. All items in the folder will be included. Others can be added later.

Create from *List View*

▶ In *List View* of any folder of Sources or Nodes, select one or more items and **Right-click > Create As Set**. Name the new set. Items can be members in more than one set.
▶ If the set already exists and you wish to add to it, select one or more additional items from any *List View* of sources or nodes, then **Right-click > Add to Set > [selected set]**.

Create sets of cases based on attributes (Advanced Find)

▶ In the Find bar immediately above *List View*, select **Advanced Find** (Figure 6.14). If you can't see your Find bar, go to the start of the **View** ribbon and check against ☑ **Find**.

(Continued)

(Continued)

| Look for: | ▾ | Search In | ▾ | interviews | Find Now | Clear | Advanced Find | x |

Figure 6.14 The Find bar, immediately above *List View*

If you are filtering cases on one attribute only:

▶ Go to the **Intermediate** tab. Choose to **Look for: Nodes**.
▶ Check against **Classified items where > Select**.
▶ Expand + the relevant classification and select the desired attribute. **OK**.
▶ Use the adjacent drop-down lists to identify which attribute values you wish to filter on, and in what way.
▶ Click on **Find Now**, and cases that match the criterion will be shown in *List View*. Select them to create as a set (so they remain available in Collections once you change the content of the *List View*).

To filter on more than one attribute at the same time (e.g., to find all males over 40):

▶ Go to the **Advanced** tab. Choose to **Look for: Nodes**.
▶ To **Define more criteria**: Under **Interaction**, choose **Attribute > [Selected attribute]**.
▶ Use the **Option** and **Value** drop-down lists to choose the criterion for the first attribute (Figure 6.15).
▶ Click **Add to List**. Repeat these steps as many times as needed (once for each criterion).

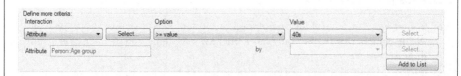

Figure 6.15 Defining criteria to select cases using Advanced Find

✓ The cases that will be found will meet *all* the specified criteria (there is no OR option).
✓ Although you might have a reason to make a set on the basis of an attribute (usually so you can set the scope for a query), don't try to make sets do the work of attributes – attributes have greater functionality and are more flexible in their use. So, if you can apply the value or characteristic or feature to *all* the data in a case, then you would use attributes of the case to do so, not sets.

Viewing a set

▶ To view any set you have created, go to *Navigation View* > **Collections** > Expand + **Sets**. Members of a selected set will show in *List View* as aliases (shortcuts).

✓ Deleting an item from a set will not delete the item, just the shortcut to it. If you open an item from a set and modify it, however, you are modifying the actual item.

? Search Help for *Advanced Find*, and for *Create and manage sets*.

Using a set to scope a matrix coding query

As well as placing a set as an item in the rows or columns of a matrix coding query, you have the option of using a set to scope a query – to limit the sources or nodes NVivo looks through when searching for data that meet the criteria in the rows and columns of the query.

Scoping a query to a set of sources and/or nodes

Near the bottom of the Matrix Coding Criteria tab, the default option is to search **In > All Sources** (see Figures 6.12 and 6.13). To restrict the scope of the query to a set:

▶ Select the drop-down arrow next to **All Sources > Selected Items > Select > Sets** folder (not the check box) > **[your set]** > **OK**.

You just changed the scope of the query to look only in your selected set, rather than all of your sources.[5]

✓ Whenever you alter the specifications for a query, it is wise to return to the General tab to rename the query (or change its description) to reflect these changes. If you change the name before going to Query Options, the changes will be reflected also in the name given to saved results from the query.

---

[5] If your scope is a set of cases, NVivo will search through and report from all of each of the sources that contain text relevant to each of those cases rather than specifically and separately at what is coded at each case node. For matrices based on AND (finding intersections of coding) this is not a problem, but it becomes a problem for any of the NEAR (in same scope) options when cases are part of a focus group, or comprise more than one source. Check your results carefully (e.g., by reviewing the coding density bar for cases, with stripes showing for the nodes selected in the query), and consider employing the alternative options described under cross-case analyses and/or theory-building in Chapter 11.

Overview

It is not unusual to need the same kind of information stored in a number of different ways within NVivo, so you can use it in different situations. At first this may seem confusing to the novice user, but as you gain experience with the management tools of the software, you will begin to appreciate the flexibility this provides.

Table 6.1 provides a summary overview of these different tools, how they function, when to use them, and how to apply them. An example of how they might be used in a study with complex sources of data is then provided. The application of folders, sets and cases, along with regular nodes, for scoping and filtering queries and models will be explored further in later chapters where you will start to use them regularly as tools for refining analyses.

Example: Managing a complex set of data

You are intensively studying the course of events over a period following a traumatic, life-changing event for a (necessarily small!) sample of people, who are defined as the cases for the study. You have data from multiple time periods and multiple sources available for each case. The question is how best to organize and manage the data so analysis within and across cases can be facilitated.

Your data sources comprise:

- *multiple interviews with each case, obtained at different time periods;*
- *notes from group meetings where multiple cases may have been present, with these notes comprising both your observations of the group as a whole, and contributions by particular cases;*
- *interviews with professionals who deal with individual cases of interest to you;*
- *interviews with caseworkers who are responsible for one or more cases who fall within your sample;*
- *interviews with family caregivers;*
- *notes from observations of each case interacting with his or her family;*
- *demographic data (age, gender, education, etc.) for each case; and*
- *measures of level of functioning for each case at the beginning and the end of the data collection period.*

Consider some management strategies which might be employed for such a situation. These are suggestions only; they are not prescriptive, and they will vary depending on the exact nature of the data and the questions to be asked of it.

(Continued)

Table 6.1 Folders, sets or cases: which should I use?

	Folders	Sets	Cases
Viewed in …	Sources	Collections	Nodes
How many can a single source be in?	One only	More than one	Usually in one only for any particular classification.
Primary purpose	Visual organization. Sorting and management of files.	To allow any combination of documents and/or nodes regardless of their location.	Identifying units of analysis. Locating attribute data about those units.
Additional purposes	Scoping a query. To rapidly include a number of documents as separate items in a matrix coding query.	Scoping a query. To treat multiple documents or nodes as a single (combined) data item in a matrix coding query.	Filtering in Find, for a query or a model. Within case analysis (setting as a scope). Across case analysis (as items in a matrix).
Scoping a query (identifying which data are to be searched)	Can select one or more folders	Can select one or more whole sets (as items within the Sets folder).	Can select one or more cases, folders of cases, or sets of cases based on filtering by attribute.
Included in a matrix coding query rows or columns as …	Member items	Single entity (usually). Option to display individual members in results.	Individual case nodes. Groups based on a combination of attribute values (i.e., as a set).
Special features	Right-click on selected folder to Create as Set.	Right-click on selected set to Create as Node.	

(Continued)

- *Do not create cases as you import the documents!*
- *Create a document folder for each type of data (individual interviews, group sources, notes from observations, etc.).*
- *Use sets to identify the category of person who was the source of the data (e.g., professionals, family members, caseworkers).*
- *Create a folder with case nodes for each of the target cases (the traumatized individual). Code all of the interviews for each case, and those of the professionals and family caregivers associated with them to his or her case node, also caseworker interviews if the caseworker deals only with that case.*
- *Create a classification for those cases (e.g., Cases), and assign it to each of the case nodes.*
- *Data from group meetings (if headings have been used to identify different speakers within the documents) can be auto coded to relevant case nodes. Interviews with caseworkers who covered multiple cases, or meetings where headings haven't been used consistently in the notes, will need to be interactively coded to relevant case nodes (this may not include all of it).*
- *If each document relates to one time period only, create sets for each time period, and add each document to a relevant time-period set. If documents generally include references to multiple time periods, create a node for time with subnodes for each time period, and code all material (whole or part documents) to a relevant node in that tree.*
- *Create a tree of nodes for various people to whom reference is made within the interviews (e.g., for when someone is talking about the caseworker, or a family member).*
- *Import the demographic data and other measures (e.g., of functional level) as attributes of the cases (as well as data for the traumatized individual, these could include some that describe the caregiver and caseworker who are part of the case).*

Folders, sets and individual case or thematic nodes can all be used for scoping a query. Attribute values can be used to filter cases to scope a query to a particular subcategory of cases. Case nodes, thematic nodes, sets and attributes can each be used within matrix queries to make comparisons or to identify patterns of association. A combination of matrix query and scoping will allow, say, an analysis of individual or grouped cases over time for a particular factor, or limitation of the analyses to include only the perspective of the cases themselves. The perspective of those involved with a case (e.g., a family member or case worker) can be viewed in relation to the characteristics of the case with whom they are involved.

Thus it would be possible, for example, to compare:

- *how particular cases changed over time with respect to their experience of anxiety, independence, and so on (save the set-up for a cases-by-time-periods query, and run it multiple times, changing the scope each time to each of a series of nodes);[6]*

- *the perspectives of different people involved with each case, with respect to behavioural issues, or potential for development;*
- *groups of cases based on, say, level of function in relation to behavioural issues, in the view of different people involved with those cases.*

The possibilities are determined by your questions, your imagination, and your application of the principles outlined above in setting up your data.

---

[6] Alternatively, save the result of the cases-by-time-periods query as a node tree, and intersect it with nodes representing feelings or actions, etc., to produce a three-way matrix.

7

Working with multimedia sources

Changes in the way we communicate, interact, and collect information through various media have brought with them a need to analyse such data in new ways. The emerging analytical approaches that are fuelled by and generate non-text data are pushing many researchers to rethink the way they inquire, analyse and disseminate findings. NVivo allows you to import and work with audio and video files, photographs, images and web pages, with all that they promise to the visual researcher. Because you can, however, is not always a reason why you should. We explain both the benefits, and the caveats, to working with non-text (multimedia) data.

In this chapter:

- Consider the way technology (especially the digitization of information) has changed our understanding and management of data.
- Start thinking about the benefits and challenges of using non-text data in your research.
- Prepare, import and transcribe (if relevant) pictures, audio, video and web pages.
- Link, annotate and code pictures, audio, and video.
- Install and use NCapture to collect web pages and YouTube videos.
- Export pictures, audio, video and web pages to open in Word or as html.

The promises and perils of non-text data

Increasingly, audiovisual data are being analysed in their own right, rather than simply as supplementary illustrative material, raising issues about the fidelity with which such data are represented, manipulated and reported in QDA software (Silver & Patashnick, 2011). The capacity of NVivo to allow you, as a researcher, to represent, manage, analyse and report non-text data offers both possibilities and limitations.

Why use pictures, audio, video or web pages as data?

Much current qualitative practice includes the collection of text or the transformation of data into text via field notes, audio or video transcripts, and other written sources. However, as Ochs (1979) described in her work on transcription as theory, the act of transcribing data (turning other forms of information into text) can carry with it some hidden assumptions. In her classic example, Ochs explains that when analysing the talk between adults and children, it is a common convention in her community of practice to place the text of the adults in the left-hand column of the page and the text of the children in the adjacent right-hand column of the page, with sequential turn-taking back and forth from left to right. This common convention may lead researchers to presume, more often than is warranted, that the adults are leading the conversation. In fact, as Ochs explains, in many instances the children lead the adults. This is one of the reasons why researchers may turn to audio or video data (independent of – or alongside – transcribed data): to be able to see or hear information that is unavailable, concealed, or unknowingly modified by the act of transcription.[1]

Another reason to turn to non-text data is that some research questions simply cannot be adequately investigated with text and require audio or video, pictures, or screen-captures from web pages. A study of sarcasm in executive meetings at a company's headquarters provides an example. To examine the use of this very specific form of humour in the management of power and position among executives, access to synchronized audio and/or video data allows for a far more intricate study owing to the ability to observe gestures (such as eye-rolling) as well as the audible inflections that are associated with sarcasm. Or, if you want to study the way movie marketing reifies notions of racism and sexism, consider a study of newspaper advertisements for action movies in the 1980s, where the images of hero, villain and victim are examined for their location in the advertisement and their associated demographic characteristics: the fair-skinned, would-be female victim on the bottom left-hand side of the image, the villainous, dark-skinned man tormenting her in the middle, and the heroic musculature of her white hero swooping in from above to save her. In a more contemporary vein, the capture of a carefully designed web page may be required to answer a question if you are examining, for instance, the way various political rivals are using internet marketing to create a brand that is distinct from that of their competitors.

---

[1] The camera angle, video duration, and audio-recorder sound quality (among many other aspects) also influence researcher perceptions of salient and irrelevant data. For our current purposes, however, the juxtaposition of text and non-text data will allow us to highlight the rationale for some of the methodological choices around these various data formats. We invite you to explore the rich terrain of scholarship in areas such as visual sociology for additional nuances.

As a third rationale for using these forms of data, some researchers claim that the handling of non-text data creates a more intimate relationship between the researcher and the subjects and thereby improves the rigour of the study. For example, Pink (2001) argues that the visual ethnographer who collects and investigates the sounds and images of her participants is invited more explicitly to empathize with their sensations. She acknowledges that while researchers may not be able to feel or experience the exact same things as the participants, seeing and hearing the data regularly may allow researchers to become more contextually aware of the physical and emotional realities of research participants.

Why not use audio, video, photographs or web pages?

Before moving on to the detail about how to import, manage and code such data, a few caveats are warranted about the allure of multimedia sources. There is no doubt that a vivid photograph, compelling sound bite, or graphic video clip can be used effectively to supplement textual information for the purposes of creating vignettes or presenting findings. The use of these types of media is fairly common, even when the primary data are in textual form, because photographs, audio and video stimulate our auditory and visual senses and in many ways help us to understand social settings. The issue you should address early on is whether non-text media should become an important data source, or simply an adjunct to text or a way to communicate findings. Most of the tools in NVivo, particularly those we describe in this chapter, are designed to do much more than package a few key images or sounds for the purpose of presenting findings, but if that is all you need, NVivo will do that for you too, using simpler tools such as pictures embedded into text sources, or hyperlinks to sound bites or video clips.

Using media such as the audio file of an interview is a mistake if you are confident that the transcripts, alone, will answer your research questions. While NVivo allows you to code streaming audio and video files, a project with 20 interviews will quickly become very tedious to manage, because you will review the material over and over as you code, memo, link, run queries, and examine results. You will soon be reminded of one of the reasons why we became literate: reviewing the transcript is much faster than listening to or watching the recorded audio or video, although NVivo does allow for a helpful compromise – the simultaneous examination of audio or video and the associated transcript. We see a red flag, however, when we are contacted by new qualitative researchers who want to use their audio, video or photographic data, without exactly knowing why (or if they are just hoping to avoid transcription)! This suggests it is time to pause, to review some of the literature that discusses methodological issues in the analysis of non-text data, and to pilot the procedures.

You might also reconsider your impulse to use non-text data in its original form if:

- you simply find visual data more exciting than text, or the use of media sounds 'cool';
- a photograph is of global interest (i.e., you don't need to code pixels), because you can code the entire image when it is embedded as an *illustration* in a text document;
- you are interested in some, but not all, of the data on a web page (and, for instance, you don't want word counts to be modified by page names and hyperlinks);
- ethical considerations prohibit the use of media files either because of your human-subjects guidelines or your commitment to handling the data honourably;
- leaving the data in media form will present practical problems in disseminating the results to the intended audience or in publishing them;
- you have massive amounts of media files that could become cumbersome to manage in a database.

Using images in your research

Images might be photographs, or they could be drawings, maps, computer graphics, handwriting samples, flow charts, architectural designs, company logos, or quilt patterns. This genre of data can be collected in any digital format if you plan on linking to them externally with a hyperlink, or in a range of supported formats (bmp, gif, jpg, jpeg, tif/tiff) if you want to import them, add other links, and code the images. The rationale for using either photographs or other kinds of images varies considerably, although we provide a few ideas next, to get you thinking about their potential for use in a project.

Image-elicitation techniques are used when the researcher wants to collect participant perceptions on a predefined image or set of pictures. The images are usually determined before data collection and may be used for a wide range of research purposes, including:

- supplementing interview questions with visuals to help prompt the respondent;
- determining the most appealing brand images for a specifically targeted audience;
- collecting a series of word associations for particular images (similar to a Rorschach test);
- assessing participant recall of the elements in the image.

In the spirit of a participant-directed research project (often, but not always, associated with action research), individuals might be given cameras (or use their own) to collect data prior to their interview; for example:

- homeless children taking snapshots of the people and places that provide comfort;
- athletes photographing the objects that play a critical role in their training;
- farmers taking photographs of the various stages when they tend to their crops;
- octogenarians taking pictures of the locations where they volunteer.

Images might also be used to augment other types of data in your project. In some instances you may be aware of the relevance of such data prior to starting your research, and in others you may not realize the relevance until you are immersed in the project (or learn what you can do with images with the assistance of NVivo). These images are not typically provided by the respondents, but collected in response to their observations. The types of images that can serve as supplements can vary widely, including:

- images of buildings or locations that were described by participants as welcoming, dangerous, peaceful, etc.;
- aerial photographs of a region that are compared with the participants' discussions of their perceptions of changes in the geography of that region (such as the photographs in the *Environmental Change* project);
- paths used by blind students to navigate from one place to another after a discussion of their narrative about these paths;
- magazine advertisements for the clothing items associated with school cliques after hearing various students' discussions about the values or identities associated with this attire.

In addition, drawings or graphics might be produced during the interview process to help participants work through their understandings and communicate these to the researcher verbally, including:

- an organizational chart of power relations in a corporation alongside participant discussions of their mentors and advocates;
- a diagram of family ties associated with a mother's description of the role of religion in her relationships with family members;
- a drawing of a car crash and a report of the injuries associated with that event;
- a visual model of educational barriers and the resources required by a non-traditional student to overcome them.

The diversity of image formats, the reasons you might use or collect them, and the role you and your respondents have in creating them point to the applicability of images in addressing a wide range of research questions.

Three technical options

If you are convinced images will play a role in your research, you have three options for managing them technically. These options are to use a hyperlink, embed the image in an internal, or import the image as a standalone internal. Before you commit yourself, you should probably pilot all three to determine the best fit. Determining the best option is likely to depend on several issues: the relevance of these data to your primary research questions, the degree to which you need to analyse discrete portions of the image, your personal style, and the amount of data you will be managing.

Hyperlink

In Chapter 2 we described how to create a hyperlink that allows you to connect a specific spot – an anchor – in your database (a sentence in an interview, for instance) with a file that has not been imported into NVivo. If the image has a logical connection to one of your text documents (e.g., a map someone drew can be associated with their interview transcript where they discuss the map), follow our instructions in Chapter 2 to create a hyperlink from the interview transcript to the image and see if this will meet your needs.

- Advantages: The ability to keep the item external so it doesn't take up space in the database, and the storage of the linked files in locations where you already have them nicely organized (hopefully!).
- Disadvantages: The potential to break links if you move either the database or the linked images (although you can link them again later), the inability to code the image, and the inability to export image content out of the database (because it doesn't actually exist in the database).

Embed in an imported text-based source

Simply embed your image as an illustration in a Word document (**Insert > Picture**) and import this source file, then link, code and query according to the instructions in Chapters 2–6.

- Advantages: Manage the image in a familiar text document, code the entire image to any relevant node, and export the image in both docx and html formats.
- Disadvantages: You cannot code portions (pixels) within the image or link annotations and see also links to specific locations within the image. All of these actions must apply globally to the entire image.

As a standalone imported source

The third option, importing the image as a standalone internal, allows you to treat the data quite intricately because it allows you to code pixel regions of the image as well as record and code associated text in a log. The remaining information about images in this chapter pertains to this third strategy, as it is by far the most complex.

- Advantages: The most detailed way to code and link images, and an ability to choose whether to code a region of the image, the text associated with the region, or both.
- Disadvantages: When one of the other strategies will suffice, this approach can be unnecessarily cumbersome to manage; if you code an image with this strategy, coded regions can be exported efficiently from the database only in html format (in contrast with the option above to embed it in an internal, which provides export options in both formats).

Importing the image, creating a log, and adding links

After saving the image in one of the recognized formats, import the file in the same way as for a text-based document (you will use this same strategy for audio and video data also). Before you import any of these different data types, however, consider whether you want to store them in their own folder, within the Internals area. If so, then create the additional folders before you start importing files.

Once they are imported, you will find that most of the tools you have learned to use with text can be applied also to images and other multimedia sources with just a few slight variations to accommodate differences in methods of selecting what is to be linked or coded.

- Create folders or sets of pictures, displayed as thumbnails, as a form of gallery present-ation on a topic or theme.
- Create a series of sequenced images, for example, by using a series of see also links to entire items.
- Link specific parts of a picture to part of a transcript of an interview where they are discussed (or the discussion to the part of the picture).
- Use annotations or the log to comment on what is happening in a selected region of a picture (the log can be coded; an annotation always remains linked to the image, whether viewed as a source or in a node).

While the instructions to follow will focus on linking and coding images, many of the strategies apply also to audio and video sources and so these common-alities will not be repeated when we discuss them.

Importing, viewing, annotating, and linking a picture

Import a picture

▶ In *Navigation View* select **Sources**, expand **+ Internals > [your media folder]**.

▶ If this is the first source you are importing, your *List View* will be empty. **Right-click** (in the white space in *List View*) > **Import > Import Pictures**.

▶ In the Import Internals dialogue that opens, click on **Browse** to locate your file(s). Select one or more from the same location > **Open > OK**.

✓ In *List View*, **Right-click > List View** > change the display to **Medium Thumb-nails** to see your pictures in a gallery.

✓ Open the **Picture Properties > Picture** tab, to access metadata for photo-graphic images, including the date the photo was taken, aperture, exposure time, etc.

View and adjust your picture

▶ After you import the item, go to *List View*, double-click on the icon next to the picture you imported. The image will show in *Detail View*.

With your cursor active in the open image, you will see a ***Picture*** ribbon at the top of the screen with several tools. To access these tools:

▶ Select **Click to edit** on the top margin of the image.

▶ You can now adjust the **Brightness & Contrast** or **Rotate** the image 90 degrees left or right, for instance.

▶ The area allocated to the image versus the log can be adjusted. On the bottom right-hand side of the NVivo window you will also see a slide bar that allows you to zoom in or out.

Enter a log

If you would like to write notes about some or all of the image, this can be accomplished with a log, an annotation, or a memo link.

▶ Make sure you are in edit mode. (If you right-click in the image, and the **Edit** icon is illuminated, you are able to edit. If not, select the icon.)

▶ Drag your cursor diagonally to select a region of the image (Figure 7.1).

▶ Place your cursor somewhere inside the selected region > **Right-click > Insert Row**.

▶ The log locates the region (using pixels) and you can add text in the **Content** field (Figure 7.1).

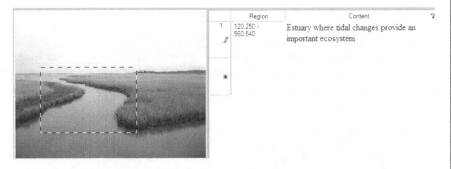

	Region	Content	▽
1	120,250 - 560,540	Estuary where tidal changes provide an important ecosystem	
*			

Figure 7.1   Picture with a newly inserted log entry

(Continued)

(Continued)

Add annotations or links to the image or log

To add a memo link, annotation, or see also link to the image or log, follow the instructions in Chapter 2 and treat the selection just as you would text from an interview transcript. In brief:

▶ Memo link: Right-click anywhere in the image or log > **Links** > **Memo Link** > **Link to New** (or existing) **Memo**.

▶ Annotation or see also link to an entire item: Select a portion of the image or log > **Right-click** > **Links** > **Annotation** (or **See Also Link**) > **New Annotation** (or **New See Also Link**).

▶ See also link to specific content: Select a portion of the image or log > **Right-click** > **Copy**. Go to another source, such as an interview or press release or another picture, and locate the passage there that refers to this part of the image > **Right-click** > **Paste As See Also Link**. Alternatively, select content from another source and copy it, then return to select a place in the image or log and paste as a see also link.

Coding an image or the log

You are able to code an image and its log in much the same way as you code a transcript (drag and drop, right-click, or select recently used nodes) – see Chapters 4 and 5 for details about coding text and working with nodes. The differences are to do with how parts of the image or log are selected for coding, and how they appear in a node.

Coding images

▶ To code a portion of the image, drag diagonally across the image to select a region (just as you did above to add a log entry). Drag this region of the image to any node, or right-click to code selection.

▶ Code part or all of the text in a log row (for images, audio or video) as you would for any other text.

✓ If you want to code an entire log row (instead of just a portion), you can select the number to the left of the row and drag this number to the node (or right-click and code). The text will follow.

Viewing a coded image

▶ Open the node in *Detail View* and you will see the pixel coordinates of the image in the **Reference** tab. Switch to the **Picture** tab on the far right margin of your screen to see the image with the coded portion illuminated (Figure 7.2).

✓ Coded text from a log entry will appear in your nodes along with the references from text-based sources.

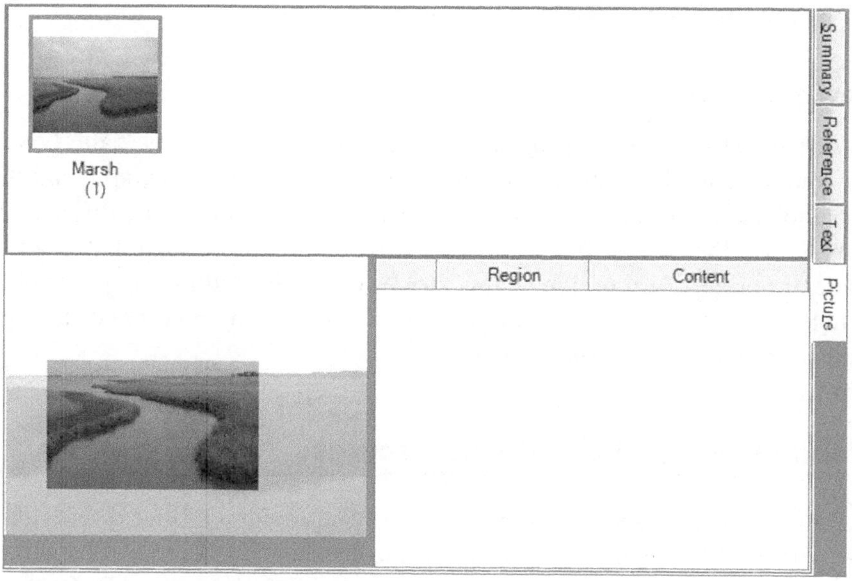

Figure 7.2 The picture tab of a node open in *Detail View*

Adding images to case nodes

In Chapter 6 we walked you through the conceptualization of case nodes and classifications as well as the attribute values (often demographics) that can be associated with case nodes, usually for the purpose of comparing subgroups in the data. Return to Chapter 6 for conceptual grounding if case nodes, classifications, attributes or values in NVivo are unfamiliar to you. You will also find detailed instructions for creating and managing case nodes and classifications in Chapter 6.

Any type of data you can import into NVivo can be regarded as a case and coded at a case node. For example, if you ask engineers to bring along photographs of their customized fish ladders (structures that enable fish to pass around artificial barriers such as dams and locks), and you import these photographs into your database, you might be examining just the image, just the log rows associated with the image (where the engineers discuss the specific features of the fish ladder), or both. These images and/or their associated log data would then be included in the case node for the particular engineer who developed the ladder (assuming that your cases are people; alternatively they could be types of fish ladders or sites where fish ladders are used).

You can place the image, the log, or both types of information from the picture source into a case (the latter would be more usual). Methods for coding images to case nodes parallel other forms of coding and of creating case nodes. Once you create the case nodes, you can classify them and add attribute values to them, just as you would any other case node (see Chapter 6).

View examples

The *Environmental Change* project makes extensive use of image data. Look in the source subfolders under Area and Township to see photographs and GIS (geographical information systems) data. Click on the number identifying a log entry to see the part of the picture it refers to (it will be highlighted with a shade of purple). Turn on the coding stripes to see the coding applied to either or both the image and its log (tab between stripes for the image and the log at the base of the coding stripe display).

Working with audio and video sources

In the introductory section to this chapter, we provided a brief discussion of the rationales for using non-text data, the reasons you may prefer media to text, and our cautions and caveats about making use of this type of data without a comprehensive understanding of the methodological implications. Instead of repeating that grounding content, we dive directly into some examples here. Audio can capture a wide range of sounds and conversations, such as emergency phone calls with a fire department, radio transmissions from fishing vessels, candidate debates, and even bird songs in the Amazon. As with pictures, this genre of data can be collected in any digital format if you plan on linking to it externally (with a hyperlink), or in a range of supported formats (mp3, m4a, wma, wav) if you want to import, add other links, and code the audio.

Video offers exciting possibilities to those engaging in community or behavioural research, where context and action can 'speak' more loudly than words. Providing a (video) camera to participants in the research so that they can film their own lives and communities changes the perspective from which the data are seen (Mitchell, 2011). Michael Rich and his colleagues had adolescents with chronic illness create video narratives that included tours of home and neighbourhood, interviews with family and friends, daily activities, and daily diaries in a study designed to have patients teach clinicians about their illness experiences (Rich & Patashnick, 2002). Working over a decade ago with 500 hours of video data, the researchers experienced limitations in computing capacity and in qualitative software that have now been overcome in a technical sense – although the question of simply working through the sheer volume of data remains.

Video may be required when the audible record cannot address the research questions (as in our earlier example of sarcasm in team meetings), or when the data have been captured already and you simply choose to retain the image along with the sound (e.g., you are studying the decibel difference between television dramas and television advertisements and want to see and hear participants discuss their reaction to this decibel change). As with pictures and audio, the video data can be in any format if handled with a hyperlink, but must be in a recognized format (mpg, mpeg, mpe, wmv, avi, mov, qt, mp4, 3gp, mts, m2ts) if you intend to import, add other links, and code the data.

! The .mov format is not supported by the 64-bit version of NVivo, and switching to the 32-bit version after having installed a 64-bit version is both cumbersome and potentially limiting of the volume of video you can store (embed) within your project.

Although audio and video are used quite differently in the field methodologically, they are handled technically very similarly in NVivo (the audio just doesn't have the image). The following screenshots and instructions will focus on video, but the instructions apply equally to audio.

Importing and managing audio and video files

Because audio and video files can be very large, and therefore impact on the performance of a project, NVivo allows for the files to be either embedded in the project, or stored in another location. As you work with your media, the interface in NVivo is identical whether media are embedded or not embedded. When the file is not embedded, the software creates a seamless link between the database and the externally located file. The critical factor with files that are not embedded is ensuring that, if the project is moved, these files travel with the project and the file paths (the links from NVivo to the videos) retain their integrity.

Importing audio or video sources

▶ Import audio and video files in the same way as you import pictures or text data.

After importing a video file, check to see whether it is embedded or stored elsewhere.

▶ **Right-click** on the file you have just imported > **Video Properties**.

▶ Select the **Video** tab. If your media file is under 20 MB, you will see it was imported as an embedded file. If it is 20 MB or larger, it was imported as a not-embedded file.

(Continued)

(Continued)

✓ You can change the options for your project to modify the size of files that will be embedded (up to 40 MB) when you import them.

✓ If you move the files and break the link, you will receive an error message if you attempt to open it from inside NVivo. Fear not, however, because as soon as you re-establish the link by updating the file location, all of your coding and links will jump back into position.

✓ At any time, you may alter the status of the file as embedded or not embedded by changing the Video Properties of the file.

? Search the NVivo Help files for *Store audio and video files* for additional information.

Playing media

When you open a video file inside NVivo, you see both a timeline (the audio wave file) and the video playback. In your research you might make use of both of these features. The variations in the wave file give an indication of rising and falling volumes that potentially tell you about, for example, the progress of an argument, or the rise in distress of a caller to the emergency line. The video, of course, reveals gestures, facial expressions and actions that are not accessible any other way. Video is being used, for example, to analyse children's play activity during assessments in a study involving early intervention with families at risk (Kemp et al., 2011). The time and kind of attention given to objects associated with literacy (such as books) compared to other play materials will be a focus of one related sub-study.

If you click in an open media file (i.e., in *Detail View*) the **Media** ribbon displays at the top of the screen. In the *Playback* group you can play, pause, start, jump to another location, and change the speed and volume of the playback, much as you would when managing audio and video outside of NVivo.

Playing media

▶ Double-click in *List View* to open your media file in *Detail View*, and from the **Media** ribbon select **Play/Pause**.

▶ In the *Detail View*, watch the blue playhead move across the timeline (Figure 7.3).

▶ Click on **Stop**.

✓ In addition to using the features in the **Media** ribbon to manage the playback, you can place your cursor on the playhead and drag it to any point along the timeline to play a different segment.

? For additional details on playing and managing the media defaults, search the NVivo Help files for *Play audio or video* and *Customize the audio or video display.*

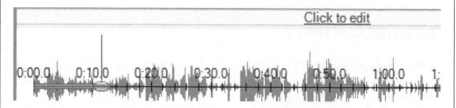

Figure 7.3 The playhead moving across the timeline of an audio or video source

Transcribing media files

Many issues surrounding transcription were discussed in Chapter 3, and a few were noted earlier in this chapter. Before you dive into transcription, consider those issues carefully, test different options, and develop a plan for your preferred strategy.

- If you plan to code directly to the audio or video timeline, rather than transcribe, you can skip to the subsequent section on coding – but remember our earlier warning that coding directly to the media timeline is not likely to save you time in the long run, and you should do so only for clear methodological reasons.
- If you do transcribe, you can do so directly within NVivo, or as noted earlier, you can prepare a transcript outside of the software and import it later.

Transcribe to the level of detail that suits you (see Chapter 3), answering these questions before you begin transcribing:

- Do you need every utterance (uhm, ah, hmm-mmm)?
- Do you need to indicate pauses or overlapping speech?
- Are there gestures you want to capture and record as part of the transcript?
- Will you be able to answer your research questions if you simply summarize rather than transcribe verbatim (especially given you have the parallel video source)?

? If you want to transcribe outside of the software, search NVivo Help for *Import audio or video transcripts* so that you format it correctly to allow synchronization with the media file.

If you transcribe inside the software, NVivo will accommodate your transcription machine foot pedals and keystrokes for start, stop, etc. Alternatively, you can use the software interface to provide commands while you transcribe. Either way, you need an orientation to the *Media* ribbon.

Transcribing in NVivo

In the *Media* ribbon, *Playback* group, you will see **Play Mode** with three different settings. You are currently in **Normal** play mode with a green triangle illuminated (Figure 7.4).

To transcribe, you will need to select the **Play Mode** on the right that is currently greyed out. To access and use it:

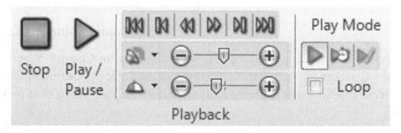

Figure 7.4   The *Playback* group of the *Media* ribbon

▶ Select the **Click to edit** bar just above the timeline of your audio or video.
▶ From the **Play Mode** options, select the **Transcribe** icon on the right ▶/.
▶ Adjust the speed and volume of the playback to suit your needs.
▶ Move your playhead to the location where you want to begin transcribing and click **Play/Pause** (or use your keystrokes or foot pedal).
▶ A transcript row appears to the right of the media where you can begin typing.
▶ Click **Pause** (or use your keystrokes or foot pedals) to remain in the same row while you correct, retype or catch up, and then **Play** to start again. Use the skip back icon ▐◀ then **Play**, to repeat the last few words if needed.
▶ Click **Stop** and then **Play** to create a new row.

Your decision about when to create a new row or stay in the existing row depends on your analytical goals. You will be able to code either selected text within the transcript row, or select the number next to the row to code the entirety. Some researchers create a new row for each speaker (to allow auto coding for cases), others divide data into similar lengths, and others identify meaningful episodes within the media based on the content.

✓ Each time you create a new row it appears at the top of the *Detail View* for easy access, but the rows will sort themselves and you can play the media chronologically whenever you like.

▶ After you pilot a few minutes of transcription, go to the **Media** ribbon > **Play Mode** > **Synchronize** (the **icon** between the **Normal** and **Transcribe** modes). While you are in the synchronize mode, the transcript will scroll into view as the media plays.

? For additional details on transcription, search the NVivo Help files for *Create audio or video transcripts in NVivo*; *Filter, sort and customize audio or video transcripts*; and *Delete, copy and organize audio or video transcript rows*.

Links

To add memo links, annotations, see also links, and hyperlinks to a media source or a transcript row, select as you would for other types of data, and apply in the usual way. To add links to the media timeline, select material the same way you would for coding (see below).

Adding audio or video to case nodes

Entire media sources can be coded as case nodes by employing the usual strategies (as outlined in Chapter 6). If a source includes more than one speaker, however, you are likely to want to code portions of the file to different case nodes. This could be achieved interactively, but will be much easier to do if the transcription has been done so that each speaking turn is in a new row, as this will allow for auto coding based on a custom field added (as a column) to the transcript to identify the speakers.[2]

Using custom fields and auto coding in a media transcript

Add a custom field

▶ Go to the **File** menu > **Info** > **Project Properties** > **Audio/Video** tab.
▶ Under **Custom Transcript Fields**, select **Audio** or **Video** and use the **New** button to add new fields.

(Continued)

---

[2] It is being assumed in these instructions that the case coding is for speakers. If you are using some other unit of analysis (e.g., site or event), simply substitute that for 'speaker' in these instructions. Up to ten custom fields can be added for various types of labels that might apply to an entire transcript row, for example, to identify critical content in the row to facilitate (auto) coding to thematic nodes.

(Continued)

▶ Edit to provide a name, such as *Speaker*. Click on the + to assign the name.

▶ Open the media in *Detail View* to see the new field.

✓ Any fields that you add will be applied to all media of that type within this project.

Auto code speakers to create case nodes

In *List View,* select your audio or video source > **Right-click** > **Auto Code**.

▶ Select the **Available Transcript Field** containing your case names (e.g., Speakers) and use the arrow to move right, under **Selected Transcript Fields**.

▶ Identify the **Location** and **Name** for where the auto coded (case) nodes are to go. **OK**.

You can now classify your case nodes and add attribute values to them, just as you would any other case node. See Chapter 6 for more details.

Coding media files

As with the picture data, you can code either the media or the transcript, or both.[3]

Coding a media file

▶ To code the transcript, simply handle it as you would any text and use your right-click or drag-and-drop options. As with image files, if you select a row number it codes the whole transcript row.

You have two options for selecting portions of the media timeline for coding:

▶ If you know the time count you want to select (because it has already been transcribed or because you just played it), click and hold on the timeline where you would like the episode to begin, and drag as far as you need. You will see that your cursor is marking off a blue box around the selected region. Release and your box is complete.

▶ Alternatively, go to the *Media* ribbon, *Selection* group and click to **Start Selection** or **Finish Selection** as the media plays. Again, a region in the timeline will be marked off with a blue box.

▶ Code the selected region by placing your cursor inside the blue box and coding as you would normally (drag and drop or right-click).

---

[3] Doing both can double your counts for some displays.

Viewing coded media

When you code a portion of a media source and then open the node, you will be in Reference view and so you will see only the time range identified alongside any text you coded at the node.

▶ To see the range of media and play it, choose the appropriate tab (Audio or Video) from the right side of the *Detail View*, and then **Media** ribbon > **Play**. The episodes or clips coded at that node will be played consecutively in chronological order.

Viewing coding stripes for images, audio, and video

Coding stripes were introduced in Chapter 4 as a way of checking what coding you were applying to text. With images and media files you can use coding stripes to see a visual of your coding, but with a new feature – shadow coding stripes. Because you are potentially coding two forms of the same file, NVivo will show you the coding on the parallel forms, using a solid line for the primary form being viewed, and a hatched line for parallel coding in the secondary form.

You can turn on coding stripes, for example, to show **Nodes Most Coding** or **Nodes Recently Coding** for your image or media files just as you would for any text. Turning on coding stripes will provide a visual of where and how you have coded the actual media timeline (horizontal stripes below the timeline) and the transcript rows. At the same time, you will see hatched stripes below the timeline to indicate a parallel portion of the transcript that was coded, and hatched stripes adjacent to the text to indicate a parallel portion of the media that was coded. As for any coding stripes, use your right-click menu to access additional viewing (and coding) options.

Figure 7.5 shows the parallel coding stripes in Max Coltheart's interview in the *Researchers* project. You might also look at the video interviews in the *Environmental Change* project, and at the image file under **Internals** > **Area and Township** > **Aerial** > *Cartaret with boundary and county names*. In the image file, you need to click on Image or Log at the base of the coding stripe display to see the alternative views.

Accessing and using web-based data

In this section we will show you how to download and work with a web page or YouTube video in NVivo, but if you are planning on analysing a social media dataset, you should turn to Chapter 9, where you will find instructions on how to turn Facebook (wall posts for a user, page or group), LinkedIn (discussions and comments), YouTube (comments), and Twitter data into an NVivo dataset.

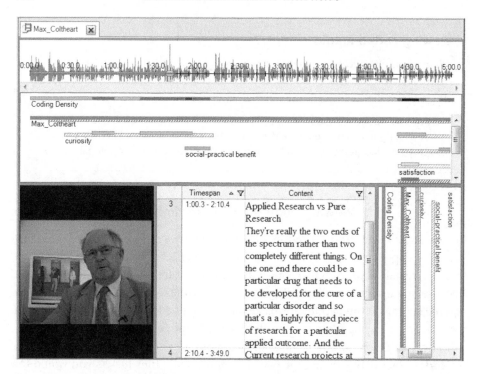

Figure 7.5   Coding stripes with shadow coding on a media file (Interview with Max Coltheart, Federation Fellow and Professor of Cognitive Science, Macquarie University. Permission for use granted.)

Web pages and YouTube videos may be a core of your study, because you want to look at the way various companies present themselves to the public, or at how people make judgements in talent quests. Or you might unexpectedly want to capture a web page because one of your interview respondents mentioned some curriculum guidelines that she found on another college's web page, or a video that inspired her to take up singing. Regardless of your reason for capturing these web pages, you will be able to code content on the page or in the video, as well as follow embedded hyperlinks, once you've imported it into NVivo.

An initiative in a palliative care project involving doctors, hospices and hospitals had as a goal to improve the coordination of end-of-life care between these service providers. Assessment of whether this had been achieved or not involved examining how frequently each website provided a link to one of the other organizations, and how accurately and thoroughly they explained the services of the other organ-ization. Being able to capture and code the content of each organization's website facilitated this evaluation.

Getting started with web pages and YouTube

Installing NCapture

NCapture is a module provided with NVivo for the purpose of capturing web-based data using Internet Explorer or Google Chrome for analysis within NVivo. When you open one or other of these search engines (depending on the choices you made at installation) you should see the NCapture button in the toolbar (Figure 7.6).

If you can't see the NCapture icon in the toolbar of Internet Explorer, check if it is listed under Tools. If you can't see it on the Chrome toolbar, click on the Customize and Control icon at the far right of the toolbar, select **Tools > Extensions,** and see if it is listed there. If NCapture for NVivo is included in the list for either of these programs, it is installed. If not, go to the QSR website to download and install.

? Search Help for *NCapture* if you're having any problem with installation of or access to NCapture.

Figure 7.6 NCapture icon showing in the Internet Explorer Command bar

Capture a web page or YouTube video

✓ NVivo has created a default destination folder (called NCapture) in Documents to store captured data, ready for importing into NVivo.

▶ Open the web page or video you want to capture for importing into NVivo.

▶ While you have it open, click the NCapture button on the Toolbar or (in Internet Explorer) select **NCapture for NVivo** from the **Tools** menu.

The NCapture window opens, indicating that the web page will be imported as a pdf (Figure 7.7), or providing options for importing the video with or without comments (Figure 7.8). If you capture the comments as well as the video, they will be treated as a social media dataset, similarly to those from other social media sites as described in Chapter 9.

(Continued)

(Continued)

▶ In either case, you can add a description for the item and a memo if you wish. Both will be imported with the web page or video.

▶ Add nodes for coding, although you should be mindful that the entire page or video will be coded at these nodes.

▶ Save in either the default location or select a location[4] > **Capture**.

Import and view a web page or video

▶ In *Navigation View* > **Sources** > **Internals** > **[your folder for NCapture downloads]**.

▶ In *List View* (for both web page and video), **Right-click** > **Import** > **Import from NCapture**. NVivo will convert the download for you.

▶ **Browse** to identify the folder where you stored the captured data. All available captures will be listed.

▶ **Select captures to import** by choosing one of the three radio buttons and checking against available captures as required > **Import** (Figure 7.9).

Figure 7.7   Collecting a web page with NCapture

---

[4] Internet Explorer defaults to the NCapture folder created by NVivo in Documents. Chrome defaults to your Windows Downloads folder, so for Chrome in particular it is recommended that you take care to specify a preferred location for the file.

Figure 7.8 Collecting a YouTube video with NCapture

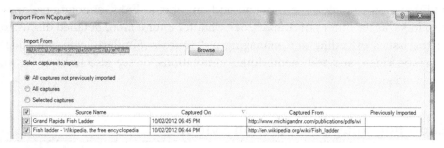

Figure 7.9 Selecting an NCapture file for importing as a web page

▶ Open the imported file in *Detail View* (e.g., Figure 7.9). The whole of the web page or video will have been captured, beyond what was immediately visible on the screen.

! You must be connected to the internet to open a YouTube video in NVivo.[5]

(Continued)

---

[5] Those with limited internet access should be aware of the demand on their service when transcribing or coding a YouTube video.

(Continued)

Figure 7.10   A web page converted into a pdf and opened in NVivo

Linking and coding your web page or video

The hyperlinks in the imported web page are accessible with a **Ctrl+click**. In addition, you can code the file, and add any memo links, annotations, or see also links, as for other pdf sources. See Chapter 8 for a more detailed discussion of the issues in coding and managing pdf sources. Similarly, you can code a YouTube video, and add memo links, annotations, or see also links as for any other video.

Exporting images, audio, and video

After you link and code your image, web and media data to your satisfaction, you can export it in several ways.

1   Print any source directly from the screen. For example, with the view from Figure 7.9 open and selected in your *Detail View*, **Right-click > Print >** choose the elements you wish to include in the printout > **OK**.

✓   NVivo will show a print preview first, for you to check, as the output may not appear as you expect it to, especially when you have coding stripes turned on.

2   Export the data from any source or from any node where it has been coded. Select any source or node(s) in *List View*, **Right-click > Export > Export Source** (or **Export Node**).

a   If you select to **Export > Entire Content**, the contents of the node will be saved as an html file, with tabs for Summary and Reference views and also for each type of content (e.g., text, video, pdf, picture).

b   If you change the **Export** option to **Reference** view, the contents of the source or node will export as a Word file (defaulting to docx, but with other options) showing coded text and pdf passages. For coded image, audio or video sources, you will see only the pixel coordinates, time stamps, or the coded log or transcript rows, and not the image or the video contents.

c   In both forms of output, coded passages from pdf sources will show as highlighted regions within the context of the relevant page.

Consider also using image files within a model, which can then be printed or copied and pasted into other programs. Images stored on your computer can be used as fill for icons within a model and shown with connectors to other items. Alternatively, use connectors between a series of images to take the viewer on a photographic journey through some aspect of your data.

8

Adding reference material to your NVivo project

Reference material of many kinds and from a variety of sources plays a part in any research project, including a qualitative project. NVivo's suite of tools can be useful for working with this type of data. You can code, reflect on, write memos about, and query reference material just as you do with an interview, focus group, or set of pictures. To assist this process, you can import portable document format (pdf) sources, web pages captured with NCapture, or notes and articles stored in your bibliographic database (EndNote, RefWorks or Zotero). While NVivo is *not* a substitute for the referencing functions provided by a bibliographic program, it does provide a rapid way of bringing the literature you have been gathering and reading into your project, so you can refine your analysis of that literature and quickly access relevant material when you are writing your review or report.

In this chapter:

- Consider the ways you might work with reference material within NVivo.
- Discover the potentials and pitfalls of importing and working with pdf sources in NVivo.
- See what options NVivo provides for importing reference material from a bibliographic database and from web pages.

Using reference material in your project

Reference material has the potential to play multiple roles in a qualitative project, where it might be used for one or more of the following purposes:

- as preparation during the initial planning stages of a project, from which the outcome will be a literature review;
- to build a framework for design and analysis;
- as a source of sensitizing concepts and potential nodes;
- as a source of contrast, for comparison with your data;
- to frame the debates (or camps) in your field of study;
- as your primary data source, as in a systematic review, metasynthesis or analysis of trends or patterns using academic literature or other reference material.

Employing NVivo for working with literature is most appropriate when you are undertaking an analytical task with the literature, or you are creating a database that you will return to again and again because this is a core area of research for you. If you are doing a one-off review of a set of literature, consider the alternative of just using the facilities provided by Word (through use of heading styles, the Document Map available in the Navigation Pane, and Outline view) to record and organize notes from your reading. Place the notes under headings, jump to particular headings as needed using the Navigation Pane, and sort your text using Outline view. Use your bibliographic software to identify relevant articles (e.g., via keyword searches) and to add the reference list.

Including literature and other reference material as background data

Beginning a project by reviewing what is already known on the subject of your research is a well-established practice, as is reviewing the implications of relevant theories for your topic, and methods others have used to investigate it (Bazeley, 2013; Boote & Beile, 2005; Hart, 1999). Adherents of some qualitative traditions have promoted the alternative understanding that it is better to begin data collection without such prior investigation of the literature so as not to prejudice emerging understanding from informants or participants in the field. Even in these traditions, however, there has often been a shift back to seeing value in viewing the literature as a source of stimulation and/or sensitization throughout a project (e.g., Charmaz, 2006; Corbin & Strauss, 2008; Silverman, 2010).

In a practical vein, working with notes from literature or other archival sources in a project can be a good place to start developing skills and ideas using NVivo, as these are readily available while you finalize plans and gain the various approvals necessary for gathering your own data. Coding articles and any notes you made while reading articles facilitates the development of a literature review, and will provide a basis for making comparisons with what you find from your own data. Don't delay until you have already written a literature review: one of the points of this exercise is to use NVivo to assist you in moving from rough notes to an organized review.[1]

Using reference material as your source of data

Qualitative researchers are not limited to interviews and focus groups for their sources of data! We have worked with researchers doing innovative research with newspaper articles, blogs, web pages, company reports, poetry and novels – a nearly infinite variety of reference material. These sources are analysed for trends and patterns over time or across types of sources, for narrative or discourse, in all the ways you might analyse any other kind of data.

> Jannet Pendleton, at the University of Technology, Sydney, used media releases and newspaper articles as her primary sources of data for her doctoral study of the public relations campaign conducted by a pharmaceutical company to have a newly developed (and expensive!) vaccine added to the recommended list for childhood immunization in Australia. Using NVivo, she was able to trace the development of the campaign over time, and the way in which materials contained in media releases from the company, especially human interest stories, were incorporated more or less directly into subsequent newspaper articles.

The overwhelming amount of information now available to both academics and practitioners has led to increasing adoption of meta-analyses, systematic reviews, and metasyntheses of the literature, to filter, condense and extend what has been learned through all those individual research projects (Barnett-Page & Thomas, 2009; Dixon-Woods, Agarwal, Jones, Young, & Sutton, 2005). These differ from a literature review in that they are designed to generate new information. Your approach to this kind of analysis of the literature can take either of two major pathways (Bazeley, 2013). In an aggregative review the findings of various studies are summarized with conclusions based on overall patterns, while an interpretive review approaches the literature as data to be analysed and theorized. While a bibliographic database will allow you to search for keywords, and sort and group your reference material, bringing that literature into NVivo has the potential to add value, regardless of your approach to the literature, through use of its more sophisticated searching, coding and querying tools. Here are some examples.

---

[1] If you have already written a review but it lacks organization, you might find it helpful to import the review and code it, as a way of seeing structure in what you have written.

Pat has a project that comprises pdf articles as well as abstracts and notes made while reading mixed methods literature (much of it pre-dated being able to readily access electronic pdfs or to link those with EndNote) in which she has coded all the material relating to the paradigm debates in mixed methods research, as well as other topics and issues. Because each source has a date attribute (year of publication), it is possible to sort the coded material on paradigm debates, for example, by decade (or a shorter period if desired), to trace changes in the way researchers have written about that issue.

Kristi has a project comprising pdf articles about qualitative researchers' understandings of the advantages and disadvantages of using QDAS. While some of the articles claim to be research-oriented, they contain considerable references to expository materials from other authors. Therefore to more accurately distinguish 'research findings' from 'expository literature', she created a node for each type, and while reading the articles she coded the referenced material to the appropriate location. After doing this, she ran a matrix coding query on the benefits and problems of using QDAS (columns) by whether the literature cited was research or expository (rows). By doing so, it became evident that when researchers identified potential problems with QDAS in the narrative of their own research publications, they consistently cited a single expository article by Coffey et al. (1996) rather than any actual research that confirmed these potential problems.

In Wickham and Woods' (2005) article documenting their literature review process for their doctoral theses, they identify several benefits of using NUD*IST (now NVivo). One benefit was the way their coding of the literature pointed to gaps in the research in order to develop pertinent research questions. One of these students coded literature to a node for 'the role of government', and after reviewing these roles became aware that 'government social responsibility' was a missing strand. This concept was included as a question to be addressed by the research.

Reference material in NVivo

In many ways, working with reference material is no different from working with any other form of text (standalone, or transcribed alongside various media). Sources are imported, searched, annotated, linked, coded, and reflected upon like any others. The major difference from other material is that most of it is likely to be in the form of pdf files, often with embedded tables and figures, rather than Word documents. If it is in the form of research literature, it is also likely to be more structured than information from an interview, for example, and will contain author-defined sections that can be compared across the literature (abstract, background, methods, findings, implications).

There are three major sources of reference material that you will potentially work with in NVivo:

- your bibliographic database, stored in EndNote, RefWorks or Zotero, which will contain references with abstracts, notes, other metadata (reference type, etc.), and possibly attached sources (usually but not necessarily in pdf);

- pdf sources, not part of a bibliographic database;
- pages downloaded from the internet using NCapture.

You might also import notes you have stored in Word files, in OneNote, or in Evernote.[2] For guidance on importing from and working with OneNote or Evernote notes or pages, search for *OneNote* or *EverNote* in NVivo Help, where the alternatives for selecting parts or all of your pages to import are very adequately described. As with much other data in this chapter, files are converted to pdf sources on import.

Importing, coding, and viewing pdf sources

Shortly we will show you how you can import pdf sources as part of your bibliographic database, but sometimes you will have pdf sources that are not part of such a database, or sources (web pages) that NVivo converts to pdf on import. As well as showing you how you can import and code a pdf source, this section will cover issues faced in dealing with any kind of pdf material, regardless of how it is created or imported.

Pdf sources can be in either of two formats, with different implications for how you work with them.

1　Most downloaded pdf files will appear as normal text (or text and images) that allow you to select content in the usual way by dragging with your mouse pointer (although the resulting highlighting of the text in some might appear rather uneven and broken). Scanned data might also appear this way, if it has been scanned to pdf, rather than scanned as an image. Most scanners also come with additional software for converting a pdf to regular text using optical character recognition (OCR) technology. OCR can be used, also, with scanned handwritten responses, as long as you're prepared to check the results.
2　Some scanned and downloaded pdf material will appear more like an image, as if the page has been photocopied or photographed. One of the hints that you are working with this format is if you cannot select ranges of characters within text when viewing it as a pdf in Adobe Reader before you import it. In some cases, you can convert a scanned image to text using OCR software before you import it (there are some free OCR conversion programs available on the web). Alternatively, you will need to select text by region, similarly to the way you would work with an image file such as a photograph (see Chapter 7). You will not be able to use word or text search queries in this type of source, and retrievals will be similar to those for images.

We suggest that you store literature in one or more folders separately from other data sources – one if you are happy to have it all together, more than one if you want to separate items by their format (of the two outlined above) or, alternatively, by the type of material they contain (e.g., web pages, industry reports, peer review articles). The issue of where to store pdf files in your project can be especially important now that web pages collected with NCapture are converted into pdf files when they are imported. Because the symbol for a pdf file in NVivo is the same regardless of whether the data source is a web page or an article, and regardless of whether you can select text or only regions, the storage location and naming convention you provide to these files might influence your efficient management of the data.

Importing a pdf source

Pdf sources can be imported like any other source (*Navigation View* > **Sources** > expand + **Internals** > **[your literature folder]** and then *List View* > **Right-click** > **Import** > **Import PDFs**).

- If you highlight text in your pdf using Adobe Reader (or similar, i.e., before importing it), those passages will remain highlighted when you import the pdf.
- Comment markers attached to the text remain visible after import, but the comments are not.
- Pencil marks and text boxes on the text will be visible, but they cannot be selected.
- When selected and coded text is retrieved from a node, none of the added markers remains visible (unless you **Open Referenced Source**).

Sources that are scanned image files, or that protect their text from being copied in Adobe Reader (format type 2 above, without OCR) can be imported and coded by region, but you will not be able to select the text in the usual way for coding, annotating or linking.

Selecting and coding text in a pdf source

In this section we focus on more traditional sources such as articles, chapters and reports. In most cases (format type 1 above), sources can be annotated, linked and coded like other sources, as described in earlier chapters. Additional issues that arise with web pages are covered in the final section of this chapter.

Selecting text for coding in a pdf source (format type 1)

You will be able to select text for drag-and-drop coding or coding using the right-click menu in the normal way for both regular text in paragraphs and for text in articles with columns. Depending on the source and circumstances, however, you may find some specific issues arise in relation to selecting (and viewing coded) text.

- If your text selection runs across a page break, it is likely to include the footer and header text.
- When you select text in a pdf source in NVivo you will notice in most sources that there is a space between lines and sometimes between the words in the text (Figure 8.1a).[3] If your mouse pointer lands on that space when you go to drag the passage to a node for coding, it will change to a cursor rather than pointer, and when you click to drag, the original selection will be lost.
- Text selection is unstable under some circumstances. In particular, if you have to scroll your node list to locate a second node, the selection is lost (use right-click to code to multiple nodes at once as an alternative).
- When working with tabbed text (e.g., where speakers are set apart from what they say) or text with line numbers, take extra care to ensure all required characters are included (Figure 8.2a). If you find you cannot select correctly, switch to region selection for that passage (as for format type 2, see below).

In general you will be working with regular paragraphs of text, and you should not experience significant difficulties in selecting, coding or viewing it.

Viewing coded text from a pdf source (format type 1)

Standard paragraphs of pdf text do not pose any issues with regard to viewing coded material. Depending on the nature of the source, however, you may find that when you view what you have coded, the message in the NVivo Help file for pdf sources will apply: 'NVivo tries to determine the order of text on a pdf page; however when you select text, you may find that the text on the page is not sequenced as you expect.' This warning will apply if you look at the Reference tab view of the coded text for non-standard paragraphs of data, as spacing and line breaks in the original are likely to have been reconfigured to some degree. If this creates a problem, the safer option for viewing is to select the PDF tab, where coded text will be shown in its page context. Figure 8.1 illustrates these alternatives, with text involving multiple short lines of speech.

Coded text with line numbers, and sometimes tabbed text (for speakers), is reordered when seen in the Reference tab view (Figure 8.2b), rendering that view not useful if line numbers are needed.[4] The PDF tab view is better (Figure 8.2c), although on those not-so-common occasions where you might wish to code text on to further nodes while viewing it in a node, you will need to select it from the original source, as you will not be able to select a line number with its adjacent text from either this or the Reference view in a node.

---

[3] This is a characteristic of the pdf format, whether viewed in NVivo or a pdf reader.

[4] Although it did not occur on this occasion, the same problem can be experienced with tabbed speaker names, where all are moved to the start of a coded section.

Allison: To get married.
Caitlin: I think that these days a job to everyone is more important than being mar-
  ried and that's what it's coming down to. People would rather, you know, have a
  job.
Mathew: We need jobs to afford a bloody marriage.
Caitlin: Rather than say "Oh, I want to get married," people are saying "I want a
  job."
Shane: I want a job!
Meagan: Ahm, I want to have kids and have a job.
Allison: What about marriage?
Meagan: And marriage too, but that's way down the track, I'll have kids first,
  thanks.

(a) Text selected in the imported pdf

<Internals\\Warr QI 2005 focus groups> - § 1 reference coded [0.35% Coverage]

Reference 1 - 0.35% Coverage

Allison: To get married. Caitlin: I think that these days a job to everyone is more important than being
mar- ried andthat'swhatit'scomingdownto. People wouldrather,youknow,havea job.
Mathew: We need jobs to afford a bloody marriage. Caitlin: Rather than say "Oh, I want to get
married," people are saying "I want a job."
Shane: I want a job!
Meagan: Ahm, I want to have kids and have a job. Allison: What about marriage? Meagan: And
marriage too, but that's way down the track, I'll have kids first, thanks.

(b) Reference tab view of coded text

Allison: To get married.
Caitlin: I think that these days a job to everyone is more important than being mar-
  ried and that's what it's coming down to. People would rather, you know, have a
  job.
Mathew: We need jobs to afford a bloody marriage.
Caitlin: Rather than say "Oh, I want to get married," people are saying "I want a
  job."
Shane: I want a job!
Meagan: Ahm, I want to have kids and have a job.
Allison: What about marriage?
Meagan: And marriage too, but that's way down the track, I'll have kids first,
  thanks.
Caitlin: Oh, I sort of don't know, yeah, I want to have kids but that won't be until the
  future, and I want to own a house one day and sort of have work, work in a full-

(c) PDF tab view of coded text

Figure 8.1 Selection and retrieval of text in a pdf source

Source: Warr, D. J. (2005). 'It was fun ... but we don't usually talk about these things': analyzing
sociable interaction in focus groups. *Qualitative Inquiry, 11*(2), 200–225.

```
1   Allison:    To get married.
2   Caitlin:    I think that these days a job to everyone is more important than being
3               married and that's what it's coming down to. People would rather, you
4               know, have a job.
5   Mathew:     We need jobs to afford a bloody marriage.
6   Caitlin:    Rather than say "Oh, I want to get married," people are saying "I want a
7               job."
8   Shane:      I want a job!
9   Meagan:     Ahm, I want to have kids and have a job.
10  Allison:    What about marriage?
11  Meagan:     And marriage too, but that's way down the track, I'll have kids first,
12              thanks.
```

(a) Text selected in the imported pdf

```
1 2 3 4 5 6 7 8 9
10 11 12 13 14  15
Allison: To get married. Caitlin:
I think that these days a job to everyone is more important than being married and that's what it's
coming down to. People would rather, you know, have a job.
Mathew: We need jobs to afford a bloody marriage. Caitlin:
Shane: I want a job!
Meagan: Ahm, I want to have kids and have a job. Allison: What about marriage?
Meagan: And marriage too, but that's way down the track, I'll have kids first, thanks.
```

(b) Reference tab view of coded text

```
1   Allison:    To get married.
2   Caitlin:    I think that these days a job to everyone is more important than being
3               married and that's what it's coming down to. People would rather, you
4               know, have a job.
5   Mathew:     We need jobs to afford a bloody marriage.
6   Caitlin:    Rather than say "Oh, I want to get married," people are saying "I want a
7               job."
8   Shane:      I want a job!
9   Meagan:     Ahm, I want to have kids and have a job.
10  Allison:    What about marriage?
11  Meagan:     And marriage too, but that's way down the track, I'll have kids first,
12              thanks.
```

(c) PDF tab view of coded text

Figure 8.2 Selection and retrieval of text in a line-numbered pdf source

There is one further potential limitation with pdf sources that you need to understand. If you copy and paste text from a pdf into a Word document, you will find, in most circumstances, that there will be paragraph breaks at the end of each line.

- In NVivo, the effect of these paragraph breaks is to remove the opportunity to mean-ingfully view the paragraph surrounding a segment of coded data (e.g., when you select the text > **Right-click** > **Coding Context** > **Broad**). Instead, view the context of a coded passage using the PDF tab which will show the full page as context, or use Open Referenced Source (select the text > **Right-click** > **Open Referenced Source**).
- Paragraph breaks at the end of each line will also impact your ability to run a query that looks for words or codes that co-occur within the same paragraph (NEAR options). It will not impact on your ability to locate passages coded by *node x* AND *node y*.

Importantly, however, pdf text *can* be coded and retrieved, if care is taken, in one form or another that will allow for review and for most if not all the analysis options you are likely to want to use. Additionally, word frequency and text search queries will work with text in these pdf sources.

Selecting a region for coding in a pdf source (format type 2)

▶ With a pdf open, go to the **Home** ribbon, *Editing* group, under **PDF Selection**, choose **Region**. You will then be able to select and code regions within your source (Figure 8.3), with similar results to selecting a region within a picture.

✓ Use this approach also if you wish to select a table or a figure within any pdf source.
✓ Annotations and see also links are applied to the region, just as they are for pictures.
✓ Retrievals of coded text will show as coordinates for a region in Reference view; in PDF view they will appear in a similar way to retrieved pictures, as a highlighted region within a page.

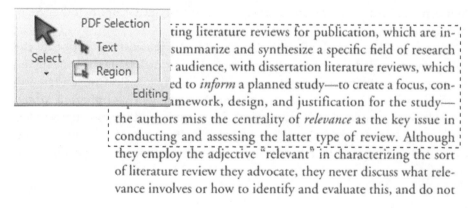

Figure 8.3 Selecting a region of text for coding

Pat comments: I've always made notes from my reading of the literature (having started my academic career well before photocopies were readily available), and so my mixed methods database is almost entirely composed (at this stage) of notes I've made. These days, because I am now making notes from an electronic version, I often copy and paste passages of text from the article into my notes (making sure to note the page references). What always bothers me about the way people use things that can generate large volumes of information in any automatic way, such as downloading bulk citations to EndNote from a web search, or printing off reams of statistical output from SPSS, or importing a stack of articles into NVivo, is that it is extremely difficult to get the time and motivation to then go through them in any meaningful way. If you import only the notes you've made, with their relevant copied passages, you have a useful and manageable set of literature to code and to write from, without the issues associated with pdf sources and without the clutter of unused reference material.

Importing reference material from bibliographic software

Most academic and student researchers now have access to electronic databases of articles through their university or college libraries. Typically, they will also have access to bibliographic database software to store citation details for their reference material, with EndNote being one of the most common.[5] Any researcher who has not started storing their reference information using bibliographic software is strongly advised to do so – buy it if you have to! Even if you use it at a basic level only, it is well worth the cost (if any) and the effort to learn enough to set up your reference library in it. At a basic level, a bibliographic database will help you keep track of all your reference material, and it will format your reference list for you when you are writing for publication. You can also search reference material by keyword, author or any other field, or for content.

As noted in the introduction to this chapter, NVivo will not duplicate the functions provided by your bibliographic software, but rather, it is designed to supplement them by facilitating searching, coding, reflecting, and analysis using your literature sources. Data of this type can be imported at any time during your project, and there is no problem with importing further sets of reference material in this way during the course of your project, even if those happen to include some references that you have imported already.

---

[5] Instructions to follow will focus on EndNote. Check Help for minor variations if you are using RefWorks or Zotero.

When you import literature from bibliographic software, NVivo will place

- attached files into a designated folder under Internals;
- the citation for any references without attached files into Externals;
- abstracts, and any notes you have recorded, into a memo that is attached to the internal or external record for that reference.[6]
- Other fields in the bibliographic software (e.g., publication year and author) will be recorded by NVivo as source attributes, with values attached to any associated records stored in any of the Internals, Externals and/or Memo folders.[7] This is one of the few occasions in NVivo where you are likely to make use of *source* attributes for comparative analyses, rather than node attributes.

Transferring literature from a bibliographic database

Preparing to import

▶ **Select** the references you want from your reference database, to import into NVivo. Your selection might be based on a keyword, a combination of keywords, or some other sorting feature of that software.

? If you are unsure how to select references, check the Help files in your bibliographic software.

! If you want to import the original pdf (or Word) files as you import the reference information, make sure that you have **attached files** to all your selected entries in your bibliographic software; that the attached files are in the locations pointed to within the software; and that this location will be available as you import the database into NVivo.

▶ **Export** the references you want from your bibliographic software in a format that will be recognized by NVivo. These are:

  o EndNote – export as .xml
  o RefWorks – export as .ris
  o Zotero – export as .ris

(Continued)

---

[6] The abstract needs to have been copied into the Abstract field in your database – NVivo will not extract it from the article. Similarly, notes need to have been written in the Notes field.

[7] Bibliographic material in versions 9 and 10 of the *Environmental Change* sample project was imported with a very early release of version 9, after which substantial changes were made to the import process and storage locations. For a more up-to-date example, look in the *Researchers* project.

(Continued)

✓ NVivo will recognize already imported references and provide options for ignoring or updating those.

Importing and managing your literature in NVivo

▶ In *Navigation View*, **Sources > Internals**, expand to select the folder you have created for storing literature sources.

▶ In *List View*, **Right-click** (in the empty space) > **Import > Import from EndNote** (or Zotero or RefWorks). The import dialogue in Figure 8.4 will open.

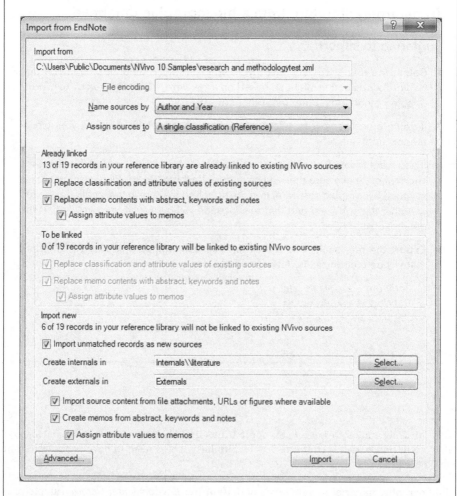

Figure 8.4   Selecting options in the import dialogue for reference material from EndNote

> ▶ Change the default for **Name sources by** to **Author and Year**. This is so that the author and year of publication will show in the node at the top of each coded passage – the kind of information you will need when writing up from your literature. NVivo will add the database record number for the source to the name, as well, to assist with Cite While You Write functions.
>
> ▶ Keep the **Assign sources to** as **A single classification** – otherwise you will create an unworkable set of classification sheets, with one for each type of worksheet (publication) you have included in your bibliographic database.
>
> ✓ If you have already imported some of these references, NVivo will recognize them and will not reimport them. You have the option of choosing to update them, however, if you added notes or other details within your reference database since first importing them.
>
> ▶ Note where NVivo is going to locate the files, and modify to your preferred location.
>
> ✓ Unless you recorded the abstracts or made notes, or the original articles are attached to the reference, then there's not a lot of point in importing those references into NVivo for coding or searching.

Viewing, coding and analysing your reference material

Reference material imported from EndNote, Zotero or RefWorks can now be viewed, coded, annotated and linked in the usual ways, subject to the above provisions regarding pdf sources. Notes and abstracts in Memos as well as original source material (e.g., articles) in Internals will have source attributes attached to them, allowing for their use in matrix coding queries to generate comparisons of coded material.

> ✓ If you wish to compare content over time, you are likely to need to combine years of publication into sets of years (e.g., decades). For this you will use an Advanced Find (see Chapter 6), using the Advanced tab to set multiple criteria when you need to get, say, all references including and after (**>= value**) 1980, but before (**< value**) 1990. If you are using this comparison often, and also constantly updating your references, it will probably be simpler to add another attribute to the classification sheet, because your sets don't automatically update when you add further sources to your database.

It is possible you will want to do relational analyses using coding queries based on your reference literature, asking questions like: Is the way authors define self-management associated with their understanding of what constitutes good care? More often, however, analysis and reporting from reference literature will involve fairly straightforward techniques of summarizing key points in relation to material on a topic stored in a node, or perhaps of viewing what is in that node sorted by values of an attribute associated with the source of the reference material.

In Kristi's study of qualitative researchers' conceptualization of 'transparency' in the qualitative research process, she wanted to examine the degree to which discussions of transparency were implicit (use of the term with no attempt to define it), simple (a brief definition or explanation of the term), or explicit (elaboration regarding dimensions of transparency such as the purpose, ways to achieve it, or potential problems with pursuing transparency). As she reviewed articles in her NVivo database, she gave each pdf an attribute value of implicit, simple or explicit, in order to be able to run a matrix coding query on these values by whether they used QDAS or not.

Capturing web pages with NCapture

Increasingly, web pages are being used to provide background information for research projects. NCapture, which accompanied your NVivo 10 software, is a browser extension for Internet Explorer or Google Chrome designed to capture web pages and convert them to pdf format within NVivo, so that they can be coded and analysed in the same way as other pdf files. These might add to the reference material for your project, or comprise data sources for analysis.

The technical procedures for downloading web pages and importing them into NVivo as pdf sources were covered in Chapter 7 in the context of accessing multimedia sources. The process is exactly the same for accessing web pages that might contain useful reference material.

Linking, coding and viewing coded web pages

When you use NCapture to download a web page that is long enough to run over several screens, the whole of that 'page' will be included in the capture, so the resulting pdf will comprise multiple pages (i.e., the capture is not limited to what will fit on a single page). Additionally, hyperlinks within the web page will convert to NVivo hyperlinks (and so can be accessed using Ctrl+click). Memo links, annotations and see also links can all be applied as for other text and image sources. The text of web pages can be searched using the word frequency query or a text search query.

When it comes to coding, however, if your web page is set out with text and images in frames and boxes rather than in neat columns, you will have problems selecting text, similar to those discussed earlier for pdfs, and as a consequence you will have problems also with viewing coded text. Figure 8.5 provides an example of a downloaded web page, to illustrate the points being made below.

- Text selected and coded within a section on the left-hand side of the downloaded page can be retrieved in the node relatively well in Reference view as well as PDF view.

Figure 8.5   Web page 'captured' as a pdf source in NVivo

Note: Downloaded from http://nsmnss.blogspot.co.uk/ on 30th September 2012.

- If you try to select text in a column on the right-hand side of the page in order to code, you are likely to include a large section of text from the left-hand column as well. This is particularly so if there is a break between lines in the text you are trying to select. When you view your text in the Reference tab of the *Detail View*, the additional text from the left-hand column will be inserted between the sections of the text you intended to code. For example, using the page in Figure 8.5, when selecting the text on the right beginning with 'New social media, new social science?' (as text), the date at the bottom left of the page followed the heading, and then, because the paragraph ran across a page break, the whole of the article on 'Using Quant Methods' was selected at the same time and, in Reference view, was inserted before 'explore this question'.
- While you can move smoothly across page breaks inserted into the web page by NVivo when viewing the source document, this does not happen when viewing coded text in the PDF view of a node. In that view, you will jump from one page to the next, sometimes losing continuity in the process (page breaks in NVivo are based on regular page lengths, not content).
- Selecting by Region rather than Text will solve selection problems to some extent – as long as you don't want your selection to cross an NVivo page boundary (see the selected region around the same right-hand-side article in Figure 8.5), and, of course, your only option then for viewing the coded data in a node is through the PDF view.

✓ Once a page is converted to pdf, you cannot edit it. If what you want from the web pages is reference-type information for your study, you might consider copying and pasting the required text and pictures into Word as an alternative to downloading the page with NCapture, as that will allow you to 'tidy up' the layout (and remove unwanted text) so that selection of text for coding is no longer a problem.

In summary, while working with literature and related sources in NVivo offers great promise, our advice is to tread carefully, testing all alternatives before you commit to any one approach.

9

Datasets and mixed methods

NVivo was designed primarily as software for the analysis of qualitative data, but the tools it provides go beyond simply managing complex projects with multiple sources of often diverse data to having those different data combine in a mutually informative way. You have already seen how to use attribute values in combination with coded text to compare subgroups in your sample (Chapter 6). Now you will discover how to import and work with a dataset in NVivo as a way to facilitate the process of combining open-ended text responses with demographic, categorical or scaled data from fixed-response questions – one of several strategies for mixing methods.[1] A *dataset* in NVivo refers specifically to a set of data that usually includes both text and numeric data, with both types of responses having been entered into Excel or similar software. Such data are typically gathered through a structured interview or questionnaire, although web surveys and social media sites provide new, additional options for creating datasets that can be analysed with the assistance of NVivo.

In this chapter:

- Discover ways in which NVivo can support mixed methods research.
- Learn how to manage mixed qualitative and quantitative data obtained through structured questionnaires, web surveys, and social media websites.

Combining data types in research

Combination of methods employing different data types 'has a long standing history' in evaluation research where both outcome and process are being considered; indeed, 'most real-world evaluations pose multiple and diverse

---

[1] This chapter draws on previous published work, especially Bazeley (2006, 2010a).

questions that cross paradigmatic boundaries, so evaluators tend to be pragmatic in drawing on methods' (Rallis & Rossman, 2003: 493). Combining data
and methods, particularly at the stage of data analysis, has a lesser history
however, with many mixed methods researchers reporting difficulty in 'bringing together the analysis and interpretation of the quantitative and the qualitative
data and [in] writing a narrative that linked the analyses and interpretations'
(Bryman, 2007: 10). Lack of tools for all but the simplest forms of data integration has contributed significantly to this problem. In mixed methods
research:

> Integration can be said to occur to the extent that different data elements and
> various strategies for analysis of those elements are combined throughout a study in
> such a way as to become interdependent in reaching a common theoretical or
> research goal, thereby producing findings that are greater than the sum of the parts.
> (Bazeley, 2010a: 432)

Strategies for integration

Strategies for integrating mixed forms of data in analysis for which NVivo has
the potential to make a contribution[2] include:

- Use of one data source to complement or expand on the understanding gained
  through another, such as when qualitative responses gained through open-ended
  questions in a survey or follow-up interviews are used to help the analyst (and the
  reader) understand the meaning of responses to categorized or scaled data items.
- Use of one form of data to shape or inform the analysis of another.

*Harden and Thomas (2005) used qualitative themes to guide analysis and synthesis
of both qualitative and quantitative findings about children's food preferences, and
Jang, McDougall, Pollon, Herbert, and Russell (2008), in a study of school success,
found when they refactored scaled data based on key qualitative themes that they
were able to generate results that were more interpretable than those from a purely
quantitative factor analysis.*

- Use of data in combination for comparative purposes, as discussed in Chapter 6.
  Demographic, categorical or scaled data are imported as attribute data to define
  subgroups for comparison with respect to how often, and in what way, associated
  qualitative data vary.
- Use of qualitative data to create and record new attributes for use as a basis for comparison of qualitative data.

---

[2] NVivo was used for some but not all of the studies referred to in this section.

A study was designed to better understand and provide for safe travel from home to work for adults with a range of communication and mobility issues. In interviews, family members and employers discussed the level of mobility of these adults as they journeyed from home to work: they could be highly mobile (i.e., few transportation issues), somewhat mobile (i.e., some sporadic difficulties), or problematically mobile (i.e., consistent difficulties). These characteristics were turned into attribute values for the purpose of comparing members of these three groups according to other rich, qualitative codes.

- Conversion of qualitative to quantitative data, for inclusion with other variables in statistical analyses. This might be generated in the form of dichotomous variables, based on the presence or absence of a code for a case; as a 'measure' based on the frequency with which a code is used within a case; or as a score applied by the researcher to capture the intensity with which the category captured by the code has been expressed. These data are generated using a cases-by-nodes matrix (see Chapter 11), with either presence or absence of coding or number of coding references showing in the cells. The matrix can be saved as an Excel file, ready for direct import into statistical software for analysis.

Happ, DeVito Dabbs, Tate, Hricik, and Erlen (2006) categorized a large amount of observational data to combine with physiologic measures on weaning lung transplant patients from ventilators. They were then analysed to produce statistical trends and visual displays.

- Combination of qualitative and quantitative data to create blended variables that can then be converted to attributes and used in further analysis.

In Lynn Kemp's (1999) PhD study of the community service needs of people with spinal injuries in New South Wales, she found a mismatch between need and care delivery. While her quantitative data revealed a desperate shortage of community services, the qualitative data spoke of people feeling ambivalent about whether they would access services they had most complained about not having. She was able to import the codes reflecting feelings about services into the project's statistical database and blend them with the quantitative variable that reflected the current use of services, to create a four-category variable that combined use of and desire for services. Subsequent quantitative analyses suggested that the qualitative ambivalence to services was the response of the people with spinal injuries to the apparently arbitrary distribution of community services, rather than its being

(Continued)

(Continued)

based upon their need for the service, defined either quantitatively or qualitatively. Data from policy documents, however, clearly indicated that services were legislatively mandated to be allocated according to need. Once again, there was dissonance. This time, the newly created use-desire variable was added to the qualitative database as an attribute and used in combination with service satisfaction scales to compare respondents' qualitative responses about the beneficial and detrimental effects of services. When re-analysed qualitatively, the quantitative arbitrariness of service provision was, in fact, not so arbitrary. Services were allocated on the proviso that persons with spinal injuries adopt life plans which met the expectations of service providers, demonstrated by being 'just right', that is, being not too independent, nor too dependent, and evidenced in demonstrating suitable levels of gratitude and humility.

- Use of content-analysed qualitative data as the basis for visualization strategies, including cluster analysis and multidimensional scaling (see Chapter 10).
- Combination of qualitative data with visual and/or geographical data.

Hume, Salmon, and Ball (2005) explored the relationship between children's environmental awareness and their level of physical activity. They used children's maps of their home and neighbourhood, while levels of activity for each child were measured using an accelerometer. The data in the maps were analysed qualitatively to identify what was important to the children. Descriptive themes were then quantified in terms of the frequency with which particular objects and locations were included to create 11 variables. These were then analysed statistically in association with different intensities of physical activity for boys and girls.

- Application of social network analysis to data matrices generated through cross-tabulation of qualitative data.

Exchanges recorded between a group of health professionals involved in making assessments of patient needs were coded for who initiated each instance of communication and to whom it was directed. The content of the communication was also coded. Matrices showing who communicated with whom in particular ways were exported to UCINET for social network analysis, to reveal which professional group was central and who was isolated in relation to the types of issues being discussed.

Structured survey data

Structured surveys comprising both pre-categorized and/or scaled questions and open-ended questions are one of the most common ways in which mixed methods data are gathered (Bryman, 2006). In its most elementary form, integration of data occurs in structured surveys where a pre-categorized response to a question is followed up with a request to respondents to provide comment, explanation or illustration for their answer. Comments, explanations and illustrative material assist the researcher to interpret what each category of response really meant to the survey respondents. Sorting entire comments by associated categorized responses to a parallel question is a relatively simple task in any spreadsheet or database. Analysis in such cases, however, rarely extends beyond identification of broad patterns in the text in relation to respondent groups with, perhaps, the identification of anomalous responses for further investigation.

Using NVivo to analyse mixed format survey data allows you to take analysis further than is possible using a spreadsheet or other database software. The flexibility of the coding system in NVivo means the detail of the text material is readily coded into new emergent concepts or categories, rather than simply being sorted by the question asked. Text stored in these new coding categories can also be viewed comparatively across demographic subgroups, or in relation to responses to parallel categorically coded or scaled questions, for example, when a comment follows a question with fixed-response alternatives. Text viewed also in relation to coded responses to other text-based questions allows you to see connections between the issues that were written about. While doing so has always been possible in NVivo, the introduction of the datasets featured in more recent versions simplifies the task of preparing and working with this form of data.

As well as contributing to understanding the quantitative responses, when data are matched in this way, instances where individuals go against a trend can be readily identified and explored in detail. These cases might be outliers on a statistical measure, deviant cases in qualitative terms, or cases where there is an apparent contradiction in the data from the different sources. When contradictions or other anomalies arise from an exercise in combining data types, this has the potential to stimulate analytical thinking beyond simple illustration. The cause of the contradiction or anomaly might be explained methodologically (an important insight in itself), new substantive understanding could result, or it could create the need for further data collection in order to resolve emergent discrepancies (Bazeley, 2009).

What does a dataset look like?

A dataset is a table of data containing both qualitative (open-ended) and quantitative (pre-categorized) fields (e.g., Figure 9.1). It is often the result of a download from an on-line survey. In addition, NCapture, a browser add-on for Internet Explorer or Google Chrome, can collect data to which you have access from Facebook, LinkedIn, Twitter, and comments on YouTube. These data are converted into a dataset when you import them into NVivo.

Data for cases are entered in rows of a dataset, one row per case, while columns define fields for the data being entered. In Figure 9.1, column A lists the names of the cases, while other columns match questions that were asked. Cell entries in columns E–G contain short verbatim text responses to structured questions. Cell entries in columns B–D contain demographic information relating to each case. They might be used also to include alternatives selected to show responses to pre-categorized questions, 0/1 data indicating selection of an alternative from a list, or a score from a scaled test, rating, or visual analogue scale. Potentially, also, text cell entries might contain summarized contents from longer interviews, perhaps including 'pithy' quotes.

	A	B	C	D	E	F	G
1	Responc	Township	Generation s Down East	Age	The natural environment Down East is	The water quality Down East is	Commercial fishing Down East is
2	DE046	Straits	1	52	beautiful, clean, full of life, rare on the East coast, the main attraction, even for the local people	apparently very good	an important way of living, heritage and generations handed down to family as well as making and mending fish nets and decoys for hunting
3	DE047	Smyrna	3 or more	42	Special environment for wildlife + hearty people	still in good shape	almost gone
4	DE048	Sea Level	1	49	one of the most scenic in the world	clean and inviting	dying, fuel prices, foreign competition, encroachment by fishermen from other state (FL), and lack of customers for custom made fishing boats are hurting the comm. fishermen.
5	DE049	Marshallberg	1	56	not polluted & is clear + clean.	good quality for marine reproduction	in danger, Fuel costs and markets there seems to be plenty of seafood.

Figure 9.1 Data from a survey prepared using an Excel spreadsheet[3]

---

[3] For convenience when entering and viewing data, select columns that will contain text data then **Right-click > Format Cells > Alignment tab > ☑ Wrap text.**

Managing data in a dataset

These instructions assume you are familiar with the layout of an NVivo database and basic concepts and functions in NVivo, as described and demonstrated in previous chapters, especially Chapters 1, 3 and 6.

Preparing a dataset in Excel

Although your survey data can be prepared in any table-based software, each dataset you want to import into NVivo needs to be saved in one of the following formats:

- Microsoft Excel spreadsheet (.xlsx or .xls);
- tab- or comma-delimited text file (.txt).[4]

Data in the first column (usually, though not essentially) will identify your cases. Each record (case) must be on a separate line. If you want to match other data with the survey data, it is essential that the names you use for identification exactly match the case names for the other data. The order in which they are entered is not important, and it is possible to select any column as the column that contains the case names.

Column headers must be entered in a single row (row 1). These will become either attribute names or the names of topic nodes in your NVivo database. Each attribute or text field must be in a separate column.

Cell entries primarily comprise text or numbers. If you include images, or audio or video extracts, NVivo will store these as sources in a separate folder in the same location as the dataset, with an icon inserted into the cell as a shortcut that points to the source. Cells can be left blank.

! You cannot add further data to a dataset source after import – although you can add additional data to the same cases by importing a second dataset (or other sources) and coding it at the relevant case node(s).
! You cannot edit fields in a dataset after it has been imported – although you can annotate them, e.g., if you find an error you want to correct, and you can change an attribute value *after* it has been assigned to a case.
! You cannot select multiple worksheets from within a spreadsheet, so the data you want to import must be gathered into a single worksheet – or import the additional data as another dataset.
! Case names for each row are best kept unique (if you do have two lines of data for one case, the data in the classifying fields must agree).

---

[4] To ensure you have the data laid out appropriately and to facilitate import, we would strongly recommend importing a .txt file into Excel before importing it into NVivo.

Not all of your quantitative variables will be relevant to the qualitative analysis. It is your choice as to whether you (a) keep them in the version of the dataset you import into NVivo in case you change your mind about their relevance (or because it might be useful to refer to them when viewing a particular case sometime) or (b) decide to remove unnecessary 'clutter' from this version of your dataset. For example, if you have scaled measures that have been constructed from a string of subquestions, then for NVivo you need to keep *only* the final scale measure and *not* the subquestions used to create the scale.

Importing and viewing a dataset from Excel

The steps for importing a dataset will be outlined for data prepared in Excel. Importing a text (*.txt) file involves almost identical steps (search Help for *Import data from spreadsheets and text files* for details). Steps for importing a social media dataset follow.

Importing a dataset prepared in Excel

▶ Go to *Navigation View*; select **Sources > Internals > [your subfolder]**.
▶ In *List View*, **Right-click > Import > Import Dataset**.
▶ **Step 1**: **Browse** to locate the Excel file > **Open > Next**.
▶ **Step 2**: If you have more than one sheet with data, select the sheet that you require > **Next**.
▶ **Step 3** provides an opportunity for you to change any qualifiers (e.g., the date format), but this is usually not necessary.
▶ At **Step 4**, you *must* check that NVivo has correctly read the **Analysis Type** for the data in each field of your dataset. A *codable field* is one that contains qualitative responses, designed to be interactively coded; a *classifying field* contains attribute data, designed to be auto-assigned to cases. (Your column with case names is also a classifying field.) Because NVivo scans only the first 25 rows to determine the type of data in a column, the type sometimes needs correction. For example, when importing the dataset shown in Figure 9.2, Pat had to change *ARecognition* to a decimal with 2 decimal places, and *activity* had been read as a classifying rather than a codable field, so the type of data for it also had to be changed. In this step you can elect, also, to not import particular fields: in Figure 9.2, the tick was removed from the **Import Field** checkbox for *AApproachability* and *approachable*.
▶ **Step 5**: Rename the dataset source file within NVivo if you wish > **Finish**.

! You cannot change the field type after import, so it is critical you select the correct type as you are importing!
! Any pairing of T, F, Y, and N will be considered Boolean fields by default and will be converted to 1 and 0 during import unless you change the **Data Type** from **Boolean** to **Text** at Step 4 of the import process.

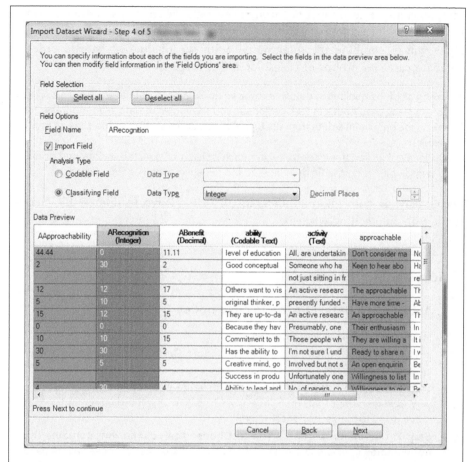

Figure 9.2 Checking the Analysis Type for each field when importing a dataset

✓ Carefully check your imported file before proceeding to code it, so you can delete and reimport if something isn't right – or create a pilot dataset with just a few rows of data to test how the import and auto coding will function with your data, before you import your main file.

? If you have problems importing your dataset, search Help for *Import data from spreadsheets and text files* for additional information.

Viewing the dataset in NVivo

▶ After import, use the tabs on the right margin of the *Detail View* to display the information in **Table** or **Form** view.

Auto coding cases and assigning attribute values from a dataset

While it may seem that NVivo could or should easily handle this dataset file and immediately allow you to make comparisons among the groups in your sample, you will need to work through several series of steps in order to transform this file into components that NVivo can effectively manage. These steps allow you to combine the quantitative with the qualitative data in order to compare cases (or groups of cases) later. The steps are:

1 Taking all of the qualitative data in a row and coding these data to a case. This will give you as many case nodes in your project as you have rows of data in your dataset table.
2 Taking the quantitative data from the same row and adding them to the case as attribute values.
3 Optionally (but recommended), taking each column of qualitative data and coding it to a node based on the field name (i.e., the question asked or topic covered).

Fortunately, as with many other kinds of data, NVivo facilitates this clerical work with auto coding wizards.

Auto coding the dataset

1. Auto coding dataset rows to case nodes

▶ In *Navigation View*, select **Sources**.
▶ In *List View*, **Right-click** on the dataset > **Auto Code**. This will open the Auto Code Dataset Wizard.
▶ **Step 1**: Select to **Code at nodes for each value in a column**. (This is NVivo's very obscure way of saying 'Code rows'! Fortunately, the diagram in the dialogue helps to clarify this description.)
▶ **Step 2**: Use the drop-down arrow to **Choose the column that contains the node names** (this is usually the first column in the dataset). These will be used to name your cases.
▶ You probably do not need to create a hierarchical structure for these case nodes (and it is *not* recommended that you do so). The window at the bottom of the screen provides a preview of the case nodes that will be created. At this stage they are shown under a parent node created by the wizard, named to match the dataset. **Next**.
▶ **Step 3**: The wizard will show you the columns that have codable text in them. Usually you would select all of them as this is the text that will be coded to each case node. If they are not there already, move them to the right, under **Selected columns**). **Next**.
▶ **Step 4**: Choose to locate the new case nodes under a new or existing parent node or in a new or existing folder. Or if your case nodes already exist, and the names match exactly those that will be created from the survey, then select an existing location (i.e., where the case nodes currently reside) as the location for coding the new content. The content will be added to the existing nodes. **Finish**.
▶ Locate and view the case nodes you just created. Each should indicate that a source has been coded to the case, with the number of references matching

the number of cells coded at each case. Open one in *Detail View* to see its qualitative data.

2. Classifying nodes and creating attributes from a dataset

Preparation

! The wizard to assign attributes from the dataset will do so only for an existing classification. If you do not yet have the classification you plan to use, you will need to create it before using this wizard.

To create a new classification (if necessary):

▶ Navigate to **Classifications > Node Classifications**.
▶ In *List View*, **Right-click > New Classification**, and then provide a **Name**. That is all you need to do at this stage.

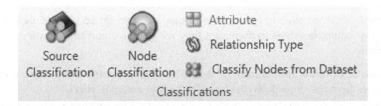

Figure 9.3 *Classifications* group in the ***Create*** ribbon

Start the 'Classify Nodes from Dataset' wizard

▶ Go to **Sources**, and in *List View* select the dataset. From the ***Create*** ribbon, *Classifications* group, select **Classify Nodes from Dataset** (Figure 9.3).

Assuming you have already created the case nodes using the **Auto Code Dataset Wizard**, as outlined above:

▶ **Step 1:** The wizard is showing the kind of classifying fields (attributes and values) that will be added to your cases.
▶ **Step 2:** (Figure 9.4) Select to classify nodes **Under > Existing Node** or **Existing Folder**.
o **Select** the **Name** of the parent node or folder where your existing case nodes are located.
o Remove the tick next to ☐ **Create nodes if they do not exist in this location**.
o Check ☑ **Update the classification of existing nodes**.

(Continued)

(Continued)

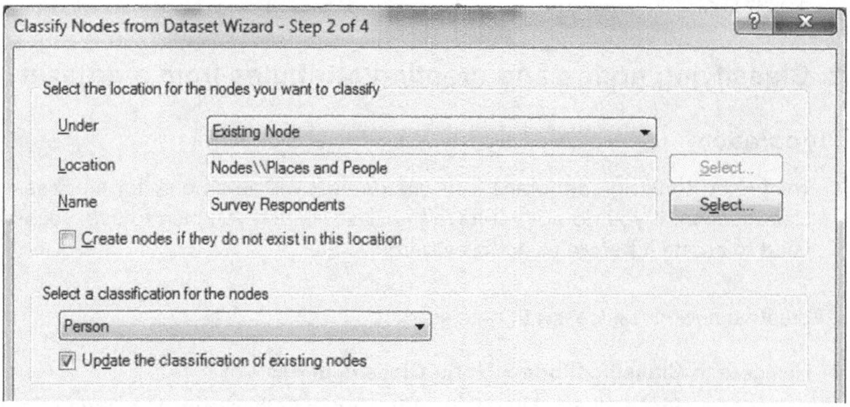

Figure 9.4 Locating the nodes to be classified

✓ If you have not already created the nodes, you can do so via this wizard, and assign attribute values to them, but they will not have qualitative data coded to them.

▶ **Step 3: Choose the column** (of the dataset) **that contains the node names:** select from the drop-down list (usually the first column). **Next**.

▶ **Step 4:** (Figure 9.5) **Choose the columns containing attribute values for your** (case) **nodes.** From the **Available columns**, select the ones you want to be included (ignoring the one with case names), and use the arrow in the middle to move them right, so they appear under **Selected columns**. You can select more than one at the same time using **Shift+click** or **Ctrl+click**.

If you have attributes with integer or decimal values, you can choose to **Map and Group** the values of those attributes as they are set up. This will make them more useful for matrix coding queries. For example, if you want to change something recorded as a continuous variable to an attribute using categories, you would need first to **Map** the new attribute by changing its **Data type** from Integer (or Decimal) to Text. Then **Group** categories as you see fit. (In Figure 9.5 the age range, originally 32–81, was modified to 30–89, to allow NVivo to group the ages in a more standardized manner.) **OK**.

▶ When you have finished making any modifications you might want, **Finish**.

✓ It is important to check your work, by selecting one or two of your case nodes (in *List View*), then **Right-click > Node Properties > Attribute Values**.

? Search Help for *Classify nodes from dataset*.

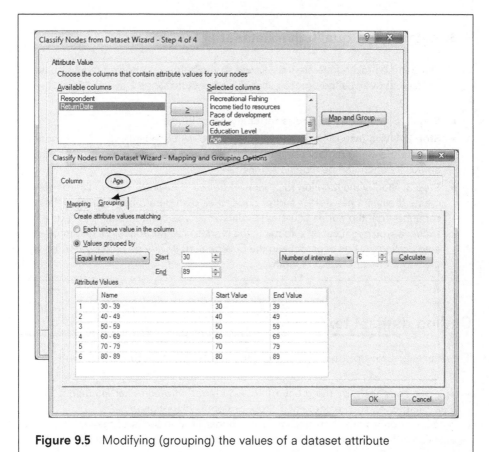

Figure 9.5 Modifying (grouping) the values of a dataset attribute

Auto coding dataset 'codable text' fields

There is one more time you might want to run the auto code dataset wizard before you start working through to interactively code thematic text from your dataset. You can auto code the data for each field (each usually holding responses to a particular question) to nodes for the questions being asked or the topic or issue being written about. This will then allow you to (a) code within just one question at a time; (b) run a text query or other form of analysis within just one question; and (c) easily compare responses to different questions, if that becomes an analysis issue. It will also mean you can do some rapid analyses before you code interactively, by comparing responses to particular questions for different subgroups in your sample.

✓ Nodes created this way should be placed in a separate location from those created through interactive coding.

---

3. Auto coding qualitative dataset fields

The steps to be taken here are very similar to those for auto coding rows to case nodes (see above), as the process uses the same Auto Code Dataset Wizard.

▶ **Step 1**: Select **Code at nodes for selected columns**.
▶ **Step 2**: NVivo (usually) will automatically select all codable fields. Check those that are there and modify using the arrows to add or remove as you wish. The default location can be modified in the next step.
▶ **Step 3**: Modify the location for your new nodes, if desired. You would normally create them in a new folder and/or under their own parent node, to keep these separate from the nodes you create yourself as you work through the text. For example, you might set up a folder in the Nodes area for nodes created through auto coding (as has been done in the *Environmental Change* project) – or move them into one afterwards. **Finish**.

Coding dataset text

There are several options for coding the qualitative data in dataset cells.

- You can code them by using any of your preferred strategies for interactive coding (see Chapter 4), such as drag and drop, or right-click options.
- Where responses are short and/or fairly standardized in terms of the words used to describe different aspects of the topic, you might code them using text search queries (see Chapter 5).

✓ If your dataset has large cells so that the display is awkward to manipulate in either Table or Form view, you will find it easier to code the data by either (a) opening the case nodes – if the focus of your analysis is on the respondents or sources of data, or you need to understand any response in the context of that person's other responses; or (b) opening the question nodes – if your analysis focus is on the issues raised by each question. You can code data to other nodes from either of these places.

When coding dataset text (or very structured text of any sort), avoid the temptation to create a series of codes under each question to capture the responses to just that question. In most surveys or interviews, this will lead to considerable repetition of codes, as many of the same issues will come up in response to different questions. This, in turn, will create a problem of not being able to get a comprehensive understanding of any one issue because text about it has been spread across several nodes – and you will have created an unmanageable ('viral') coding system. You need to have all your data about any topic or issue together in one place, as outlined in Chapter 5. This is why we suggest storing the auto coded question nodes separately from your other coding. If necessary, you can always check which question prompted a particular answer by hovering over the coding density bar, retrieving the context (**Right-click > Open Referenced Source**), or using a matrix coding query.

Importing and analysing a social media dataset

The capacity of the software to make use of social media sources is too new for us to have broad experience of how this might be used, or for a lot of examples to share with you, so we will mostly leave that to your imagination! Using NCapture, you can download the following kinds of data from social media sites:

- Facebook: wallposts for a user, page or group.
- LinkedIn: discussions and comments from groups that you belong to.
- Twitter: tweets that are public or from people who have granted you access to their private tweets.
- Comments associated with a YouTube video.

In his research to investigate the co-created spectator experience of the London 2012 Olympic Games, Paul Emery of La Trobe University Business School gathered information covering a breadth of spectator experiences that included all Olympic events from different viewing locations. Data for the study included questionnaires, interviews, observations, diaries, operational management plans, as well as social, print and electronic media sources.

Within the 24 hours following the opening ceremony, more than a thousand tweets were captured from the BBC London 2012 social media site. NCapture was used to convert these into a dataset for analysis in NVivo 10. The dataset was auto coded to identify individual responses as cases with associated demographic attributes. Each tweet was then individually coded as to whether it was positive, negative, mixed or neutral in tone towards the opening ceremony. The content was analysed with codes including, for example, references to humour (e.g., Mr Bean; the Queen meeting James Bond), 'wow' factors (e.g., the industrial revolution) and the element of surprise (e.g., who was going to light the Olympic flame).

Data could then be sorted and queried. Attitudes could be matched with content, and questions could be asked, such as how UK females differed from those from overseas in their opinions. These social media findings could then be compared with those from other sources, to add to the breadth and depth of data for appraisal.

In social media files gathered by NCapture, fields containing posts or comments are automatically defined as codable fields, while those containing user names, hashtags or biographical data are predefined as classifying fields. NVivo establishes how each field is treated, and the layout of the files. Because each site differs slightly in the way the data is laid out, and they differ from a regular spreadsheet, for example, in having information about the same topic spread across two fields (the original post and the comments that follow), the steps for working with these kinds of data are a little different from analysing a regular spreadsheet, and from each other, although the general principles for the four media types are the same.

Capturing and importing a social media dataset

The steps for capturing and importing a Facebook, LinkedIn, Twitter or YouTube database differ from those for an Excel or text file. The process is similar, however, to that for capturing web pages, to which you were introduced in Chapters 7 and 8.

Capturing the data

As with web pages, you first capture the discussion data from the internet and save them as a source file in a folder in your regular Windows filing system. Only then can you import the file into NVivo, where it becomes a dataset.

▶ Open your browser (Internet Explorer or Google Chrome). Check that you can see the NCapture icon in the toolbar, or alternatively that NCapture for NVivo is available under Tools. (If you are having trouble with installation of NCapture, or seeing the icon, search NVivo Help for *NCapture*.)

▶ Sign in to Facebook, LinkedIn or Twitter, and locate the wallpost for a user, page or group (Facebook), discussions and comments from groups that you belong to (LinkedIn), or tweets that are public or from people who have granted you access to their private tweets (Twitter).

▶ Click on the NCapture icon in the toolbar or select **NCapture for NVivo** from the **Tools** menu.[5] The download dialogue shown in Figure 7.7 will open, showing the **Source type** (e.g., LinkedIn Discussions as Dataset) and **Source name** for the page you are downloading. For YouTube, if you check the option to download Video and Comments, the comments will be saved as a social media dataset accompanying the video.

▶ Add a description to the source (and a memo as to what it is about if you wish). These will be imported by NVivo at the same time as the dataset.

▶ Check where the program is saving the data file. Internet Explorer will default to the folder established for NCapture within Documents, but you can navigate elsewhere; Chrome will default to Downloads unless you change it.

---

[5] You will be asked to authorize NCapture to gather the data on the first occasion you use it within each social media site (in recognition of the potential privacy of the data). After you authorize it once, you will not be asked again.

Importing the social media dataset

▶ In *Navigation View*, select **Sources > Internals > Right-click** to create a sepa-rate Internals folder for social media data.

▶ In *List View* for your social media folder, **Right-click > Import > Import from NCapture >** locate and select the source(s) you want to import.

! Do *not* select Import Dataset! NVivo will convert the download to a dataset for you.

▶ By default, NVivo will match imports that are downloads from the same user or group and merge them. Merging datasets allows you to update an earlier import. Optionally, you can turn this off by unchecking ☐ **Merge matching social media datasets** at the base of the dialogue.

? Search Help for *Import from Facebook* (or *LinkedIn*, *Twitter* or *YouTube* as needed).

Auto coding the discussion threads and users in the data

The most useful way to auto code social media data for analysis is to code the content of posts to nodes for discussions (threads) and to create case nodes from the usernames. For all forms of social media, Option 1 in Step 1 of the **Auto Code Dataset Wizard** will achieve both of these goals, and in addition, will automatically classify the usernames and assign attributes to them based on biographical data downloaded with the dataset (illustrated below).

✓ Create a special Node folder you can use for storing auto coded data from social media sites to keep the auto coded nodes separate from your interactive (thematic) coding. Specify this as the folder to store the new nodes at Step 3 of the Auto Code Dataset Wizard.

In datasets downloaded from *Facebook* and *LinkedIn*, usernames will be recog-nized and matched for original posts and following comments, even where these are recorded in different columns of the dataset. Discussions (LinkedIn) and conversations (Facebook and YouTube) will be arranged under the username of the original poster in nodes identified by the post topic, with both the original post and all following comments included in the node (Figures 9.6 and 9.7). Each of these also creates a branch coding data to usernames. For a *Twitter* data-set, Option 1 of the **Auto Code Dataset Wizard** creates a tree of nodes also with two branches, one based on usernames, and the other on hashtags used in the tweets.

You can either leave the structure as it is in your social media nodes folder, or, because the nodes for each social media site are arranged in two separate branches, you might keep the discussions, conversations, tweets or comments branches in your social media folder, but move the usernames to your cases folder (as in the *Environmental Change* sample project in NVivo).

When you open and view the node for a discussion thread, if you select **View > Coding Stripes > Coding density only**, you will be able to hover to see who contributed each individual post or comment (Figure 9.7). You will, of course, also be able to code, annotate or link the content of the post and comments.

Name	Sourc
⊟ ◯ LinkedIn	0
⊟ ◯ Discussion	0
⊟ ◯ Aidan T.	0
◯ Mixed methods thesis, how	1
⊟ ◯ Albert E.	0
◯ Best Practices for Sequenc	1
◯ Is it best practice to include	1
⊞ ◯ Angela G.	0
⊞ ◯ Betty C.	0
⊟ ◯ Username	0
◯ Adam B.	1
◯ Ahmad A.	1
◯ Aidan T.	1
◯ Albert E.	1
◯ Alex L.	1

Name	Sources	Refere
⊟ ◯ Twitter	0	0
⊟ ◯ Username	0	0
◯ AmarooCruises	1	4
◯ CaptainAhab1313	1	15
◯ JervisBayWhales	1	7
◯ Jjarbow	1	2
◯ TamboiQueen	1	9
◯ WildAboutWhales	1	216
◯ cee_m_cee	1	13
◯ kiffgee	1	1
⊟ ◯ Hashtags	0	0
◯ whaleon	1	251
◯ newywhales	1	1
◯ whales	1	12
◯ NPWS	1	2
◯ whalewatchingspe	1	1

Figure 9.6 Auto coded node arrangements for social media data

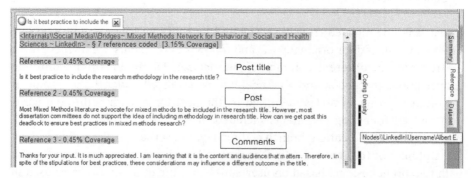

Figure 9.7 Viewing text and contributor in an auto coded LinkedIn discussion

Classifying social media data

As noted above, usernames are automatically given a classification based on the source of the data, with attributes also automatically assigned based on data in other classifying fields in the relevant dataset (Figure 9.8). This is done as part of the auto coding process, so that you do *not* have to run the separate wizard to classify the nodes from the dataset. Moving the subtree of usernames from one node folder to another after closing the wizard does not interfere with this process.

? For further information, search Help for *Analyzing social media data.*

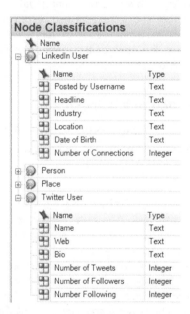

Figure 9.8   Automatically assigned node classifications and attributes for social media usernames

Analysing datasets and other mixed data types

Coded data from a dataset can be analysed along with any other coded data for the same purposes and employing the same strategies as for those other data (see Chapters 10 and 11). Additionally, when you work with datasets, attribute data generated from the classifying fields of the dataset are linked, through the case nodes you created, with the coded qualitative data from the text-based (codable) fields or with the discussion threads for social media. This linkage of data types makes possible mixed methods analysis strategies that integrate different forms of data. Whether you are working with datasets or with a combination of statistical survey data and matched qualitative sources such as notes from observations, interviews or focus group data, there are three basic underlying strategies for these methods (Bazeley, 2006).

1 Analyse each set of data separately, using them to complement each other when you write the results and conclusions, or perhaps using one to 'test' your conclusions from the other.
2 Use the quantitative data as attributes in combination with the coded qualitative data, to generate comparisons of what was observed or said, based on the demographic characteristics, categorical responses, or other scores in the quantitative data. For this you use a matrix coding query with nodes in the rows and attribute values (or sets) in the columns, as described in Chapter 6.
3 Convert the qualitative coding to quantitative variable data, for statistical analysis, or for export to an existing statistical database for use in combination with other statistical data you collected. You will use a matrix coding query to export quantitized qualitative data, but with cases defining the rows of the matrix, and nodes in the columns to create a case-by-variable table.

Combining quantitative and qualitative data

The process for achieving this is described in Chapter 6. The following illustration shows how dataset material might be used in this way.

In a study of discrimination experienced by female physicists, respondents provided both categorical (yes/no) responses and written examples and comments about being treated differently, being harassed, or experiencing discrimination at various stages of their student and work careers. Matrix coding queries were used to sort the examples and comments for each of these according to whether the respondent gave a yes or no response to the categorical questions. A participant-based understanding of harassment and discrimination could then be provided to illustrate the meaning and significance of the distribution of yes/no responses. Of particular interest were inconsistent responses, where the example given did not reflect the yes or no categorical response selected by the respondent. When is harassment (or discrimination) 'acceptable', that is, not felt to be sufficient to warrant a 'yes' response, and yet is noted as an example? How is this different from harassment that is considered unacceptable?

For example, 'occasional sexist remarks from staff members' were considered harassment by some respondents but not by others. Was it the nature or level of the harassment that was different, or was the assessment of harassment in these more marginal cases something to do with who the respondents were? Did those who provided inconsistent responses differ from those who provided consistent responses, either demographically, or in their other categorical or text responses? Is there anything unique about respondents who reported but also rationalized things that others found objectionable? One of those who was not concerned about occasional sexist remarks perceived the situation as being 'unavoidable – they can't help noticing a woman in a "man's" job'. Another suggested:

You are obviously more conspicuous than the average male. People will tend to notice you more. Some will be nicer to you. Some will patronize you. Some will find you easier to communicate with. Some will feel less confident of your technical ability. But whether these things amount to discrimination I don't know. I feel strongly that once people get to know you, their level of respect for you is based much more on whether you can do your job or not than on whether you are male or female.

These two respondents had differing levels of qualification, but perhaps it was relevant that, in contrast to many other respondents, each was older and married, and each passed it off as a natural consequence of being in an obvious minority. It was those who were younger and single who were statistically more likely to report harassment – differences which prompted a further series of questions to guide and deepen analysis.

Converting qualitative data

As noted above, conversion of qualitative coding to a quantitative form is readily achieved using a straightforward matrix coding query with cases and nodes, to create a case-by-variable table suitable for importing into any statistical database. The principal issue that arises is what form of numerical output to select as content for the matrix cells. This can be modified in the matrix display by selecting, via your right mouse button, **Cell Content**, and making your choice from there.

- The safest option is to choose to show presence or absence of coding for each case at each node as 1 or 0, respectively (**Cell Content > Coding Presence**). This makes no assumptions about the continuity or strength of the data for each code-based variable (Bazeley, 2010a).
- Alternatively, to assess the possible importance attached to any code-based variable, you could show the number of passages or words coded at each node for each case (**Cell content > Coding References** or **Words Coded** or **Duration Coded**). The 'accuracy' of this will be impacted by: whether you tended to code short excerpts or long comprehensive passages; for media files whether you have coded both the wave file and the transcript; and most obviously, by the relative verbosity of your interviewees (or length of other data sources).

Once you choose the form of output you want, conversion is a simple matter of exporting the matrix as an Excel file, ready for importing into a statistical database.

In a study of court awards of compensation to be paid by insurers for injuries received from motor vehicle accidents, the primary data were judgments made by the judge or arbitrator deciding each case. These quite unstructured judgments, which varied in content and length, included a review of the factors considered in determining the amounts awarded. The primary analysis was designed to derive an understanding of the process of judges' decision-making about compensation in

(Continued)

(Continued)

these cases, but because the amount awarded was known, it was possible also to test how relevant particular considerations were in determining the quantum of the award. Where the text of the judgment included discussion relating to, say, the veracity of the plaintiff, the regularity of his or her previous employment, the nature of the injury, whether the medical assessments were those of a treating doctor or one brought in especially by the insurance company, or whether there was conflicting medical evidence presented, that part of the text was coded at appropriate categories in NVivo, regardless of where it occurred in the document. The presence or absence of such coding for each case then could be exported as an Excel file, and imported directly to a statistical database (e.g., SPSS) and added to the variables already there (which included some facts about the court case and the amount awarded). Statistical testing could then be used (once data from a large, consecutively drawn sample were aggregated) to assess whether these considerations, either singly (using t-tests) or in combination with existing quantitative variables (using multiple regression), were associated with the level of compensation payout.

Writing from mixed methods data

Integration using different but complementary sources best occurs at the stage where results are being composed, well before final conclusions are drawn (Bazeley & Kemp, 2012). Reporting then reflects the input of all sources and methods throughout, and usually in these circumstances is best arranged by the issue or aspect of the topic being discussed. This reflects that the topic prompted and guided the study, not the methods used to gather or analyse the data.

10

Tools and strategies for visualizing data

Visual tools play a significant part in analysis. They allow us to see large amounts of data condensed into a single page. Visual summaries of data in charts, graphs and diagrams, generated within the software's database, help us see patterns and relationships in data. Creating a model, with its relative positioning of objects of different sizes and placement of connectors between objects, helps us to see who or what is involved, their relationships and their relative importance, and perhaps even causal pathways. Visualization strategies assist in early working with data, as well as in later analyses and with presenting your results.

In this chapter:

- Explore the range of tools available in NVivo for:
  - o case analysis
  - o cataloguing and conceptualization
  - o exploring relationships
  - o building theory.

- Understand the potential benefits of using visualization tools in your research through the examples provided.

Why visualize?

Prehistorically, when cave drawings, rock art, and the like were used to record events, writing was based on drawing. Somewhat more recently, William Playfair (1759–1823) created what are still the best-known statistical graphics for summarizing data (the bar chart, the pie chart, and the time-series line graph). He saw a graph where data points are plotted and patterns revealed as helping to understand nature, and therefore of use to both science and commerce (Dickinson, 2010).

Purposes for using visual analysis techniques

Visualization provides 'an ability to comprehend huge amounts of data', 'allows the perception of emergent properties that were not anticipated', 'often enables problems with the data itself to become apparent', and 'facilitates understanding of both large-scale and small-scale features of the data' (Ware, 2000: 3). When you construct a visual model, it forces you to clarify your categories and concepts and to think through the links between them. In the process, in NVivo, you always retain access to the qualitative data that support the visualization. Miles and Huberman (1994: 91) famously wrote: 'You know what you display'. At the same time, a model is an effective tool for communication of your central understanding to an audience.

Visual tools in NVivo are of two broad types:

- those that provide a visualization of data from within the NVivo database, such as charts and graphs; and
- models that you construct by connecting shapes and/or project items.

✓ As you work with visualizations, always write about what you learn from them into your project journal.

Our approach in this chapter

In Chapter 2 we took you through the basics of creating a simple model in which to map your thoughts about your project. We suggest you review those basics before proceeding here. Our approach in this chapter will be to focus more on how you might use the various visual tools provided by NVivo to support your analysis, and less on the details of the routine steps to achieve these, where the latter are adequately covered in earlier chapters or in the program's Help files. Non-routine steps will be outlined as necessary.

? In particular, we point you to the group of Help files listed under *Visualizations*, and to the associated video tutorial that can be accessed from the Welcome screen of the Help files.

NVivo offers a range of visualization possibilities – from simple pie charts based on (demographic) attributes, and bar charts showing the top 20 nodes in a document, through more complex three-dimensional charts based on matrix results or other combinations of nodes and attributes; to multidimensional clustering or visualizations. We will be drawing on our own and others' projects, including the *Researchers* project that is available on the companion website, to illustrate these possibilities.

! All visualization techniques should be treated with caution as it is very easy to gain a wrong impression from a simply generated visualization that is built on a range of complex knowledge and assumptions.

Saving models

Models that you create are automatically saved when you save your project, so you can return to them at any time to review what you constructed. Additionally, you can archive a copy of your model by saving a copy as a static model. In so doing, you retain a historical record of your evolving ideas while being able to continue to develop them on the dynamic copy of the model.

Case analysis using models

As you complete your work in reflecting on, annotating, memoing and coding a source document that relates to a case, you will find several visual tools useful to help you review what you have learned from that case. Use these to create and illustrate a case summary – or just to stimulate some final reflective thoughts.

Chart the coding on the source

A chart of coding for the source will show you the 20 nodes used most often for coding the selected source, in order of frequency according to the proportion of the source coded by each node (Figure 10.1). It provides a

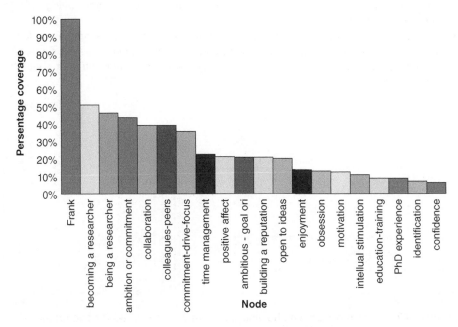

Figure 10.1   Chart of coding for Frank showing top 20 codes used

quick overview of the important topics and concerns raised within that source.

▶ With the source selected in *List View*: **Right-click > Visualize > Chart Document Coding**.

✓ Double-click on a column to access the text at the node.

Alternatively, **Right-click > Visualize > Graph** will show *all* the nodes used in coding the source, including those saved in the Queries Results folder (and these, in turn, include cells of matrices). This circular display can become very large, making it difficult to take in, and there is no order or sequence in the arrangement of the nodes in the display.

View the source with coding stripes

▶ With the source showing in *Detail View*, go to the **View** ribbon > **Coding Stripes > Nodes Most Coding**.

The stripes for the nodes you have used will be set out across the screen, adjacent to text where they were used, in order of frequency of use (Figure 10.2).
  Things to consider from this display include:

• Have you used multiple nodes, as needed, to code the various elements of what is going on in each passage? This has important implications for your being able to query your data in a satisfactory way.
• Are there nodes that often seem to appear at the same time, indicating they code the same passages? These might provide the basis for coding queries based on intersections (*Node x* AND *Node y*). If they appear together often, what is different about the times when they don't appear together?

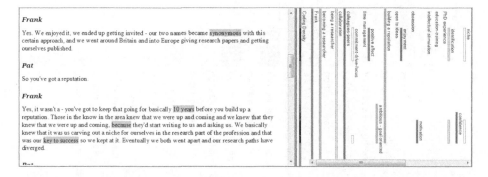

Figure 10.2   Frank's document showing nodes most often used for coding as stripes

Modelling a participant case

Try visualizing how you see this case, using a model (Figure 10.3). In building models, you gain the best sense of how the nodes might fit together to tell a story – the story of your research question from the perspective of this participant or case.

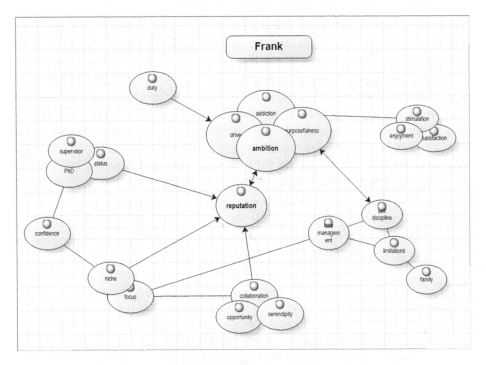

Figure 10.3   A case map for Frank, showing the centrality of ambition and reputation as driving forces in his life

---

Modelling a case

▶ In a new model: **Right-click > Add Project Items > [your source] > ☑ Items coding > OK**.

▶ Click anywhere to deselect all the items in the model.

▶ Select just the icon for the source and **Delete**.

▶ Move and connect remaining nodes to represent how you see the case. Delete unwanted items.

✓ If the case you want to model is distributed across multiple sources or comprises parts of a focus group, use a **Group Query** to **Look For** the nodes (**Items Coding**) the case (**Scope**), restricted to your thematic nodes (**Range**). Save the finds as a set, import the set with its members into the model, remove just the set icon (leaving the members behind), and then proceed as above.

When your case is an organization – using model groups

Model Groups show on the right of your screen, whenever you open a model. Some of these are built into the program, others can be custom designed by you. They allow you to specify groups of items and links within your project that can be viewed or hidden on request. If you have no need to use them for a particular model, and need the space, you can turn the display on or off in the *Model* ribbon, by unchecking the ☑ **Model Groups** box at the far left of the ribbon.

When you include case nodes in your model, then model groups based on node classifications will be activated automatically. These groups are based on attribute values and are used to show or hide the presence of cases with particular attributes within your models. Similarly, if your model contains items linked by relationship nodes (example provided later in this chapter), then the Project Groups area will contain a list of relevant relationship types to allow you to show or hide items related in particular ways.

Additionally, items can be identified as belonging to particular custom groups which are devised and named by you. Once you determine the basis for a custom group and identify its content, the contribution of that group to the overall model can be clearly viewed.

? Search Help for *Model groups.*

Imagine you are studying communication patterns within a company. You identify a series of cases – people working at different levels in the company – and you draw connectors between them to indicate who speaks to whom. Use position in the model to indicate at which level each person is working (e.g., manager, supervisor, worker). Use connectors to identify formal communication channels and use a custom group to capture the formal communication network. Repeat this for the informal communication network, as a second custom group. Perhaps some of those in these networks wield particular influence – they are the powerbrokers – identify them by giving their icons a distinctive style. When you view the model for a custom group, you can see where the powerbrokers lie in the networks, and compare whether they are most active in their formal or informal networks. With project groups activated (by using case nodes rather than sources to identify people) you can also compare the formal and informal networks (and powerbrokers) in relation to demographic and other attribute values.

Apply styles to items in your model

Styles are set up for your current project through **File > Info > Project Properties > Model Styles**, or you can apply colour to multiple selected items using the **Fill** and **Line** options in the *Home* ribbon. Apply styles (such as line, text and fill colour) to the items in your models, for example, to distinguish environmental conditions from personal factors, or positive from negative outcomes. Or use styles to distinguish between conditions, strategies and consequences. Use different styles applied to arrows to suggest mediating influences as distinct from direct influences, formal from informal communication channels, positive from negative impacts, or other differences in connections relevant to the issues of your project.

Building on case models

If you use the modeller to visualize each case as you complete coding of it, you will build up quite a series of models. Review and evaluate those models, identifying commonalities and differences across the cases. Look for patterns in how you are constructing the models; check out which nodes keep reoccurring, which seem to be pivotal in the models, and whether any are associated strongly with some types of cases but not others.

Grouping and conceptualizing

Sorting concepts to build a hierarchical code system

In Chapter 5 we provided advice for constructing a tree-structured system for your nodes, to facilitate further coding and analysis. If you made your initial nodes without thinking about structure (which is usually recommended) then using the modeller to sort those nodes into groups can really assist the process of structuring. The visual display, the kinaesthetic activity of rearranging nodes in the display as

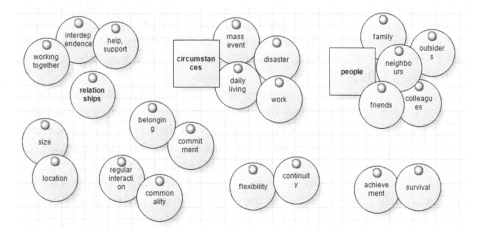

Figure 10.4 Sorting nodes into 'trees'

you explore alternatives, and the software feature that allows you to have only one copy of any node in a model all work together to help you see those that might belong in the same tree. Figure 10.4 shows an arrangement in progress of nodes relating to people's descriptions of their experience of being part of a community.

Sorting nodes

▶ In a new model, **Add Project Items**, selecting all your thematic nodes (i.e., ignoring case nodes and auto coded nodes).

▶ Do not add associated data, so they come in without any connections showing; **OK**.[1]

▶ Move the nodes around the screen to make clusters based on their being the 'same kind of thing'.

▶ Add shapes, if necessary, to provide names for the clusters you create.

✓ This arrangement, when reasonably complete, can be used as the basis for designing a hierarchical (tree-structured) coding system. You can't reorganize nodes directly from the model, so to transfer what you learned through this exercise back to your coding system, you will benefit from printing a reference copy of the model (**File** menu).

Building (theorizing) the structure of a concept

Concepts are foundational to all research. If you are interested in thinking deeply about and theorizing the structure and meaning of a concept, then make use of the strategy outlined above for structuring a coding system to help in that task. Gary Goertz (2006) lamented the lack of theorizing about concepts, arguing that theorizing should precede measuring. He proposed a multidimensional and multilevel structure for concepts in which the top level names the basic idea; the second level comprises dimensions of that concept (the elements that make it what it is); and a third (or sometimes fourth) level identifies indicators for the concept (observable items that point to those dimensions and allow you to measure them).

One approach to theorizing a concept is to use your data and a constant comparative process to prompt some analytical thinking about its dimensions before you go about identifying things that might serve to indicate these. Comparative strategies for developing new nodes (see Chapter 4) or for 'breaking apart' the data contained in nodes (see Chapter 6) can assist in this process. Another approach is to abstract from observed data to develop dimensions that encompass the concept. This approach was used by Pat in a study of academics' concept

---

[1] Clicking **OK** in this dialogue when you are not adding any associated data seems counterintuitive, but if you click on **Cancel**, you are thrown back to choosing the data to import.

of research performance. Responses to questions about the characteristics of researchers who excelled in various ways were coded descriptively for content. The descriptive nodes were sorted using the modeller, in association with queries to check associations and overlaps between them. This allowed experimentation with different arrangements, with each change leading to further reflection on the definition and meaning of the dimensions being developed and a further detailed examination of the data. Occasionally the content of nodes was recoded to ensure a sound basis for the dimensions and for placement of each indicator. This quite exhaustive process led to a detailed description and a model of research performance showing the theoretical relationships between the structural layers (Bazeley, 2010b). For further guidance on concept development and the structure of concepts, see Bazeley (2013), Becker (1998), and Goertz (2006).

Using the coding system to demonstrate the structural properties of an experience

Your coding system can help you to see the structure of the phenomenon or experience you are investigating.

Ian Coxon is a design researcher at the University of Southern Denmark, with a passion for understanding everyday human experience. For his doctoral thesis at the University of Western Sydney, he used a hermeneutic phenomenological approach (based on Gadamer) to explore users' experience of 'new mobility vehicles' – semi-covered, two- or three-wheeled vehicles designed as a sustainable transport option. From this, he developed a taxonomy of experience to reveal the range of human factors that designers might consider (an abbreviated version is shown in Figure 10.5), and proposed that this, with the phenomenological methodology he used, provided a model for further design-related investigative research.

THE BODY ~ SOMATIC EXPERIENCE

    Sensorial stimuli: taste, sound-hearing, smell, touch, sight;

    Comfort

THE HEART ~ AFFECTIVE EXPERIENCE

    Negatively valenced affect (7–1): sense of revulsion … lack of emotion

    Positively valenced affect (1–7): excitement of danger … mystical moments, joy, elation

THE HEAD ~ COGNITIVE EXPERIENCE

    Conation – reflective thought (doing): heightened awareness, physical tension …

    Cognition – reflexive thought (thinking): personal identity, detachment …

OUT THERE ~ CONTEXTUAL FACTORS

    Environmental/ Regulatory/ Social/ Existential/ Corporate factors

Figure 10.5 Using the coding system to build a taxonomy of experience

Usually it is easiest to present a visual overview of the coding system by exporting or printing the *List View* of your nodes from the screen (**Right-click** on a node in *List View* > **Export** or **Print List**). While you can import the relevant components of your coding system into the modeller as a hierarchical display by adding nodes as project items, with their 'children' as associated data, this is not a particularly useful form of display for this purpose.

Comparative analysis with charts and graphs

Matrix coding query results, particularly those comparing coding at a node for subgroups, convert easily to charts (Figure 10.6), to give you an alternative view of your data.

! Charts based on comparisons involving attributes are not adjusted for the differing numbers of cases that have each attribute value and so they can very easily give a false impression of the distribution of responses across groups.

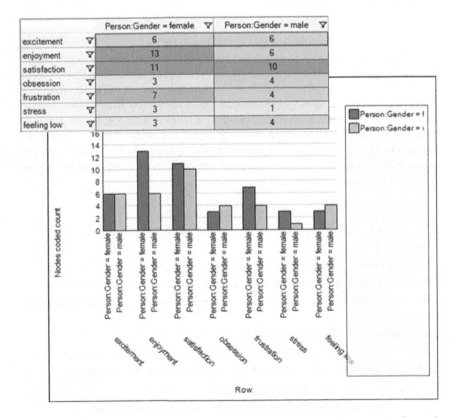

		Person:Gender = female ▽	Person:Gender = male ▽
excitement	▽	6	6
enjoyment	▽	13	6
satisfaction	▽	11	10
obsession	▽	3	4
frustration	▽	7	4
stress	▽	3	1
feeling low	▽	3	4

Figure 10.6 Comparing emotional experiences associated with research for males and females

Create a chart from a matrix

▶ In *Detail View*, ensure your table contains the values you want to show in a chart: **Right-click > Matrix Cell Content**.

▶ Select the **Matrix** tab on the right margin to convert your table to a chart.

▶ Go to the **Chart** ribbon and use the drop-down options to change the *Type* of chart to use (bar, column, heat map, radial[2]), and also to modify the *Title* and the *Labels* to suit your purposes.

✓ Two-dimensional (2D) charts (e.g., grouped column) are less 'jazzy' than 3D charts, but they are much easier to interpret!

From the **Explore** ribbon, click on **Chart > Charts** to open the Chart Wizard to discover added charting possibilities in NVivo. You will probably find, however, that the charts generated directly from *List Views* of nodes or sources or from query results are more useful (and easier to create) than most others created through the wizard.

? Search in Help for *Charts* for guidance on the different charting options.

✓ You can usually change the options in an 'automatically' generated chart, either through the **Chart** ribbon or the right-click menu.

Using interactive modelling to compare cases

Philip Thomas, in a study for the Cooperative Research Centre for Sheep Industry Innovation at the University of New England in regional New South Wales, wanted to know if the farmers who adopted one kind of innovative animal husbandry practice also adopted another, and if so, what were the characteristics of those who adopted both practices, compared with those who adopted only one or neither. Of the 48 farmers in the sample, 29 adopted the practice of scanning their ewes each season to detect those which were not pregnant, pregnant, or pregnant with multiples, so they could cull or regulate nutrition accordingly. Additionally, 22 were employing measures to reduce resistance to drenches used for worm control. Figure 10.7 shows the kind of display that can be generated from his data, to assist in answering his question about adoption of innovation. Furthermore, because case nodes were used to represent the farmers, switching cases on and off using node classifications in the model groups allowed rapid visual assessment of whether adoption of these practices was potentially related to any of the demographic or other attribute values recorded for them.

---

[2] Radial charts require at least three categories in the columns to produce meaningful output.

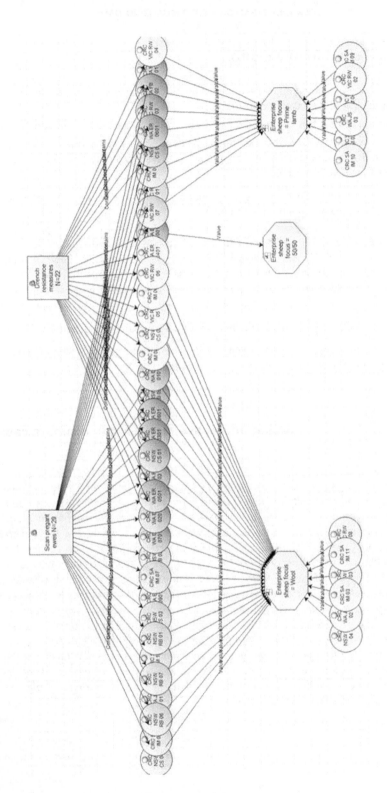

Figure 10.7 Interactive comparative modelling of cases

To obtain these kinds of displays requires a degree of persistence and patience, but the result can be very rewarding both for analysis and as a presentation tool.

Creating an interactive model of cases

▶ Using the **Group Query, Look for > Items Coding:**

  ○ **Range** = the nodes for which you want to compare cases (usually just two).
  ○ **Scope** = the cases you want to consider.

▶ Expand **+** the finds for each of the nodes you selected, then:

  ○ select the cases in each group and **Right-click > Create As > Create As Set**, one for each group.

▶ Create a new model, undock the View, and (temporarily) turn off Model Groups.

▶ **Add Project Items** > select the two sets of cases you just made. **Add Associated Data > Set members > OK**.

The resulting display will show the cases ordered by whether they were included in just Set A, both Set A and Set B, or just Set B. This may be sufficient for your purposes. In any case, if you pull the icon for Set B below the cases, you will be able to tell more easily which cases were in which groups. At this point, you should apply a distinctive colour to each of the resulting three groups – this is essential if you add attribute values to your display.

✓ If your display is too wide for the screen, use the zoom slider (at the lower right edge of the screen) to adjust it.

▶ Turn on ☑ **Model Groups**, and expand **Node Classifications** for the appropriate classification type (you can adjust the width of this pane).

▶ Expand an attribute of interest, and remove or add ticks in the right-hand-side check boxes to hide or show cases that have been assigned particular attribute values. (Wow!)

Add an attribute to the model

If one attribute is of particular interest, you can add its values to the model (Figure 10.7). This will have the added benefit of also showing those cases not coded at either of the original pair of nodes.

(Continued)

(Continued)

▶ Move the Set B icon back up to the top of the display.

▶ **Add project items > Node Classifications >** select the attribute values of interest (limit to 2 or 3 values of the same attribute at most, or your display will
become uninterpretable). Do not add associated data at this stage. Ensure the
attribute icons are located below the case nodes.

▶ Select the icons for the attribute values > **Add Associated Data >
Associated data from project**, and check ☑ **Nodes with attribute value
assigned**. (Optionally, you could display only the links to the currently showing cases.)

▶ Readjust the location of the set and attribute value icons, e.g., with set
icons above the cases, and attribute value icons below the cases. Move
the icons for the additional (uncoded) cases from the ends of the display
to under the relevant attribute values (Figure 10.7 provides a suggested
arrangement).

✓ Continue to review associations with other attributes by turning them on or off
in the model groups, or check back to the data for particular cases (Open Item),
as you contemplate what your display is telling you.

Explore relationships via the modeller

A *relationship* in NVivo is a record created by the researcher to show how two
entities or concepts relate. These might be people or ideas or abstract concepts.
Optionally, it is also a pointer to evidence for the relationship, such as text, audio
or video. Your coding system is not designed to show associations such as who
communicated with whom about what. These kinds of connections – the type
that build theories rather than categories – need to be identified using queries,
or they can be directly recorded using a relationship node (perhaps as a result of
running a query). If you use relationship nodes, you can easily obtain a visual of
the interconnected relationships using a model, and if you have coded evidence
of the connections between the items at the node, this evidence can be instantly
accessed from inside the model, and examined in its original context.

Relationship nodes record a connection of a specified kind between two project items, for example, *encourages, impacts on, communicates with,* or *loves*. The
relationship can be a simple association, or it can have one-way or two-way
(symmetrical) directionality. Thus, using a relationship node, you can record
saltmarshes impact on water quality as a directional relationship, *Betty is married
to Ken* as an associative relationship, and *shames goes with depression* as a bidi-
rectional relationship.

Recording relationships

To set up the kinds of relationships you will use in your project (and the modeller):

▶ Go to *Navigation View* > **Classifications** > **Relationship Types**.
▶ In *List View*, **Right-click** > **New Relationship Type** > provide a **Name** and choose a **Direction**.

To create and code to a relationship node:

▶ Select *Navigation View* > **Nodes** > **Relationships**.
▶ In the associated *List View*, choose to create a **New Relationship**, and select items and other details as required.
▶ Add coding to this node in the usual ways[3] – or leave without coding.

Kristi provides an example of how using relationship nodes in the modeller fosters alternative explanations of data. In her example, Rosa is a peer mediator. Hector, one of her peers, is interviewed to ascertain which peer mediators he turns to, and the characteristics of mediators that either encourage or discourage him from asking for help:

Interviewer: Tell me about the peer mediators you are comfortable turning to when there is a problem with another student.

Hector: Well, I like Rosa because she cares about people, you know? Like, she'll listen and she doesn't ever want to see anyone's feelings hurt or nothing, and she's sometimes like a class clown so she can make people laugh.

These data might be handled in several ways to answer the primary research questions, and are likely to be flagged (or coded) as Positive characteristics: Listening and Positive characteristics: Humour. In the end, the researcher might present a claim (assuming a more comprehensive dataset and more detailed examination) that peer mediators in this school who are known as humorous and outgoing tend to be more actively sought than more introverted mediators. The relationship tool, however, provides additional opportunities to look at alternative explanations. A relationship is created in NVivo (Figure 10.8). Hector seeks assistance from Rosa, and the direction is one-way.

(Continued)

---

[3] Because drag-and-drop coding to a relationship node requires that you change the *List View*, this is one of those times when using the right-click menu (**Code Selection At Existing Node**) is likely to be faster.

(Continued)

New Relationship   ?   X

From	Nodes\\Cases\\Hector	Select...
To	Nodes\\Cases\\Rosa	Select...

Type

Name	seeks assistance from	Select...
Direction	──────────► One Way	
Description	Stories in which actors describe turning to another actor for help in the mediation process	

Color   None   ▼

OK   Cancel

Figure 10.8   Construction of a relationship between two items in NVivo

When a relationship is placed in the modelling tool in NVivo, you obtain a graphic display (Figure 10.9).

Figure 10.9   Visualization of a relationship in the modeller

Because NVivo is keeping track of all possible relationships (identified by the researcher) in the project, it can generate a more complex social network map based on all pairs (Figure 10.10).

Participants identified positive mediator characteristics, but something new has become evident through the mapping that was not articulated as a relevant characteristic by the participants themselves: gender. Among the four actors, the boys are never turned to for assistance. Conversely, the two girls receive requests for assistance from at least two other actors in the network.

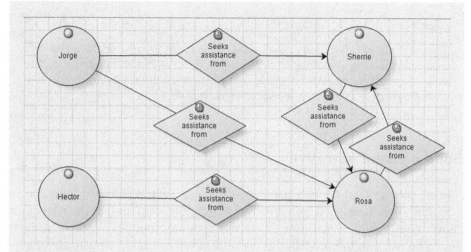

Figure 10.10 Visualization of multiple relationships in the modeller

This is an overly simplistic example, but the potential power to reveal an unanticipated pattern is clear. This pattern may lead to additional data collection, a re-examination of the coding structure, or team meetings to gather new researcher perspectives.

The next unexpected pattern is revealed through an additional, two-step process. First, the relationship between Hector and Rosa is a node and therefore a potential container for evidence, instead of being just a simple statement that 'Hector seeks assistance from Rosa'. Text can be coded at the relationship node. If the researcher returns to the model, a right-click on the relationship (the diamond) between Hector and Rosa will allow him or her to Open Item, to reveal the coded text.

Second, instead of stopping here, there is a further step that allows the researcher to right-click on the coded text and select Open Referenced Source, and be taken immediately to the quote in the context of the full interview. An examination of the additional context below the original coded quote in this case reveals an alternative, more complex pattern. Hector approaches Rosa for assistance because she listens and she's fun – but not always:

> Maybe it's different if it's like an ongoing issue, and I can go to her when I see her in a class or in the hall, but not just like when someone like Adam starts saying things, just to be a jerk while we're working on a project in class. ... If it's guys around, I may not say anything, because they'd tease me for not sticking up for myself, but if it was mostly girls, then they're more likely to stick up for me for some reason, so they wouldn't pick on me if I brought in Rosa.

(Continued)

(Continued)

The presence of other boys in the social context may be a barrier to a boy who would otherwise seek assistance from a girl mediator. Again, this potential pattern may lead to additional data collection, a re-examination of the coding structure, or team meetings to gather new researcher perspectives.

Build a visual narrative

Images can be used as fill for project items or shapes that are included in a model. This means, if you have photographic data that tells a story or shows a sequence of activities, such as an interaction between children at play, you can use the modeller to create a visual narrative with those images (Figure 10.11).

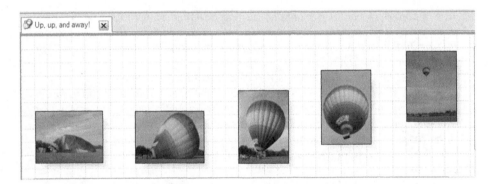

Figure 10.11   Creating a visual narrative

Mapping connections – building theory

Use the modeller as a tool to visualize theoretical connections in your data. Create a new model and add one or more project items, with or without associated items, then adjust the display to tell a story from your research. Some of the suggestions below show simple, quick records of ideas that come up while you continue to code or review data, others will require deep thought and will probably undergo numerous revisions. Seeing something in visual form and working with the visualization both serve to prompt analytic reflection and development. Part 4 of Bazeley (2013) provides multiple examples of the use of visual modelling to progress analysis that is designed to build explanatory theory and develop or demonstrate theoretical coherence.

Modelling theoretical associations

▶ Record theoretical groupings of categories and concepts. Store these also as sets so you can use them in further models or analyses (Figure 10.12).

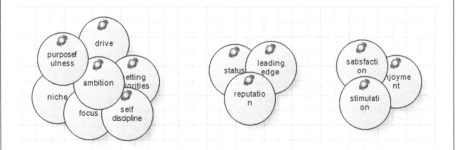

Figure 10.12 Grouping related concepts

▶ Map specific connections between nodes, to reflect processes or associations you noticed in your data (Figure 10.13).

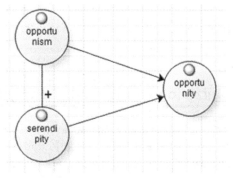

Figure 10.13 Noting theoretical associations

(Continued)

(Continued)

▶ Organize categories around a central explanatory concept. Note the inclusion of sets with their members as part of this model (Figure 10.14).[4]

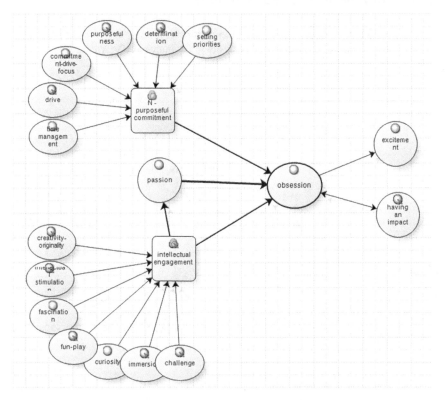

Figure 10.14 Mapping evolving theoretical connections

Exploratory visualization using cluster analysis

Cluster analysis provides an overview of the structure of the data, allowing you to gain some distance to supplement your thematic understanding arising from close reading of your nodes (Guest & McLellan, 2003). NVivo's clustering tool assesses the similarity of either sources or nodes, based on either (a) the similarity of words used in those sources or coded to those nodes, or (b) the similarity of coding that has been applied to the text or images in those sources or nodes. Those similarities are then presented as a horizontal or vertical dendrogram,

---

[4] A red cross indicates the node text is no longer accessible because the node has been merged or deleted since the model was constructed.

graphed in two- or three-dimensional space (using multidimensional scaling), or as a circle graph, accompanied by a list of the statistical measures of association between all items in the display. Clustering data based on similarities in content or coding of qualitative data is generally best used in an exploratory manner, to provoke ideas, rather than as explanatory evidence of association.

Imagine you wanted to gain a preliminary view of whether the academic and professional literature sources in your project deal with the same issues or not. A cluster analysis of those sources, based on word similarity, will show whether or not these sources fall neatly into two main clusters, based on the language used in relation to the topics covered. Later, when you've coded them, you could cluster them on the basis of their coding, to see whether the two groups actually cover the same issues even if their languages are different, or if the issues are different.

Figure 10.15 shows a simple example, created from a cluster analysis of the *nodes* used for coding data about different aspects of the natural environment in the *Environmental Change* project, based on the words found in any of the coded material (select nodes in *List View*, **Right-click > Visualize > Cluster Analysis of Nodes**). Two displays are provided initially – a dendrogram and a summary of the correlation coefficients used to create the dendrogram (columns in this can be sorted by clicking on the header row). Clearly this diagram

Node A	Node B	Pearson ▽	
Nodes\\Natural environment\Water quality	Nodes\\Natural environment\Environmental imp	0.484135	
Nodes\\Natural environment\Habitat	Nodes\\Natural environment\Ecosystem service	0.452668	
Nodes\\Natural environment\Water quality	Nodes\\Natural environment\Environmental cha	0.442685	
Nodes\\Natural environment\Environmental ch	Nodes\\Natural environment\Ecosystem service	0.40437	
Nodes\\Natural environment\Landscape	Nodes\\Natural environment\Environmental cha	0.400106	
Nodes\\Natural environment\Environmental im	Nodes\\Natural environment\Environmental cha	0.392465	
Nodes\\Natural environment\Water quality	Nodes\\Natural environment\Ecosystem service	0.383477	
Nodes\\Natural environment\Habitat	Nodes\\Natural environment\Environmental cha	0.377993	
Nodes\\Natural environment\Habitat	Nodes\\Natural environment\Environmental imp	0.329755	

Figure 10.15 Dendrogram and associated statistics based on clustering nodes by word similarity

suggests that renewable energy was spoken about very differently than other aspects of the local environment (perhaps it belongs elsewhere in the coding system?). It also suggests other links which could be followed up by examining the text at those nodes (available as a right-click option from the display) or by running a coding query to review intersecting text.

If you examine the statistical summary for the cluster analysis, you will see that *water quality* is closely linked with *environmental impacts* and is drawn to show that, but it is almost as closely linked with *environmental change*, which is drawn in a different cluster. In cluster analysis, the presence of quite close links can be hidden by higher-level links. Nevertheless, Guest and McLellan (2003: 189) argue that 'cluster analysis provides a useful alternative [to the complexity of interpreting multidimensional scaling graphs] as it presents data in clearly defined clusters in two-dimensional space, rendering a quick and easy visual tool for interpretation.'

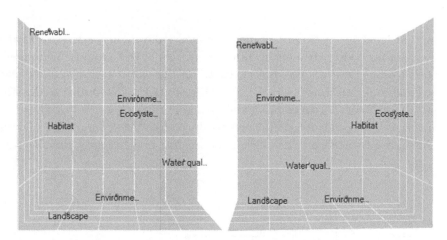

Figure 10.16   3D cluster maps of features of the natural environment, based on word similarity

The alternative of using multidimensional scaling to view the associations in 3D space has the advantage that it affords the possibility of seeing both a third dimension and clusters not necessarily apparent from the dendrogram (with the cluster diagram open in *Detail View* > *Cluster Analysis* ribbon > **3D Cluster Map**). Note the different perspectives gained when you use your mouse to rotate the 3D cluster map, shown in Figure 10.16. The relative statistical associations between *water quality*, *environmental impacts*, and *environmental change* become more evident than they were in the 2D dendrogram, with water quality positioned between the other two on the vertical dimension.[5] Note also how the positioning

---

[5] If you're in a mood for experimentation, use a word frequency count to get a tag cloud for the text in each of the nodes that are found to be most similar using cluster analysis

of *landscape* and *habitat* changes markedly, for example, when the dimensional perspective is changed, indicating that they share commonality on one level (for one horizontal dimension), but tend toward opposite poles on the other.

Overall options for gaining a multidimensional perspective on your data (with some cautionary notes) include:

- Cluster sources or nodes on the basis of word similarity in NVivo, as has been demonstrated above. Words included in your stop list will not be included in the calculations.
- Cluster sources or nodes on the basis of coding similarity in NVivo. In this, NVivo is looking at what other nodes any of the requested nodes are coded at, and also looking for similarities in the distribution of those. This will include all nodes, of any kind, including case nodes, thematic nodes, auto coded nodes, and results nodes.
- Cluster words (the top 100) generated from a word frequency query, based on the pattern of distribution across the sources or nodes searched.
- Export a case by variable table (from a matrix query of cases by nodes) from NVivo to Excel to then import into a statistical program. Run cluster analysis of the variables (nodes) based on their distribution across the cases (this is the more traditional format for data to which cluster analysis is applied).[6]
- Create a similarity matrix in NVivo by adding the same list of nodes to both the rows and the columns, being careful to specify the context in which they should be found to co-occur. Export the matrix (via Excel) to SPSS or a similar statistical program to run multidimensional scaling based on the similarity matrix (Bazeley, 2010a, 2013).

✓ Whenever you are viewing a cluster diagram or multidimensional scaling plot, you should also review the summary statistics.

Overall, then, you have two choices of strategy in approaching these kinds of tools:

- Because these visualizations are quick and easy to generate in software like NVivo (and can be fun to play with), use them just as a way of sparking ideas, without putting too much weight on the results obtained. If these visualizations lead you to explore some aspect of your data that then becomes profitable for your analysis, it is the evidence you gather in that further exploration that will support your conclusions, not the clustering.
- You can engage in a serious statistical endeavour, using the evidence gained through the calculations done either by NVivo or a follow-on statistical analysis to build a case for a conclusion – but if you are going to do so, then you will need to have a much more thorough understanding of what you are doing with the particular approach you choose to take. Your first stop should be to consult the Help files where an explanation is given of how the calculations are made to generate the cluster diagrams.

---

based on word similarity, and compare the lists. Group query will give you an equivalent comparison if you are comparing on the basis of coding similarity.

[6] For most statistical programs, you will need to open the data in Excel first, and add a variable name to the first column.

? Search Help for *Cluster analysis* and in particular for *How are cluster analysis diagrams generated?* Technical specifications used in creating clusters can be found at http://forums.qsrinternational.com/index.php?showtopic=4600.[7]

Guest and McLellan wisely concluded:

> Cluster analysis can be both a useful and a powerful tool, but its use must be tempered with common sense and in-depth knowledge of the raw data. Interpretation is only as good as the procedures that precede it (i.e., code development and application), and applying structure to an unfamiliar data set will have little meaning for even the most seasoned researcher. Used properly and solidly grounded in the data, cluster analysis can help provide meaningful structure to QDA and thematic interpretation. (2003: 198–9).

Exporting models and visualizations

Models are saved within the software, in either static or dynamic format. They can be copied and pasted into other applications (e.g., Word or PowerPoint), printed from the screen, exported as a picture (jpg) or exported in svg format for direct application on the web, viewing with Adobe software, or possible reconfiguration in Microsoft Visio. Charts are not directly saved within NVivo, but they also can be copied and pasted into other applications, printed from the screen, or exported as picture or pdf files.

Concluding comments

How much you will use visualizations of these various types in your work as a qualitative analyst will depend on your personal style as much as on the tools available. Some (perhaps those whose desk is covered in highlighters and sticky notes) might prefer to work on paper. Some (those who can never follow a map?) prefer not to work visually at all. Others will always go for the visual option, and will love the capacity to manipulate the visual displays as their ideas change and develop. And a few (like Pat) will initially struggle with visual modelling but then be won over. Many of the ideas presented in this chapter could be developed further, making more use of colour and style and model groups, for example.

The key advantages of doing this kind of work in the software (especially in model building), are (a) the flexibility you have in moving items around or changing specifications (remembering that you can archive versions along the

---

[7] You will need to sign in as a member on the QSR Forum to access the file attachment to this message.

way); (b) the direct two-way translations between project items and visualization tools and (c) the connection you have with project items, so you can always reach down into the data that support whatever it is you are seeing on the visual screen.

To borrow an idea from Lyn Richards, imagine presenting your findings to a stakeholder using the modeller. As you walk your audience through the model, using (custom) model groups to turn on and off various parts of the display, with a right-click you can take them to a view of the source data, perhaps with an embedded hyperlink to a sound bite or video clip. You could show through a series of windows (making sure they were all undocked before the session!) how your ideas developed, so they can see how you reached your conclusions – and so on. At the very least, from our experience, presenting your findings in a good visual model or chart (copied and pasted to your paper or presentation), supplemented by explanation, is always acceptable to an audience, whether that audience be academic, professional or commercial. They (along with Miles and Huberman) will appreciate the ability of a model or chart to tell a lot in a small space.

11

Using coding and queries to further analysis

Like almost everybody who writes about qualitative analysis, throughout this book we emphasize that analysis is ongoing. You begin by reflecting on and refining your research questions with the knowledge that your approach may (and probably will) change as the analysis unfolds. We began the book with modelling, memoing, annotating and linking to help you build skills in NVivo that will help you state, revisit and revise your ideas. An early portion of the analytical process usually includes coding, so we also provided two chapters on the ways coding can promote (and sometimes detract from!) moving forward with analysis. We also introduced some of the queries you might employ early in the analysis, and we did this to get you into the habit of checking and rechecking the associations in your data as you progress, rather than waiting until the end to 'test' the associations. Nonetheless, queries often become particularly useful toward the end of the analytic journey to help sort through the nodes and/or attribute values you constructed in the project. This chapter helps you think comprehensively about the query tools available in NVivo, so you will be better able to turn to them when you need them.

In this chapter:

- Think about what you are aiming for in your project.
- Review the range of queries available in NVivo, and the features they have in common.
- Consider ways of building on nodes for further analysis.
- Try different strategies for developing theory based on case analysis and/or associations between nodes.
- Learn how to approach building reports to suit your needs.

The analytic journey

Start your analysis with a question, a concept, a puzzle, and explore from there. Write as you go, and small questions will build into bigger ones. Explore, test, check back into your data and into your disciplinary literature, building up until you reach an integrated picture. The secret to analysis is in asking questions of the data, and then thinking through how you might pursue ways of answering them from the data. If you've stalled in the approach you're currently using, go back to the methodological literature seeking fresh stimulation. Read other studies using the same methodology, even if they are on an entirely different topic, for further ideas on strategies to use. Read theory, and wonder how it might inform your study. Check out Part III of Richards (2009), Parts 3 and 4 of Bazeley (2013), and Chapter 10 of Miles and Huberman (1994) for a wealth of practical strategies for searching, querying, displaying and seeing your data as you seek to move your project forward and bring it to a conclusion.

Bazeley (2013), in particular, addresses the issue of how to move forward if you reach the point of saying 'I've coded all my data. Now what do I do?'[1] by proposing a three-step process to apply to each of the categories or concepts you have developed: describe, compare, relate. In brief (to summarize three chapters!): working with one node at a time, write a description of what you found about that concept or category. Compare how different cases or sub-groups talk about it – all the time asking questions and challenging the data. Why did this group respond differently? Use this to prompt ideas about relationships in and across your data. Use queries to check those out. By the time you complete this with a selection of your nodes, you are starting to build a web of understanding and the beginnings of theory.

Where are you going?

Confirming your goals for analysis provides an essential foundation for this last step in the analytic journey. By now, you should have a strong sense of where you are heading, what you are expecting to achieve, what questions your project will answer, and what will bring it all together. Outcomes of your work with your project might include:

- 'Thick description' – a term popularized in the ethnographic writing of Geertz (1973) to convey deep understanding of a culture or experience. Thick description goes beyond details of spoken content to include wider semiotic analysis and attention to context. It is more than simply reporting what you observed or what your participants said.

---

[1] We hope you will avoid this problem, because you've been memoing and linking and modelling while coding, and so your analysis is already well under way.

- Theory development – qualitative analysis is typically described as being an inductive process. Your task, as a theory-builder, is to work at identifying and making sense of the patterns and relationships in your data; theory will not emerge on its own. Theory is often small and local to start with; as your work extends and grows, so will your theoretical sophistication.
- Theory testing – less frequent as a primary goal for a qualitative project. NVivo's query tools do allow, however, for extensive testing of hunches or hypotheses which have been brought to the project or developed within it.
- Practical application – in policy analysis, situation analysis, needs analysis or program evaluation.

The question now is: How can you use your coding system and the queries provided by NVivo to move towards your destination?

Queries in NVivo

Searching and asking questions of your data is managed primarily through seven different query tools in NVivo, some of which you have used already. When you ask a question, NVivo searches through your data to locate all the text references, picture regions, and media extracts that meet the criteria you set in your query. The different types of queries have a common architecture, but they allow you to construct and find data to answer the unique questions arising in your project. Before we deal with specific options, however, we will review the general structure of queries in NVivo.

What do queries do?

As a starting point, you should know that each query has two main components:

1 The query: the customized language you use to ask a question.
2 The results: the data NVivo presents to you after you run a query.

When you go to **Queries** in *Navigation View* you will find two subfolders, Queries and Results. Your task is to point to the data in your project that can help answer your question (craft the query), and NVivo's contribution is to select and sort the data for you (generate results), often with a degree of complexity which would be prohibitively cumbersome when working manually. Depending on how you set your preferences, additional information can be collected during a query, including the context surrounding the results, the source file for each 'find', how many finds there are in each source, and the percentage of each source that satisfied your criteria. Your follow-on task, then, is to review the data found by NVivo, and interpret it in relation to your question. NVivo will not produce a neat p-value (as if such should be considered adequate in any case)! As with any analysis (quantitative or qualitative), your results will only be as good as is allowed by the combination of your skill in coding, linking and reflecting within the database, your ability to ask relevant questions (to run appropriate queries), and your capacity to interpret – and challenge – the output.

Saving queries and saving results

The query (the language you craft) and its results (the data that satisfy the criteria in your query) do not automatically save or update, which may sometimes present a reason to save them, and sometimes a reason to delete them. We generally recommend saving the query as you start to work with NVivo so you can see what you were asking the software to do for you, and in the event you want to use it again. (If they start to clutter your system, you can easily delete them.) For instance, if you added Sue's third interview to the project yesterday, and the query you created a month ago is looking in the third round of interviews for Juan, Laura, Muriel, Petra and Richard, you can return to the saved query and examine and tinker with the instructions to include Sue's third interview in the query along with everyone else's.

Results of queries are provided in 'preview' mode by default, which means the results will appear on the screen but will disappear when you close them. Generally speaking, the results are intended for rapid perusal and then deletion. However, some might warrant saving as a way to log and review your trajectory in the database, or because they deserve to be in your coding system. As you work with a few queries, you will become more comfortable with your decision either to save the queries and results or to leave the defaults and let them 'disappear' after you are done with them.

Iterative searching

When you save the results of your queries as a node (or nodes), they can be reflected upon and used iteratively in further queries. You might start with a simple question, perhaps about the level of association between two categories, but then go on to seek further clarification or detail. Is it true for everyone? Does it depend on some other factor also being present? What characterizes the cases where this is not true?

▶ Run the first search with a different scope to see whether this association holds only for some subgroups within the sample.
▶ Enter the saved results from a first query as a data item in a further query.

As you progress with your project and grow in sophistication in using the query tools, you will be able to make your questions increasingly targeted, detailed and specific – providing your node system and project structure allow it.

Keeping track of conclusions

Saving the results isn't enough! Make a practice of immediately recording what you learn from each investigation, even if it 'doesn't produce anything' (nothing is always something). Making these records as you go will save you enormous amounts of time, in three ways:

- You won't find yourself running the same query again because you can't remember what it found.
- Recording what you learned from the query will prompt you to ask further questions, and so facilitate your searching and analysis process.
- The record provides the basis for your results chapters. It's always easier to start writing results when you have something already written down, regardless of how 'rough' it is.

✓ Avoid printing off endless text reports from your data. That is just a way of deferring thinking, and the mounting volume will quickly prove daunting.

You might choose to record your emerging understanding in a special memo in NVivo, where you can create see also links to the evidence that supports that understanding. Alternatively, if you are close to the end of your project, create a results document in Word, and use headings liberally to identify the bits and pieces of ideas you are recording. Drop your ideas (notes or quotes) under a heading, and when you think you're done on that topic, try turning them into prose.

Common features in queries

NVivo has selections built into every query that help you create the specific instructions. The following orientation may help you understand some of the common features of a query before we explain the different queries in greater detail.

To create a query

▶ In *Navigation View*, make sure the **Queries** folder is selected.
▶ In *List View*, **Right-click > New Query > [your choice of query to run]**.

Add to project

As you are learning NVivo and building your skills in the construction of queries, one move to help you keep track and go back to tinker with the query later is easy! Check the box next to **Add To Project** (Figure 11.1). This instructs NVivo to save the query so you can adjust and improve it if you realize after looking at the results that it wasn't exactly what you wanted. Saving the query cannot harm your database, so if you aren't sure, do it anyway.

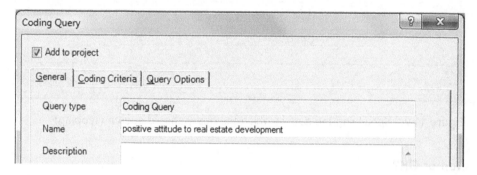

Figure 11.1   Saving a query

Three (sometimes two) main tabs

In most queries, you will see three tabs as soon as you select ☑ **Add to project**:

- General: In this tab you name the query (make it as explicit as possible), and optionally also provide a description to remind you of what the query was designed to do.
- ... Criteria: Depending on the query, this tab presents you with several windows for adding the specific instructions. This is the place you do most of the work to think through the question you are asking, the components in your NVivo database, and the specific data you want to retrieve.
- Query Options: This tab (present in four of the seven queries) provides a range of options for managing your results – whether you want to just preview or save them, where and in what form to save them, and the extra information to include with them. Alternatively (or as well), results of all seven queries can be exported once they are displayed.

Scoping to selected data

All queries additionally offer the option to specify which sources or other data items (such as nodes or sets) the query should look through, and whether the search should be restricted to coding undertaken by a particular team member. This is usually at the bottom of the query window (Figure 11.2).[2] This

---

[2] In coding queries, the keyword indicating you can select where to search is *In*; in text-mining queries, the keyword is *Of*.

allows you to add an additional criterion to the specifications for your query. In Chapter 6, for example, we showed you how to run a matrix query of nodes by attribute values and then scope the query so it only examined items in a particular set.

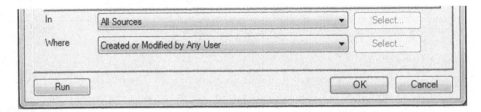

Figure 11.2   Specifying the data in which the query should search (scoping)

Run or OK?

Generally, once you set up the query, you will choose to **Run** the query. This will both save the query (if that is what you asked for) and run it. If you did not elect to save the query, the **OK** button will be dimmed. Clicking on **OK** will save the query without running it. You can open the query again from *List View* using **Right-click > Query Properties**, or run it later by double-clicking it.

Results nodes

If you choose to save the results of your query, either as you are setting up your query through **Query Options** or after you have viewed the preview (**Right-click > Store Query Results**), the program will default to saving them in the Results folder, located in the *Navigation View* of **Queries**. Alternatively, you can choose to save them elsewhere (e.g., in a folder in your general nodes area) if you want.

Results nodes provide a fixed-in-time view of your data. Regardless of where you choose to save them, while they remain in that location you will not be able to modify their content, although you are able to add or remove other coding from the text reported there. If you wish to modify what is included you will need to either (a) rerun the query with changed specifications, or (b) copy and paste the results node into your general coding system, where you will be able to add or remove coding from it.

Seven queries

We conceptualize the seven queries in NVivo according to three groups, each with a distinct primary focus. This framework is designed to give you an overview of the queries without distracting you with all of the clicks and options.

1 Text-mining queries search the text material in the database for specific words or phrases.
2 Theory-building queries help you explore the relationships among items in the database.
3 Clerical queries provide output to help you manage components of the analytic process.

The distinction we make between these three groups is largely heuristic, however, as the text-mining queries can be used to build theories and the theory-building tools can be directed toward clerical tasks. As we provide this grounding in the seven queries, we point you to other chapters where queries are presented in the context of a research activity and where, for most, you will find basic instructions for conducting them. Additionally, we point you to the NVivo Help files, which generally provide excellent instructions (so long as you know what you are trying to accomplish by following the clicks!). In the examples below, the emphasis is on using text data, although most queries can be run on any type of data that can be imported and coded in NVivo (text, audio, video, photographs, web pages, and social media).

Text-mining queries

Word frequency query

A word frequency query catalogues the words used most often in the data or a subset of the data, up to 1,000 words. For example: Find the top 20 words used to describe the natural environment in the survey responses (Figure 11.3 shows the first seven).

- Researchers usually use this to explore or map words used in the data, and this tool is often used as part of content analysis.
- This is a wide net and captures question numbers, participant names, etc. unless they are in the 'stop words' list (a list of words that should be ignored, which can be modified to suit your needs).
- Use the 'Finding matches' slider in the query to group stemmed words, synonyms, and related words in the results list.

Word	Length	Count	Weighted Percentage (%)▽
beautiful	9	22	5.58
good	4	10	2.54
need	4	7	1.78
destroyed	9	6	1.52
development	11	6	1.52
important	9	6	1.52
local	5	6	1.52

Figure 11.3 Words found using a word frequency query

- See Chapter 5 for detailed instructions for creating such a query within the context of exploring your data.

? Search Help for *Run a word frequency query.*

Text search query

A text search query searches for words or phrases you specify, with or without wildcards, in the data or a subset of the data. For example, search for *fish** to find all mentions of *fish* and also *fishing, fished, fishermen* and *fishes* (Figure 11.4).

\<Internals\\Interviews\\Richard and Patricia\> - § 11 references coded [0.89% Coverage]

Reference 1 - 0.05% Coverage

If you want a mess of seafood, like oysters, clams, crabs, you can get in your skiff and couple hours you'll have it and be back home. I mean, every now and then everyone will get together and we'll have a barbeque—something like that you know for the community building. **Fish** fry stuff like that, oyster roast.

Reference 2 - 0.08% Coverage

I started working on the water and everything I put my hand at, I made money at. There was plenty stuff in the water and I put in a lot of hours. I built two boats; the last one was a forty foot one I worked twenty years -- by this time I was commercial **fishing** on Portsmouth Island. In the summer time I'd be a shrimping, all night long and I'd come home. I'd have to go to Portsmouth. I'd get back home about twelve o'clock, one o'clock that day, get me four or so hours of sleep jump, on the boat that night, and shrimp all night, and come back the next morning.

Figure 11.4   Finds (spread to broad context) from a search for *fish**

- Researchers usually use this when they are aware of key terms or phrases and want to locate all related data (often nouns like *island* or *fishing boat*).
- Unlike the word frequency query, you can look for phrases (like "fishing boat") – indicated by the use of double quotation marks – as well as single words.
- Use the 'Finding matches' slider to look for stemmed words, synonyms, and related terms.
- See Chapter 5 for detailed instructions for creating such a query within the context of automating coding.

? Search Help for *Run a text search query.*

Theory-building queries

Matrix coding query

In a matrix coding query, pairs of items are cross-tabulated and displayed as a matrix. For example: Explore interviewees' attitudes to some aspects of the natural environment (Figure 11.5).

	A : Positive ▽	B : Negative ▽
1 : Environmental change ▽	2	9
2 : Environmental impacts ▽	0	2
3 : Landscape ▽	8	0
4 : Water quality ▽	2	3

Figure 11.5   Matrix coding query – frequencies of responses for each row–column combination

- Double-clicking on a cell allows you to access the qualitative content (both detailed content and numbers are useful products from this query). Figure 11.6 shows the text data from the cell intersecting *Environmental impacts* and *Negative*.
- Researchers most often use this to compare subgroups in the database.
- In addition to running nodes by attribute values and nodes by nodes, the query can run nodes by sets, cases by nodes, attributes by attributes, or attributes by sets.
- See Chapter 6 for detailed instructions for creating such a query using nodes by attribute values, with an example.

?   In the Help files see *Run a matrix coding query*.

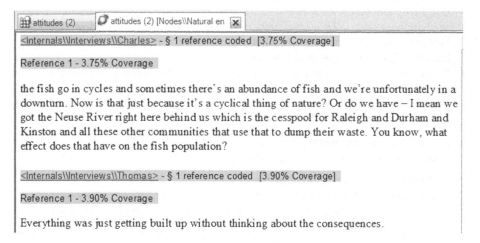

Figure 11.6   Text retrieved from the cell of a matrix

Coding query

A coding query finds text or other data in response to a single, sometimes complex question involving multiple nodes and/or attribute values. For example: Find all the data coded at *Memorable quotes* but only if the data are also in any of the selected nodes *Habitat* or *Landscape* (Figure 11.7).

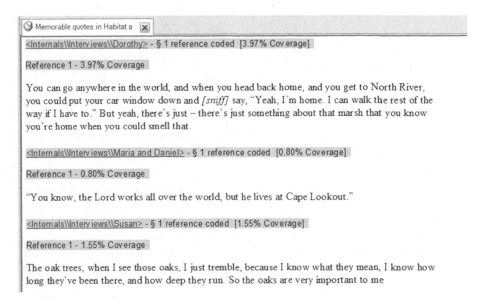

Figure 11.7 Finds from a coding query searching for a combination of nodes

- Use the Simple tab to look up a node only when it is used in a particular context.
- Use the Advanced tab to answer a complex question requiring a combination of nodes or of attribute values and nodes, such as 'Of the commercial fishermen who have lived here for more than a generation, what do they say about the changes in the aquatic habitat on the northern end of the coast?'
- If you are including an attribute so you can compare this group with others, consider using a matrix coding query.
- Boolean terms (and, or, not) as well as proximity operators (overlapping, near, preceding) can be used in combination within this query.

! In the Advanced tab, when you use the drop-down list to Define more criteria for the query, take extra care in selecting between:

  o All Selected Nodes (an intersection of data at these nodes);
  o Any Selected Node (a union of data at these nodes);
  o Any Node Where (a scoping tool allowing you to select an attribute value).

- See Chapter 4, where the coding query was suggested as a way of reconnecting nodes used to code separate aspects or 'slices' of the same portion of data.

? In the Help files see *Run a coding query*.

Compound query

A compound query finds content specified by a combination of two subqueries (text search and/or coding queries). For example: (a) find the word *fish** (or variations) near the word *policy* or *policies*, as long as they are within the same paragraph, reporting both finds and text in between (Figure 11.8); or (b) find the word *fish** in text that is coded at a combination of *Ecosystem services* and *Policy, management.*

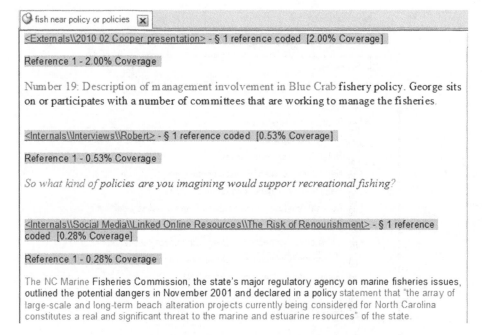

Figure 11.8   Finds from a compound query combining two text queries

- Researchers use this to find words in association with other words, or with nodes. It is also used to find specific words that are *not* already coded at a relevant node (i.e., as a check on coding).
- The query can look at the closeness of text strings, or a combination of text strings and nodes, with the latter selected using either a simple or the more complex advanced coding query.
- See Chapter 5 for detailed instructions for creating such a query within the context of checking thoroughness of coding.

? In the Help files see *Run a compound query.*

Clerical queries

Group query

A group query finds items that are associated with other items in your project and presents output in the form of lists (groups). For example: (a) see if the interview with Charles and the interview with Susan covered similar or different issues by examining a list of nodes that have been applied to each source; or (b) find a list of all the nodes that code the case *Sea Level* (Figure 11.9). You have seven different kinds of lists at your disposal.

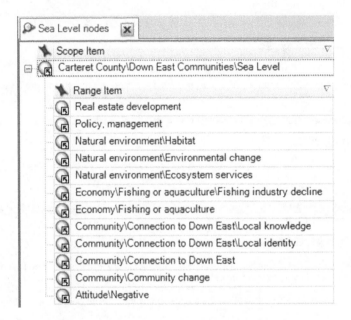

Figure 11.9   Nodes coding another node, found with a group query

- Researchers use this when they need a list of nodes coding another node, or when they want to take a step back from the data to see a summary list or to check for problems/omissions.[3]
- The output is always in the form of a list, which you can save as a set.
- Options include finding the list of nodes coding a node or source, a list of sources coded to a node, a list of see also links in a node or source, a list of sources with a particular attribute value, etc.
- See Chapter 10, where a group query was used to help build a complex visualization.

? In the Help files see *Run a group query.*

---

[3] Advanced Find allows also for finding nodes that code another node. The advantage of using group query to do this is that you are able to be more selective about what is found, e.g., by restricting the range to include only thematic nodes, or just case nodes.

Coding comparison query

A coding comparison query compares the coding of two coders (or two groups of coders) and provides output in the form of a table with the nodes of interest and the source files that were coded. For example, compare how Wanda and Effie coded at the *Habitat* node in *Barbara, Charles* and *Dorothy.*

Node	Source	S	S	Kappa	Agreement (%)	A and B (%)	Not A and Not B (%)	Disagreement (%)	A and Not B (%)	B and Not A (%
Natural environment\Habitat	Barbara	I	1	0.5743	94.47	4.16	90.31	5.53	0.49	5.04
Natural environment\Habitat	Charles	I	1	1	100	0	100	0	0	0
Natural environment\Habitat	Dorothy	I	8	0	92.51	0	92.51	7.49	0	7.49

Figure 11.10   Results from a coding comparison query

- Researchers usually use this as a process tool to discuss coding in a team and to clarify node descriptions.
- The table allows researchers to drill into the source documents to visually compare the work of different coders (via coding stripes).
- See Chapter 12 for a detailed example of a coding comparison query and its interpretation within the context of team research.

?   In the Help files see *Run a coding comparison query.*

Advanced thinking with queries

We described the overall purpose and function of queries and the general features common across queries. We also reviewed the three groups (and seven kinds) of queries provided in NVivo. For those users who want or need an overview of the many advanced and/or optional features in the queries, we also provide a resource on the companion website (see *Mapping the options in queries*) that will help you go beyond the default options in the queries to further customize your query.

Using coding and queries to further analysis

By now you should be well practised in applying strategies for reviewing concepts stored at nodes. In this section, we encourage you to push your thinking about using your nodes and applying queries to find answers to your research questions.

> [T]he move from coding to interpretation involves playing with and exploring the codes and categories that were created. … categories can be retrieved, split into subcategories, spliced, and linked together. Essentially, the codes and categories you have selected should be used to make pathways through the data. (Coffey & Atkinson, 1996: 46)

Starting from nodes, building associations

Choose a node which appears to be quite central to your current thinking about your topic. This might be selected because it is common to many documents, or because it frequently appeared as a focal point in models, or because you wrote extensive memos around it.

▶ Review the node – reading through, writing a description, recording any further ideas and questions prompted by it in a memo, refining the coding.
▶ Provide the node with a job description (What is its purpose? How is it meant to achieve that?) and then subject it to a performance review.
▶ View it with coding stripes visible. Depending on the node, you might choose to view stripes for all nodes, or refine your view to selected coding stripes (e.g., for people referred to in this context, or a set of consequences). Run a coding query to check more precisely any apparent relationships, or a matrix coding query to explore possible differences associated with contextual factors or conditions or outcomes.
▶ Create a model and place this node at its centre. Ask to see associated items (particularly any relationships). What other nodes (or other project items) should be linked to it? Write about what you are learning. If a question arises as you are writing, explore or check it immediately.
▶ Repeat these processes for other nodes which appear to have a potentially central role in your project.

If you have a number of nodes that focus around a core idea, try creating what Lyn Richards termed a 'dump node' with them – perhaps more formally referred to as a metacode. Copy each of them and merge into a new node, or if they are in a concept-based set, right-click to create the set as a new node. You might add in the results of some text searches as well, just to make sure you have all possible aspects included. Now:

▶ Scan the contents of that larger node to gain a sense of its overall 'shape' and dimensions (perhaps use a word frequency query to help). Remove (uncode at this node) any clearly irrelevant passages. Now scan it again, showing coding stripes for the original set of nodes. Do your original nodes adequately reflect the dimensions of this broader concept?
▶ Try using this new metacode in a series of matrix coding queries with attribute values and with other sets of nodes to see how it varies depending on who is the source of the comments, or the conditions under which they arise, or what strategies are being applied, or what the consequences are. This may confirm your original subcategories, or it may reveal a new way of seeing (new dimensions in) this concept. Understanding what brings about the different realizations of a phenomenon helps to create understanding of the phenomenon itself (Peräkylä, 2004).
▶ Again, repeat these processes for other sets or metacodes which also have a potentially central role in your project.

Which nodes (original single nodes, or metacodes) still 'stand up' (have the best explanatory power) after going through these examination processes? These are categories that will move you forward in your analysis as you look for ways they, with their dimensions, might link together to provide an interpretive description, enriched understanding, comprehensive model, or explanatory theory, supported by data.

Going further with cases

Some projects will focus around one case, but even where there are multiple cases, one of the reasons for taking a qualitative approach is to develop a deep understanding of each of those cases before bringing them together in either cross-case or variable-oriented analyses. It is through practical experience with multiple cases, over and above knowledge of general theories and rules, that one gains nuanced understanding of a topic and its related issues (Flyvbjerg, 2004). Whether or not you would describe your project as a case study, the methods of within-case and cross-case analysis are foundational to a range of methodologies from phenomenology through to programme evaluation (Bazeley, 2013).

Within-case analysis

The purpose of within-case analysis, as noted above, is to develop a deep understanding of a particular case. Any query can be set up to run within a single case: choose to run the query **In > Selected Items** and then use the **Select** button to identify the case (see *Scoping to selected data*, above).

▶ Use a simple coding query to review what a node looks like within a particular case, for example if you need to explore a deviant or negative case to see how and why it is different.
▶ Search for text within a case to determine whether or how a particular person used a particular expression.
▶ Use a matrix coding query to undertake within-case comparisons or to look for within-case associations of nodes, for example to explore changes over time.

Cross-case analysis

If you have been writing a summary or building a model of each case as you completed your initial coding of it, then this is a really good time to read through those summaries or to review those models, in a sense treating these now as your data – noting recurring themes, odd discrepancies, or significant concepts. Now you are indeed ready for cross-case analysis!

The dual goals of multi-case (or cross-case) analysis are succinctly expressed by Miles and Huberman:

> One aim of studying multiple cases is to increase generalizability, reassuring yourself that the events and processes in one well-described setting are not wholly idiosyncratic. At a deeper level, the aim is to see processes and outcomes across many cases, to understand how they are qualified by local conditions, and thus to develop more sophisticated descriptions and more powerful explanations. (1994: 172)

Whereas analysis based on groups of cases (comparing those with a different value of an attribute, or all the responses to situation X compared to situation Y) gives an averaged result, in cross-case analysis the comparative focus is on the individual cases, with their uniqueness preserved.

Analyses involving cross-case analysis involve using either a matrix coding query or framework analysis. We discuss each of these in turn.

Cross-case analysis using a matrix coding query

▶ Set up your matrix coding query with the required cases in the rows, and nodes or sets defining the columns. Search for content of rows AND of columns. This will find the text for each specified item (node or set) separately for each included case, and display it in table format, allowing you to compare across cases.
▶ If you want to refine your analysis by comparing what has been said or what happens at different time phases in the life of an organization, or through repeated interviews with the same participants, use time-based codes or sets to identify the columns in a matrix (with cases in the rows). By scoping the query to a particular node, you will have a comparison of how each case progressed over time for that particular issue/topic.

Thus, with cross-case analysis using a matrix coding query, you are able to:

▶ Compare cases on a specific factor, and then refine to consider an additional dimension such as time/phase.
▶ Examine and determine the significance of patterns of association in codes, for example, seeing how many (and which) cases have one or other or both of two nodes present (or three or four), and then reviewing the text at those nodes on a case-by-case basis.[4] Use the filter button on a column in the matrix results to sort the 'hits' on a particular item, and then view the other nodes to which they were coded.

---

[4] A query of this type is an alternative to using NEAR when you want to look at the association of nodes, as it ensures that you don't accidentally confuse different speakers in multi-person documents.

▶ Generate a coding table for cases that can be exported as a case-by-variable matrix for use in a statistics program.

Cross-case analysis using framework matrices

Framework matrices provide a table format designed for cross-case analysis, with cases in the rows and thematic nodes in the columns (although you can add any node to rows or columns). Cases can be displayed sorted by the values of an attribute. You can either generate a table that is empty so you can summarize the intersecting content for each cell (which will be shown to you at the same time), or you can have NVivo generate the table for you with all of the intersecting content already visible in the cell. We will outline the basic instructions for you here, but there are extended descriptions and instructions available in NVivo's Help files.

Creating and filling a framework matrix

Creating the framework

▶ In the *Navigation View of* **Sources**, select **Framework Matrices**.

▶ In *List View*, **Right-click > New Framework Matrix >** provide a **Name** and **Description.**

▶ In the **Rows** tab, select the case nodes you want to examine. Optionally select an attribute with values you want the cases to be sorted by.

▶ In the **Columns** tab, select the nodes for which you want to see and summarize content.

Data for your matrix

You are looking at an empty table with the rows and columns specified. When you click in a cell, on the right-hand side of the screen, you will see all of your data for the case whose row you have selected. This will allow you to read through and create summaries even if the data have not been coded. *If your data are coded,* then to show only the data relevant to each cell:

▶ *View* ribbon > **Framework Matrix** > **Cell Coding**.

Filling the matrix

▶ Select the first cell for which data are available. Read through the data for that cell, and type a summary into the cell. Continue to create a summary in each cell for which you have data.

(Continued)

(Continued)

▶ Create a link: As you are reading, select and copy a passage from the data that support your summary statement. Then select the part of the summary they support, and **Right-click > New Summary Link**. Clicking in the pink highlighted text (at any time) will activate the link, such that the supporting data item is shown with the linked passage highlighted.

▶ Alternatively, auto summarize to have NVivo fill the table for you: ***Analyze*** ribbon > **Auto Summarize**. This will add *all* the coded data to the cell.

▶ Export your framework matrix to Excel: **Right-click** (anywhere in the matrix) > **Export Framework Matrix**.

▶ You can edit cell contents in NVivo, or (after export) in Excel.

✓ NVivo stores the summaries you create for each cell, so that if you use the same combination of any case by node in another framework matrix, it will auto fill with that summary.

! Any changes you make to that summary will transfer across the previous and future framework matrices in which that cell combination occurs.

? Help topic: *Framework matrices.*

When data are sorted by case, in addition to seeing common patterns, you can readily identify instances where individuals go against a trend. These cases might be outliers on a statistical measure, deviant cases in qualitative terms, or cases where there is an apparent contradiction in the data from the different sources (Bazeley, 2013; Caracelli & Greene, 1993; Miles & Huberman, 1994). Whichever of these situations applies, they warrant focused attention, as it is often through exploration of such cases that new understanding is gained.

Counting and analysing text

Content coding of text for quantitative analysis is a well-established procedure. Counts of instances of a theme within unstructured text are sometimes used as a proxy indicator of the importance of that theme for a qualitative analysis. One might count the number of times an issue is raised (number of references), or the number of people raising it, for example.[5]

---

[5] The number of references shown in the *List View* of Sources or Nodes can be inflated by coding in memos, the work of multiple coders, and/or the inclusion of results nodes. If any of these is an issue, construct matrix queries (with attention to what counts are being shown in the cells) to obtain more reliable figures.

Reuben Bolt, as a doctoral student at the University of Sydney, noted that comments about racism were high in frequency in the stories told by his Aboriginal participants, but he identified other themes (such as pilgrimage, pride, and the importance of family) as prime narratives in their talk. He argued that the narrative structure to these themes within their life stories, a structure that was missing from the theme of racism, demonstrated their higher relevance for those individuals.

Counts are used often when considering aspects of discourse. Seale (1999) provides an extended discussion of their use in a qualitative context. He also has conducted several studies in which he considered the meaning given to the experience of having cancer for various groups, based on their use of particular metaphors (e.g., Seale, 2001, 2005).

Anderson et al. (2001) counted the length of passages between instances of argumentation strategies in children's discussions about various scenarios to test hypotheses about the snowballing effect of a child's introducing a particular strategy. They found, for example, that the gap between instances of a strategy diminished as it was adopted by others.

Wherever counts derived from textual data are used, care needs to be exercised in defining just what is to be counted, and in determining whether a count of cases, references or words is the most appropriate measure (Bazeley, 2010a; Sandelowski, Voils, & Knafl, 2009). The manner in which coding was applied to the text can also influence counts of passages and words.

Going further into theory-building

We recognize that talking about theory or theory building can seem slightly daunting to some researchers. The thought that your data and the analysis of them has to use, contribute to, and make sense of or build theory can halt the research process altogether. We can think about theory in terms of having and using ideas, and this seems far less daunting. Everyone can use, develop, and generate ideas. (Coffey & Atkinson, 1996: 140)

Essentially what you are looking for in developing theory is to specify patterns and relationships between concepts. Theory supports explanation or prediction. 'The acts involved in [developing theoretical sensitivity] foster *seeing* possibilities, *establishing* connections, and *asking* questions. ... When you theorize, you reach down to fundamentals, up to abstractions, and probe into experience. The content of theorizing cuts to the core of studied life and poses new questions about it' (Charmaz, 2006: 135).

Exploring associations and investigating exceptions

You were first introduced to the idea of exploring associations between concepts as a way of reconstructing the links in fractured or sliced text. In reconstructing links, you ask for text which is coded by two (or perhaps more) nodes; for example, where you are looking at the connection between such things as a context and an action, or an action and who was involved, or an associated emotional response, where both are talked about at the same time. Matrix queries efficiently check patterns in a series of associations, such as those between an action and a number of possible actors, or a series of issues and a number of possible responses to those issues. Matrix-style pattern analyses are used extensively also in case studies and evaluation research to explore changes over time, comparative outcomes, rival hypotheses, impacts for different subgroups – and for communicating outcomes.

There are times, however, when you will want to pursue a potentially interesting relationship between just two nodes. Examples might be whether institutional pressure creates insecurity, or the role of intellectual stimulation in building satisfaction with or enthusiasm for research (with implications for future motivation and performance). These kinds of queries are explored using a coding query (Advanced tab), where you look for the text that is coded by *Node X* AND coded by *Node Y*.

When you look for associations in this way, it is advisable in many instances to also check the meaning of a lack of association – what does intellectual stimulation look like when it doesn't prompt satisfaction or enthusiasm, or institutional pressure when it doesn't create insecurity, and is that any different from when both were present? At first it would seem that this could be achieved by running the same kind of advanced coding query, by changing it to ask for text coded by *Node X* AND NOT coded by *Node Y*. This type of search will find all the passages coded by the first but not the second node.

These associations are not always neatly connected, however. In asking whether being stimulated by research is a necessary condition for finding satisfaction in doing research, a clear association might be found where the same passage is coded by both *intellectual stimulation* and *satisfaction* – but there could be many more instances where participants talk about each of these separately. These instances need to be found, to determine whether an association might be present, even though each was spoken about at different times. To do so requires use of a NEAR operator in the coding query, looking for times where both nodes are present for the same case. Where cases and sources are equivalent, the search can be scoped to sources to achieve this. If you are working with a dataset, in a separate query, ask for finds NEAR > In Custom Context > Surrounding Row (i.e., the same case). If you have multi-case documents such as focus groups, however, you would be better off using a case-by-nodes matrix.[6] These strategies for finding proximity between nodes will reveal whether researchers whose text is coded for *satisfaction* also have text, somewhere, coded for *intellectual stimulation*. It is important to always carefully evaluate the results from NEAR searches, as the simple presence of both codes in the same source or case does not necessarily mean they bear any theoretical relationship to each other. Can their association be interpreted as being meaningful in terms of the question being asked? Particularly when the co-occurrence may be anywhere across a document or case rather than, say, within a paragraph or speaking turn, there is an increased likelihood of chance associations being included in the query results.

Again, it is useful (if not essential) to explore the negative cases – those cases where the association is *not* found. With searches involving nodes that are not necessarily applied to the same text, this becomes a little more difficult than finding the simple difference between one node and another (as outlined above); what is needed here is to see whether *satisfaction* exists at all for cases where *intellectual stimulation* doesn't exist anywhere in their records. There are two ways of achieving this, regardless of data configuration (continuing to use *satisfaction* and *intellectual stimulation* as an example):

▶ Run a matrix of cases by nodes, with *satisfaction* and *intellectual stimulation* as the nodes selected for the columns. The resulting matrix can be filtered on the *intellectual stimulation* column, to see more easily whether there is an associated pattern in the *satisfaction* column. Those cases where one is present without the other can then be investigated further. Checking the text in cells for this method is rather tedious if there is a large number of cases involved, although it has the advantage of providing a complete set of data for both nodes and all cases in one query.

▶ Alternatively, following the earlier searches, use a group query:

  o **Look for**: Items Coded At
  o **Scope** > select Cases
  o **Range** > select the single node *intellectual stimulation*.

---

[6] Unfortunately, the software not only reports by sources rather than cases, but also searches in sources rather than cases (a problem yet to be resolved)!

▶ Sort the results by number of **Finds** by clicking on the header for that column. Those with 0 finds are cases not coded at stimulation; those with 1 find are coded. Create two sets and use these as columns in a matrix, with *satisfaction* in the row. This will allow you to see how many of each group being compared (i.e., on presence or absence of *intellectual stimulation*) have talked about experiences of *satisfaction*, and, by looking at the text in each of the two cells, how each group talked about *satisfaction*.[7]

By the time you work through a series of queries such as these, you will be able to write authoritatively (in so far as your data are adequate for the task) about the question you raised, with your conclusion supported by both numbers and the pattern of association (or lack of it) in text responses.

Putting it together

As you were exploring patterns and relationships (associative and causal) in your data, you were constructing theory at a substantive level. You had an active role in this process – it hasn't happened on its own. From these explorations:

- Seek to understand *how people construct* meanings and actions, as preparation for understanding *why* people act as they do (Charmaz, 2006).
- Check for intervening, mediating, or extraneous factors relating to your focal concepts.
- Build a logical chain of evidence, using 'if–then' tactics: propose an if–then relation and check to see if the evidence supports it, noting that relationships have to make sense, and explanations need to be complete. 'Qualitative analyses can be evocative, illuminating, masterful – and wrong' (Miles & Huberman, 1994: 262).
- Explanations or conclusions need to have conceptual or theoretical coherence. This is a good time to draw, once again, on disciplinary literature, and to contextualize your work within that literature – perhaps to refute it, and certainly to go beyond it (Coffey & Atkinson, 1996).
- Use models to clarify what you are seeing, and eventually in synthesizing it so others can see it too. Return to your original model where you mapped your preliminary ideas about what you might find in your project. See how far you moved in your understanding of the issues you are dealing with! You might now revise that

---

[7] In the *Researchers* data, at the time of writing, 11 of 15 cases expressing *intellectual stimulation* also referred to research experiences giving *satisfaction*, while *satisfaction* was expressed by just 9 of 24 cases not expressing *intellectual stimulation* – but further checking of the text found that at least two of the latter should have been coded also at *intellectual stimulation* and therefore should have been in the first group. As noted in Chapter 4, if you miss something in coding, you are likely to pick it up at a later time, and you can remedy it then.

model – or perhaps you need to create a whole new picture of where you see your project now. Attempting to present your conclusions in the form of a model at once reveals where links are missing, and forces you to think about possible solutions or pathways.

Creating and customizing reports

NVivo provides a range of export options and standard report formats for those times when you need to have something exported or printed from your NVivo project. We referred to some of these on the way through, where we felt they would be helpful to your analysis. We do not propose to give a full digest of report options here, as they are very adequately covered in Help, but instead offer a couple of pointers to things you might consider – and avoid! – when working with reports.[8]

? First, we would point you to the introduction to reports in Help (*About reports and extracts*), and the link from there to *Understand predefined reports and extracts* where you will find a table describing what is included in each of the report options provided.

In many situations you are able to print or export your work directly from the screen. We suggested this, for example, for listing nodes; for exporting the text of a node with annotations and see also links as endnotes; for printing, copying or exporting matrix tables; and for copying or exporting charts and models. What we will consider here is:

- how to filter, run and view a predefined report, and
- how to modify a predefined report using the Report Designer.

Selecting, filtering and viewing predefined reports

With the predefined report options that are provided by NVivo, it is intended that you shape them to suit your particular needs by using the optional filters. If you simply select and run one of these reports without filtering, you are likely to generate a very large amount of useless information.

---

[8] Extracts are directly exported versions of reports in file formats (txt, xls, xlsx) designed for use in other software.

Using a predefined report

To see a description of what any predefined report provides, **Right-click > Report Properties**. Alternatively, a description of each is provided in Help.

Filtering and running a report

When you select a report in *List View*, a dialogue such as that in Figure 11.11 will open, listing the fields of the report for which you can select data.

▶ Click in a checkbox next to **Field**, and then look at the options under **Comparison** and **Select** for **Values** to help understand what filters are available, and make your selections accordingly.

✓ Watch especially to avoid inclusion of case nodes in reports involving coding, and for what node hierarchies you include in reports of attributes.

▶ Click on **OK** to run the report.

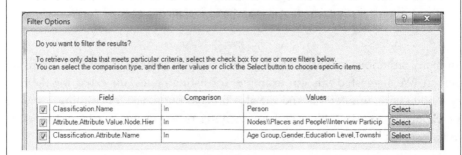

Figure 11.11   Filter options in a node classification summary report (number of cases with each attribute value)

Viewing the report

When a report opens in *Detail View*, it can be cramped and difficult to see what you have, especially if you have your *Detail View* on the right-hand side of the NVivo window. Either:

▶ Change your *Detail View* to the bottom of the window (***View* ribbon >** *Workspace* group > **Detail View > Bottom**; and/or

▶ If you want just to see the report without the report map or the preview pane, then with the *Detail View* active, in the ***View*** ribbon, *Detail View* group > uncheck ☐ **Report Map** and/or ☐ **Thumbnails** (Figure 11.12).

▶ **Right-click** in *Detail View* to **Export** or **Print** the report.

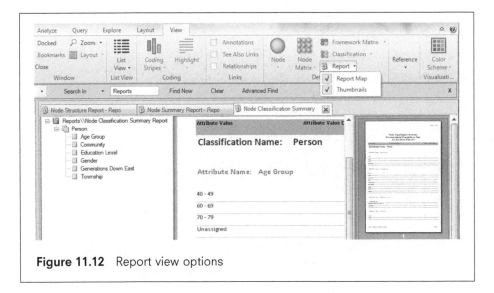

Figure 11.12 Report view options

Modifying a report in Designer

Your reporting needs will not always be met with a predesigned report. For example, we would prefer to include the Description field within any report of nodes, given its importance within any coding system, but neither of the predefined node summary reports includes this field. While building a report 'from scratch' is a daunting prospect for most of us, modifying a predefined report to remove information you don't need and include what you do want is relatively simple, especially if you're prepared to experiment a bit until you get what you want. We will illustrate using the Node Structure Report as an example.

Modifying a predefined report

▶ Select and run the report you think you want to modify, to check what it currently provides.

▶ In *List View*, select the report you want to modify, **Copy** it, **Paste** it (in the same area), and then edit the name to reflect the changes you plan to make.

! The changes you make to the design of a report become permanent within this project hence the need to work from a copy.

▶ In *List View*, select the copy of the report you want to modify, **Right-click > Open Report in Designer**. Adjust your screen so you can see the full width

(Continued)

(Continued)

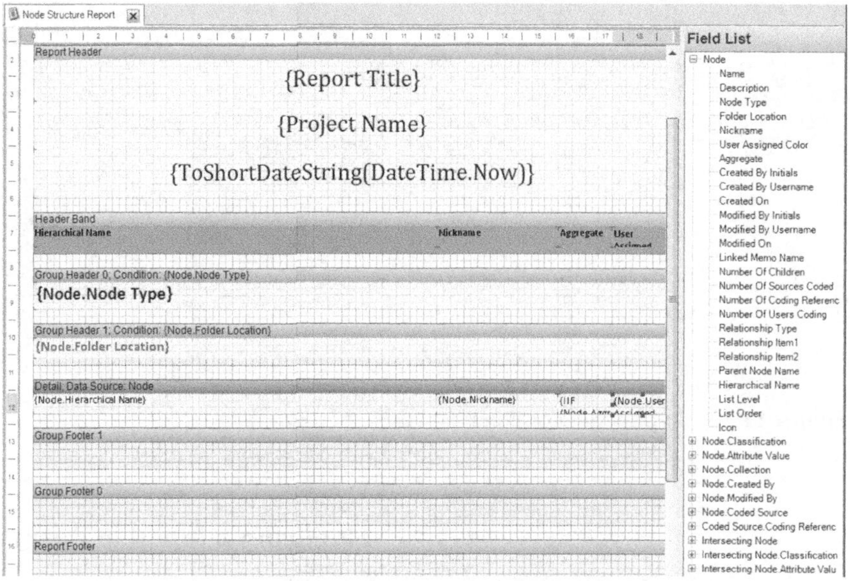

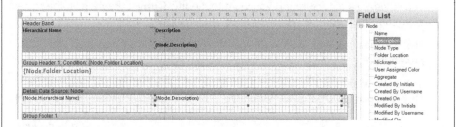

Figure 11.13   Predefined Node Structure Report open in Designer

of the report format, and on the right, the list of fields that can be modified (Figure 11.13).

▶ Click in the **Header Band** on a field you want to remove (e.g., Nickname), and **Delete**.

▶ Select the same field from the body of the report (i.e., Node: Nickname), and **Delete**.

▶ Repeat for any other fields you want to remove, including unwanted group headers.

▶ From the **Field List**, drag a selected field onto the Header Band, and also onto the body of the report. Adjust the amount of space allocated to the field by moving the handles that show when the field name is selected (Figure 11.14).

Figure 11.14   Modifying the fields in a predefined Node Structure Report

---

✓ Your new report format saves automatically.
✓ If you want to copy its format to another project: From *List View*, select the report(s) you want to move, **Right-click > Export Report(s) > select a folder to export to > OK**.
! To import a report into another project: In the *List View* of Reports, **Right-click > Import Report**, navigate to where it is stored, and select.

With some practice and experimentation, you will be able to customize a report to suit your needs, including adding company logos, appropriate headers and footers, and typeset with headings and fonts to conform to a company style.

12

Teamwork with NVivo

Whether you are in a small team working on a small project (such as a pair of students in a qualitative methods course analysing a few interviews) or a large, geographically dispersed team analysing hundreds of items from different regions, you will find many helpful tips in this chapter for planning and conducting team research with NVivo. If this is one of the first chapters you turn to in the book for guidance, it will help you think through the many implications of conducting team research with NVivo. If you are turning to this chapter after considerable experience working independently in a project, the chapter will help you think differently about the software tools. While there are tools in NVivo that are designed to support team research, others are multipurpose and their implications for team research may not yet have occurred to you. Because most of these tools are described elsewhere in the book, you will encounter many pointers from this chapter to other locations for additional instructions.

In this chapter:

- Consider three practices that should guide your teamwork.
- Learn about the three options for storing (and accessing) a team project database.
- Get started with tools for tracking team member contributions in NVivo.
- Investigate options for communicating as a team in NVivo.
- Address questions that will influence how you code as a team.
- See how to combine copies of databases.
- Consider the arguments for and against reliability testing for qualitative coding.

Getting ready for teamwork

If you are new to managing a team of qualitative researchers, you may have a general sense that multiple perspectives on the analytical process can add tremendous strength to an investigation. What you may not yet know is that qualitative research in teams, with all of its benefits, can be very challenging. One problem is the potential for inexperienced qualitative researchers to apply expectations from quantitative research where role differentiation and division of labour are much clearer, and tasks are divided across data collection, entry, analysis and reporting. Perhaps the most important principle, for that situation, is fidelity to the original design such that the hand-off points and products are standardized and predictable.

In qualitative research, this type of division of labour can be dangerous. There may be a compelling reason to change the research plan as the project proceeds, with issues up for revision including question design and sampling through to modes of analysis and perhaps even the research question itself. In qualitative research, therefore, it is critical that any differences in roles among the team are constructed alongside multiple opportunities to work together, communicate, document successful procedures, and modify processes if they begin interfering with (or fail to further) the analysis. Much of what you will find in this chapter is related to the importance of such communication and the strategies you can use to monitor and change the analytical activities of the team.

Clarity of purpose in all team research activities

The team's work with the data should be purposeful (see Chapter 2). The purpose(s) may change as the project progresses, but failing to have a clear goal can lead to a blind, mechanistic analysis. By constantly asking yourself 'What is the purpose of this activity?' and by asking your fellow teammates to also clarify their perceptions of purpose, teams are less likely to wander into unproductive 'data management' at the expense of analysis. One of the added benefits of this articulation of purpose in teams is that the often-unstated assumptions and perceptions of the lone researcher become visible, so they can be intentionally examined, altered or pursued. In teams there can also be a dangerous tendency for individuals to trust that others on the team know what they are doing in the grand scheme of the project, even though the current activity seems unproductive. This can lead to a great deal of wasted time and effort.

Piloting processes to determine if they are effective for the team

Team size, geographic dispersion, volume and variety of data, and length of project all contribute to the complexity of storing and analysing data and of coordinating the team research process. Specific questions to consider, beyond the design of the project and choice of methods, include:

- What experience does each researcher have with qualitative methods, with the research setting, or with NVivo?
- What decision-making models (e.g., consensus, democratic vote, or team leader directives) are in play to guide team progress?

- How can the geographic dispersion of the team be managed?
- What work will be done independently, in pairs, or in groups?
- What kind of access do team members have to the software?
- What is the time frame for the analysis?

Because qualitative team research with NVivo can take so many different forms based on the answers to these questions, perhaps the most important advice we have regarding this endeavour is to pilot each planned activity using NVivo. Much of this piloting will occur early on, but you will find a need to test new activities throughout the research as you move to each new stage. For example:

▶ Prepare one document and import it, before preparing all 40 or 200 files.
▶ Ask different researchers to code just one page of the same transcript to see the visual comparisons among coders and to practise merging the data and running queries, rather than having them each code an entire (different) transcript at the outset.
▶ When working with waves of data, log the process of collecting, importing, coding and managing the first wave so your management of the next wave benefits from the lessons learned (and don't assume you'll remember them when the time comes)!
▶ Run a query and some reports early on, even if you do not have enough data to make any interpretations, in order to confirm you will be able to generate the output you desire when you are ready.
▶ Take a day to pilot the process of combining databases if you plan on working in multiple copies (we provide specific instructions on this later in the chapter). This includes naming and distributing different projects to the various researchers, coding independently, collecting these databases, and importing them into a single project.

✓ Always consider making small steps first in order to reflect on them without the pressure of getting it perfectly right the first time.

Creating memos to log the pilot activities, the lessons learned, and the current procedures is an important step for most teams. Examples include:

- protocols for data collection, cleaning (e.g., reviewing inaudible portions of tapes), and storage;
- role clarifications or job descriptions;
- coding structures and definitions, along with examples and counter-examples;
- ideas proposed by team members and decisions made regarding these proposals;
- timelines or benchmarks for the phases in the research process;
- minutes of meetings;
- emerging models or hypotheses.

In addition, it can be helpful to keep a log of the structure (e.g., of your node system) as it evolves over time to help keep everyone mindful of the progress you are making.

✓ If relevant, pay special attention to the issue of team members rotating in and out of the project. A training binder helps initiate new researchers.

Leveraging strengths of team members

Differences among the team may relate to practical tasks like recruiting participants, coding, and organizing backup files. Ideally there is a match between the things people like to do, what they are competent to do, and what need to be done, but this is not always so, and it takes a good team leader or existing collaborative dynamics to appropriately leverage these strengths. Practical skills may be identified during team member selection, but sometimes these skills do not become apparent until the group is together and working on the research, especially if the members are all new to NVivo. When leaders identify and acknowledge individual strengths early, they help keep team members motivated and engaged. As processes unfold and individuals gain skills, these strengths may shift. Continuous attention to these changing contributions is an important part of managing the team.

Some of the differences will pertain to the way individuals see and interpret meaning in the data. Lyn Richards (2009) provided an activity for locating and discussing team differences in interpretation based on a strategy recommended earlier for the solo researcher (see Chapter 4). Asking team members to review a portion of the data and articulate the items or issues they find interesting, and why they find them interesting, then comparing the responses from team members, can make the researchers aware of different perspectives and widen the interpretive lens among team members. Some of these differences can be acknowledged (and perhaps promoted) early in the process. A consensus does not necessarily lead to a better interpretation of the data, though some teams may strive for consensus.

Options for storing and accessing a team project

The database for your team project can be stored and accessed in one of three ways:

1 as a single database accessed by each team member at different times;
2 using multiple copies of a database such that each researcher has his or her own copy, working independently and perhaps simultaneously until it is time to combine them into one database;
3 as an NVivo Server project where multiple researchers can access the same database at the same time if they choose to do so.

If you have only one licence for NVivo, and you want individuals to code independently, your team will work in a single database and the researchers will access the project at different times. The database will reside on a single computer (in a research office, for instance, or on a laptop), and individuals will schedule time to work in this central location. You might also use a single database even if you have multiple copies of the software, in order to avoid the extra administrative work required to merge copies of databases together (or to avoid the extra cost of NVivo Server). In the scenario of one database (one project file) and multiple copies of the software, the database can be transferred from one researcher to another as they work sequentially.[1] The primary limitation to either of these single, 'standalone' project options is the inability to work simultaneously.

If the dynamics of the project require that multiple researchers work at the same time in the database, you must either make multiple copies of the project for use on separate computers or purchase NVivo Server. When working in multiple copies of the database, several rules must be followed in order to eventually reintegrate the different work among the team members into one database (see below). If you intend to use this strategy, we strongly recommend that you read the section of this chapter on *Combining databases* very carefully before you begin (and the material between here and there might also be important to you)! The primary benefit of working in multiple copies is the ability to meet rapidly approaching deadlines with the simultaneous coding and analysis efforts of team members. The primary limitation is the problem created when individual researchers edit the contents of the sources (e.g., by fixing typos) so the merged databases contain unmerged duplicate files (and we have seen a few research teams weep and start over in this circumstance). Following a few simple rules from the outset can prevent this problem.

Alternatively, in order to support the work of multiple researchers working simultaneously, you can purchase NVivo Server. This software allows multiple researchers to work in the same database (located on a server) at the same time with no worries about the consequences of editing files. When one researcher is editing the contents of an interview, it will be unavailable to other researchers (to either code or edit), but as soon as the interview is returned to 'read only' status (which means you can still code the data – you just cannot edit the contents), it is available for multiple researchers to examine or code.[2]

Identifying which of these three strategies to use (with points to take into consideration summarized in Table 12.1) is one of the first decisions you need to make when using NVivo for a team project.

---

[1] Doing so requires excellent 'housekeeping' practices to ensure work is always done on the most recent copy of the project.

[2] More information about pricing, system requirements, and the capabilities of NVivo Server are available on the QSR website.

Table 12.1 Choosing a database storage and management strategy

Points to consider	Single project	Multiple copies	NVivo Server
You are most likely to use this strategy in a team if ...	You have only one licence for the software. You want to avoid the potential problems of merging databases. You will not be purchasing NVivo Server.	You have multiple licences for the software. Your team members need to work simultaneously. You will not be purchasing NVivo Server.	Your team members need to work simultaneously. You want to avoid the potential problems of merging databases.
Can I edit the text while I work?	Yes	No	Yes
Can we work simultaneously?	No	Yes	Yes
Can we code differently and track who did what?	Yes	Yes	Yes
Do we need to make backup copies?	Yes	Yes	Yes (they can be scheduled to run automatically).
Can we use different versions of NVivo?	Not applicable, since you are working in a single database.	Only if you convert any work done in an older version of the software to the newer version before merging.	No. All users must be in the same version.
What basic rules do I need to follow?	Change the Application Options to 'prompt for user' when you launch NVivo so that users are correctly tracked.	Unless each researcher works exclusively with different internal sources, do not allow editing of the text of those internals until *after* the projects are merged. Ensure the user is being correctly recorded for each working session in each copy of the project.	You may edit and code as you wish. If another researcher is editing a source, it will not be available to you until they finish editing. Users will need to log in, to access the server project.
What Help files will assist me?	About teamwork in a standalone project. Manage users in a standalone project.	About teamwork in a standalone project. Manage users in a standalone project. Import items from another NVivo project. How duplicate project items are handled during import.	About NVivo Server. About teamwork in a server project. Manage users in a server project. Maintain NVivo Server.

Getting started as a team with NVivo

Training together on the project

If possible, the team should engage in a day of NVivo training together, focusing on the research project in mind.

- ✓ If data have not yet been collected, generate a page of a transcript for five imaginary participants based on the research questions and the interview protocol. Simply have team members interview each other for a few minutes as a role-play activity prior to the training session.
- ✓ If NVivo skills are not already available in the team, find a trainer who is willing and able to customize training for you with these data instead of training on the sample data that accompany the software. This will help identify issues that are unique to your project and begin the process of developing guidelines for your team.
- ✓ If possible, hold your training when you start to collect data. By doing this you can more easily reap the benefits of some tips for preparing the data before all of the responses are collected.

Regardless of whether you do it before or after data collection, training will help you move forward and keep you from wasting time as you determine which work practices and software tools are the most relevant for your research. In the process, you are also likely to resolve many of the project set-up and management issues that result from the kind of complex data arrangements that often accompany team projects.

- ! If team members all lack experience with NVivo and some are also new to qualitative research, starting the process without the guidance of an NVivo expert is a mistake that is likely to cost you (in money and grief).

Creating a project shell

As a supplement to training (or as a set of issues you might request to be covered by a trainer for your team's project), we now turn to some of the core tools in NVivo that are most relevant to teams. As you work through the rest of the information in this chapter, you should create a 'shell' for your project to set up a framework for data management and team communication, and to pilot some of the activities. Especially if you plan on working in multiple copies of the database, you should think through all of the set-up activities you can accomplish in a single database before it is copied, in order to reduce redundant work. You might consider completing the following activities in a single shell before you distribute it.

Create a project shell

▶ Create a node for each coder (see Chapters 4 and 5). Later, each researcher may create nodes under their own name as a way of proposing new nodes without creating a chaotic coding structure.

▶ Create a memo for each researcher where they can later track their particular questions, issues and insights (see Chapter 2).

▶ Create a memo called *Teamwork in NVivo* as a protocol document based on early team discussion (subject to further review and comment by individual researchers later).

▶ Create and maintain an archive folder on a server or external drive to store backup copies of the database (see below).

▶ Import one or more sources (see Chapter 3), depending on how the work of coding is to be distributed among team members.

Keeping track of who did what

Now that you have a shell, you should make a copy and pilot the activities below.

Recording memos and tracking users

• With the *Teamwork in NVivo* memo open and in edit mode, add the date and time (**Ctrl+Shift+T**) to track the chronology of ideas about team protocols, and then record a comment.

• Close the *Detail View* and look at the columns that are visible in the *List View*. This is your first glimpse of NVivo's ability to track researchers. The default columns provide the initials of the researcher (hopefully yours!) who created or most recently modified the memo. This list is available for every type of item in the *List View* of your project (sources, nodes, attributes, sets, queries, models).

Identifying users

You will want to ensure that work (such as coding) can be traced back to the researchers who did it, for both audit and coding comparison purposes.

Users and passwords

Identifying and changing users

▶ *If you work on a shared computer*, the default Application Options (found in the File menu) in NVivo should be changed (Figure 12.1) to ☑ **Prompt for user on**

(Continued)

(Continued)

launch. Subsequently, each time a researcher launches the software on the computer, they'll be asked to provide their login name and initials.[3]

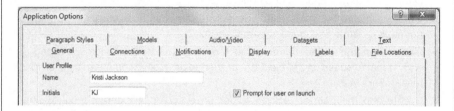

Figure 12.1   Setting the Application Options to prompt for user on launch

✓ This should be changed whether or not you have added Read/Write or Read Only password access (described below), because the user names and initials are requested when the software is launched and before opening a particular (potentially password protected) project.

▶ Exit the software completely and launch NVivo again if you are switching users on the same computer. Closing and reopening a project while the software remains open will not activate the request for the user.

! *If you are working on a solo copy of the project,* on your own computer, ensure that it is correctly registering you (and not the administrator) as the user each time you open the software. If it isn't, then follow the procedure above to prompt for user on launch.

✓ *If you are working on a server copy of the project,* you will be required to log in at the start of each working session.

If a team member has accidentally entered a different name or initials on different occasions, you can remove one of their user names and replace it with their other user name.

! Because this will change all the coding in the system done under either of those names and allocate it to the single user, it is wise to make a copy before following these steps to combine users.

▶ Go to **File > Info > Project Properties > Users**.

▶ Click to **Remove** a user, and then respond to the request to **Please select a user who will replace the user being removed**.

---

[3] Projects in NVivo Server contain a different interface for establishing users and passwords. See NVivo Help files for additional information.

✓ The system will update all of the project items (this may take a few minutes).

! If two or more users code the same passage to the same node, the reference *count* (but not the actual text) is duplicated. To obtain accurate reference counts when you have multiple users, *make a copy* of the database and merge the work of all of the users by removing all but one.

! NVivo will allow different users to enter the same initials into a single project. So, if Sylvia Blake and Sadik Botros both enter SB as their initials, you will have problems distinguishing authorship of work that is identified on screen using only initials. If this is a risk, the team leader should determine the name and initials for each team member to use prior to initiating work in the project.

Passwords

Passwords can be developed for a particular project to allow for Read/Write access, or Read Only access. Passwords are optional.

▶ With the project open, select **File > Info > Project Properties > Passwords**.

▶ Choosing the slot for the appropriate type of access, enter and confirm a password and provide yourself with a password hint.

Turning the project log on or off

Although the user names and initials in the *List View* will provide researchers with information about recent changes, they do not track each independent action in the software. A project log where researchers can trace these actions can be created for any NVivo project. This allows you to:

• track the specific activities of individual researchers, and
• identify the exact time and date that an error occurred (e.g., you deleted an important memo accidentally!) with the hope that you can reincorporate this item into your project from one of your backup databases.

Be aware of two limitations to the project log:

• The log will describe a specific event (e.g., on 02/03/2010 10:24 AM, Henry coded a passage to the *Balance* node), but it will not provide the source or the exact passage. In this regard, it is much more of a log (aptly named) than an audit.
• The log is not interactive, so while you will obtain a history of events, you cannot use the log to access specific database items to make rapid changes or corrections to them.

To turn the project log on or off once you open a project:

▶ Check or uncheck **File > Info > Project Properties > ☑ Write user actions to project event log**.

To see the log entries (or to clear the log):

▶ Select **File > Info > Open project event log**, or **Clear project event log**.

Annotations

Using annotations in NVivo (see Chapter 2) raises two issues for teams.

- Adding an annotation is not the same as editing the text. Therefore, it is safe for different researchers to add different annotations to the same document (such as an interview) in their own copies of the database. They will all be transferred into the single file later.
- Unless the researchers toggle to the **Collections** button in the *Navigation View*, it is not evident who wrote an annotation. Make sure each researcher initials (and perhaps dates) his/her annotations in the event it becomes important to quickly ascertain the author.

Use colours to flag things for team members

In Chapter 2 you learned a little about the use of colours to identify project items. Teams might find this tool useful as a way of tagging and sorting items according to researcher. If Pat is assigned ten transcripts to code that do not fall in alphabetical order in the list of sources, and Kristi is to code another ten, we can allocate a colour to each user's interviews to help us distinguish our allotted interviews. This strategy can be useful also to flag memos created by different researchers.

Keeping track of different copies of projects

At the end of Chapter 2, we walked you through the steps for saving backup copies of your projects. If you plan on merging different copies of databases later, we have a few additional recommendations about keeping track of the projects. Things tend to go much more smoothly when one person is in charge of this process and sets up some housekeeping rules.

We recommend naming copies of the project file in the following way: *project name, date, researcher*. So, for instance, if an early childhood education project with the title *ECE* is being distributed to Pat and Kristi for coding, Pat will receive a copy with the filename *ECE 2013 02 15 Pat*, while Kristi will receive *ECE 2013 02 15 Kristi*.[4] In addition to helping Pat and Kristi differentiate successive versions

---

[4] Note the use of the international date format (usually YYYY MM DD or YYMMDD). This will ensure that the list of files are sorted consecutively by date within a folder, from oldest to most recent.

of the projects, this naming convention will help the database manager distinguish different projects during the merge.

Each time a researcher backs up (copies) the project, they should modify the date in the filename of their project, so that they know which is their current version (see Chapter 2). Note that the filename (which you see in your list of files in Windows Explorer) will be different from the title of the project (which is registered in NVivo). The Welcome window in NVivo will show the title of recently used projects, with the file pathname and the date last accessed also visible when you hover over a particular title, to help avoid confusion (Figure 12.2).

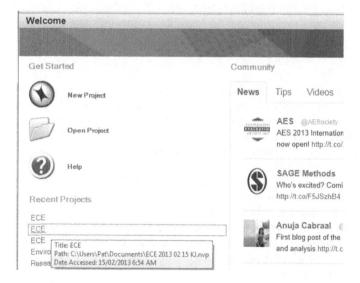

Figure 12.2   The Welcome window showing a project copied for different team members

If, when it is time to merge the files (or at any other time), you (or your database manager) would prefer to have your project title match your distinguishing filename, then you can change it by going to **File > Info > Project Properties**. Then save the project.

The most important thing here is that you develop a system for how team members should label their own backups, detail this system in the *Teamwork* memo, and then ensure that everyone is following that procedure. The approach will vary to some extent, depending on which of the three methods you are employing for managing the database, as this has an influence on how many different copies of the project there will be 'floating around'. Projects should be backed up at least once each working day.

Using NVivo's tools to facilitate team communication

Tools for recording thoughts about ongoing analysis, logging changes made in the project, and linking between items were also described in Chapter 2. Here we provide suggestions for ways to make use of them to facilitate communication in a team project.

Memos

Memos are an important tool for analysis, but they are also important for keeping track of team guidelines, decisions, activities, benchmarks, proposals for changes, issues for the next team meeting, etc. In addition to these diverse and customized ways to use memos to facilitate communication about the project, we have specific recommendations about recording node descriptions, based on our work with teams.

- If you are working in multiple copies of the database, you need a strategy to compensate for NVivo's inability to reconcile node descriptions (which essentially serve as your codebook) when aggregating copies of the database. One option is to have a memo for each researcher regarding *Node description proposals* where they log recommendations for changes that will be reviewed at team meetings and after the database has been merged.
- Make and save regular reports of node lists with descriptions (see Chapters 4 and 11), and/or record memos about changes, as a way to track changes over time and across team members. This will help keep the team from wandering back over earlier descriptions without a clear purpose or rationale. The reports and memos also serve as helpful references when you write up your methods, because they map the trajectory of your node descriptions. Have one of the researchers take responsibility for this.

Memo links

In addition to any of these 'standalone' memos, a team can also benefit from linking memos to either nodes or sources, for the purpose of creating helpful summaries for one another. Because it could take weeks (or months) for each team member to read through all of the data in each source or node in a very large project, this process of creating memo links can help the team efficiently discuss the patterns in the data. When managed effectively, this allows researchers to obtain a broad view of the entire corpus of data while also allowing each researcher to become an 'expert' in a subset of the data.

See also links

As team members interact with the data and develop questions, ideas, or things they want to discuss later with other team members, the see also link inside a memo can be a critical component of effective communication. For instance, you might write the following inside a memo called *Coding questions and recommendations*: 'I am unclear if this quote should go in the node called *loyalty* or the node called *trust*, and I'm wondering if we need to change the definition of *loyalty* so that it always involves an action or behaviour, while *trust* always involves a thought or feeling without a specific action.' By pasting the quote you are referring to as a see also link in the memo, you place all ideas for discussion in one location, with links to the quote(s) in the raw data. These can then be brought to a team meeting for resolution (print the memo with see also links as endnotes, or use a data projector to display your project) – or if the team members are working on one computer, then it can be reviewed by each team member as they work.

Use see also links to:

- point to locations that clarify your request for changes in node descriptions;
- flag places that you want to discuss because the passage is unclear or because you disagree with your teammate's coding;
- ask the researcher who conducted the interview for clarifying context;
- propose evolving theories or hypotheses to your teammates and direct them to specific examples or ask them to identify counter-examples.

Annotations

Consider using annotations to help make your teammates aware of the context. For instance, you conducted the interview and are coding the transcript as a first pass through the data. One of your interviewees says, 'It's like that awesome donation we had in year one of the programme. It breathed new life into the entire organization and everyone seemed more willing to cooperate and to compromise.' You know the 'donation' was a $50,000 gift from a former participant of the programme (a piece of information that may have come from another interview or simply from your contextual knowledge of the setting), but your teammates don't know this. You could add an annotation to 'donation' that says, 'A $50,000 gift form Gloria, a former participant of the programme'. Mindfully adding annotations to help clarify these quotes for your teammates will help them better understand and interpret the data when they encounter your interviews.

Models

In Chapter 2 we walked you through the creation of a simple model to begin mapping ideas and expectations. When working in a team, models can be an effective way of accomplishing two things at once.

- Models can hone the ideas of different researchers on the team regarding the related concepts, causal relationships (if relevant) and factors at play in the study.
- When a diverse range of perceptions are at play among team members, the Modeller can be an efficient way of presenting, exploring, and assessing the various ideas. For some learning and communication styles, this is a more effective way for teams to effectively share and explore alternative explanations.

Coding as a team

Our experience indicates that most teams vastly underestimate the time needed to meet and discuss the various ideas and differences among team members, especially early on in the coding process. In some instances, teams would be better off coding as a group in the initial stages in order to begin moving forward on firm footing. This helps the members address and discuss differing views before these differences become liabilities instead of assets to the project. While coding together may seem cumbersome at first, it could save hundreds of hours in the long run, and we know of a few teams (less constrained by deadlines!) that code all of the data in pairs or groups because of the rich discussions this promotes.

Guiding questions

Attend to the following questions early in your team planning, because they will have an effect on the choices available to you in using NVivo to code data as a team. Some of them may not be clear until you begin working in NVivo, but they should all be addressed eventually in order for team coding to evolve effectively.

- What access do team members have to NVivo (timing, duration, location, etc.)?
- What is the time frame for coding (interim and final deadlines)?
- What coding will be approached individually, in pairs, or in groups?
- Do you want team members to code familiar data (e.g., interviews they conducted) or unfamiliar data (so they are exposed to a wider range of perspectives)?
- What decision-making models (e.g., consensus, democratic vote, or team leader directives) are in play to guide team progress during coding?
- What internal benchmarks or final reports does the team need to consider or produce as a result of teamwork (e.g., summaries and coder reliability reports)?
- Who is responsible for reporting and what do they need to produce?

Attend to the following issues

- There is no magic number associated with the hours per day (or week) that lead to burnout (too much) or distance (too little), but being mindful of the potential to engage in either type of unproductive coding will help you guard against it.

- If you plan on dividing up the work, researchers may either code different documents (e.g., interviews 6–10 of 20) or sections of the interview (e.g., questions 1–3 of 12). With the former choice researchers gain comprehensive knowledge of a subset of the participants, but not all of them. With the latter choice researchers become content experts in an area of the protocol but may not have a good sense of any participant's holistic experience.
- In practical terms, it is easier to build consistency between coders by coding to umbrella nodes first, and then taking a second pass at the data to refine these into subnodes (this may serve to limit inductive coding, however).
- Beware of the potential to create purely descriptive nodes when using deductive and team coding strategies such as these, and continue to revisit the ways you might engage in rich interpretation of the data.

The thorny issue of coding context

When teams are trying to promote coding consistency among team members, the amount of contextual information to code is a frequently encountered hurdle. There are three issues to consider early in the team coding process (and you may need to revisit them as the analysis unfolds):

- the need to ensure that all team members understand coding done by another researcher;
- the information that NVivo will retrieve when you run queries with an intersection operator;
- the mechanics of the coding comparison query, because this query yields a lower score for agreement if coders select different amounts of context when they code.

There is a unique dynamic in teamwork regarding the ease of understanding the coded portions that have been removed from context. To the coder who read and coded the transcript, a brief fragment may make sense when reviewing a node, but a researcher who did not code this data may be unclear about the meaning and lament the lack of context. In Chapter 4 (see especially Figure 4.5) we explained how, with a click of the right mouse button, you are able to see either the immediate context of a coded passage (e.g., the remainder of the paragraph) or the passage highlighted in its original source. For the former option, the additional context will be temporarily incorporated into the *Detail View*, as greyed-out material.

▶ If seeing it as temporary context is not sufficient and you want to retain some or all of the context around the coded portion, then select and code in your usual way (e.g., drag and drop the additional context into the node). It will show as coded text in the node next time you open it.

The second issue to consider regarding context is the implication for intersection searches (i.e., coding queries and matrix coding queries, using AND). Because these query tools allow researchers to find text coded at one or more nodes, the amount of context chosen during the coding process has a direct effect on the results of an intersection query. It can result in no finds (when coding has been too brief), or 'false' finds where the tail end of coding for one node connects with the start of coding for another (when the coding has been too generous). Pilot some of your intersection coding queries early in the process so you can make more informed choices as a team about how much context to include.

The third issue regarding coding context is the impact of coded context on the coder comparison query results, which we detail in the final section of this chapter. When two researchers code independently and one codes the first two sentences in the paragraph to *trust,* but the other codes all four sentences to *trust,* the coding comparison query will report the discrepancy, and record a potentially low kappa score because one coder applied the node to approximately twice as much data. Before handling this and the broader, contentious issue of coder reliability and the coding comparison query, we first attend to the process of merging projects so teams that need to combine projects before running this query are able to do so. If you do not need to combine databases, you should skip directly to the section on *Comparing the work of different researchers.*

Combining databases

If you are working in a team with the project spread across several computers, you might want to combine databases early in the project to test the process to make sure it will serve your needs later, and to take stock of the way multiple coders are approaching the data. Then, you will combine databases once coding is completed in order to produce comprehensive queries or final reports.

The basic rules for importing one database into another

All project items (sources, nodes, sets, queries, models, etc.) are considered when one database is imported into another, even if one copy of the project has the item but the other does not. Projects are likely to have some combination of common and unique items. Unless you specifically ask for duplicate items to be ignored or added to the project as separate items, NVivo will combine them.

Combining databases is very easy, provided researchers are aware of some basic rules.

!   Know these rules before you start copying and working in separate projects, because failure to follow these rules may result in an inability to combine projects successfully.

When you combine projects you are opening one (the master) and importing the other (the auxiliary) into the master. Your immediate task is to decide which is the master and which is the auxiliary. If you have more than two project files to merge, only one is the master and all of the others are auxiliaries. The remainder of this section will help you prepare for the process and help you make the decision on which project should be the master.

Sources and nodes

Sources and nodes in project A and project B will merge as long as three conditions are met:

1 The nodes and/or sources have the same name.

   o *Positive* in project A is also called *Positive* in project B.
   o *Susan* in project A is also called *Susan* in project B.

2 The nodes and/or sources are in the same hierarchical location with the projects.

   o *Positive* in project A and *Positive* in project B are under the same parent node, such as *Valence.*

If the node *Positive* in project A is under *Valence* but in project B it is under *Attitude,* the two nodes will not merge. This is fairly easily resolved later as you can manually merge two or more nodes after the projects have been combined, although this can become tedious if it happens often.

   o *Susan* in project A and *Susan* in project B are in the *Internals* folder, but ...

If *Susan* in project A is directly under *Internals* but *Susan* in project B is under *Interviews* (which is a subfolder under *Internals*) the two sources will not merge. This is a much more significant problem than having two nodes that do not merge, because the coding of two, separate files cannot be merged within a database the way nodes can be merged. Therefore, it is important that one of the first things you check after a project is imported is that the sources were merged properly.

3 A third condition applies to all internal sources in the database: internals such as *Susan* will merge only if they contain the exact same text characters.

   o It is critical that *none* of the researchers edits any of the documents that are in common across the copies of the project. Researchers may code as differently as they would like, but they must not edit the text in the internal source.

If a researcher working in project A finds the word 'dove' in *Susan's* interview, and changes it to the correct word, 'love', but the researcher in project

B does not, the two versions of *Susan* will not merge, even though the documents have the same name, are in the same hierarchical location, and have the same length.

To ensure the files are not edited, explain the problem of editing text to all team members early on in the process so they are aware of the importance of this status and do not change it. Because the **Click to edit** bar is quite visible in the *Detail View* when a source is open, this is especially important. We suggest training researchers to use an annotation or a see also link in a memo to note any editing errors they find in the text, which can then be corrected once the project is fully and finally merged.

Other project items and their properties

While the nodes and sources are the primary concern for most teams when projects are merged, it is also helpful that NVivo adds any *unique* item from the auxiliary into the master. So, in addition to sources and nodes, this includes classifications, collections, queries, reports and models. Furthermore, several project properties from the auxiliary project will be added as well, such as customized fields for audio or video transcripts.

The issue is more complicated when items with different properties (e.g., descriptions, colours, aggregation settings) exist in the master as well as the auxiliary. For instance, the item descriptions (of sources, nodes, etc.) in the master project will be retained, but none of the auxiliary item descriptions will be incorporated. The master also trumps the auxiliary regarding the settings to aggregate (or not to aggregate) the nodes, the application of colours to project items, the stop words list, the default model styles, and other tools. However, if a same-named set exists in both projects, NVivo will import all set members from the auxiliary project into the master project.

? For a complete list of the way NVivo identifies and reconciles conflicts in the master and the auxiliary, search the NVivo Help files for *How NVivo determines that two project items are duplicates, How duplicate project items are handled during import,* and *How project properties are handled during import.*

Combining projects

We are assuming at this point that you are choosing to import the content of one whole project into another, to combine the work of team members.

? Search the NVivo Help files for *Import items from another NVivo project* for more information if you want to import selected items with or without content (for instance, to add the coding structure from an earlier project into your new project that will contain different data).

Final preparation

▶ Before you combine projects, first create an archive folder for all the projects you will be combining by making copies and putting them in a safe place where they will not be altered. This is especially important for the project that will become the master project, as it will be changed. All others, by default, will be auxiliaries.

Import the auxiliary project

▶ Open the master project that will be the foundation for the new, combined project.

▶ From the *External Data* ribbon, select **Project**.

▶ In the Import Project dialogue, **Browse** to locate the project you want to import > **Open**.

▶ Click the **All (including content)** option if you want to add all items in the auxiliary project to the master.

▶ Choose how you want to handle duplicate items – to **Merge into existing item** or **Create new item**. The default to merge items is by far the most common need.

▶ Click on **Import**.

When the process is complete, a report will open describing the items that were or were not imported. Do not be too dismayed regarding **Items Not Imported** in the report, because if an item already exists in the master, it is not imported. Your main concern will probably be to check that additional content in the auxiliary project has been added to the master (e.g., whether the coding Pat did to *positive* was added to the coding Kristi did to *positive*).

Check the import worked as intended

▶ First, check that all users have been imported (**File > Info > Project Properties > Users**).

Then you may do one or more of the following as a double-check with project items:

▶ Look in your sources to make sure none of them was duplicated (be careful of ignoring the subfolders, where duplicates can often hide).

▶ Open a node and turn on coding stripes by user (see below).

▶ Check your classification system contains the correct attributes and values. As an extra check, you might also go to the properties of one of your case nodes to make sure the attributes for that case are correctly assigned.

(Continued)

(Continued)

▶ Examine your sets to see if all the members are identified as expected.

▶ Look in your queries to see what has been added and organize them in subfolders if needed.

! Be aware that if a database manager engages in activities such as manually merging nodes in the new database, her initials will appear in the list view as the researcher who most recently modified an item. She will also be listed as the researcher who created the item if she creates a new node and merges existing items into that new node. Fortunately, the coding stripes for users within the text of the newly merged nodes retain the initials of the original coders.

Comparing coding by different researchers

Whether you have just merged a project together, you are working with NVivo Server, or you are working in one project where users have logged in each time they accessed the project, you may now be interested in comparing the work of different researchers. When researchers work in teams there is usually an expectation that coding should be checked along the way and at the end of the project to ensure there is an adequate level of coding agreement between team members. These kinds of checks are seen by some as an indicator of the reliability (or trustworthiness) of the coding process, and as contributing to the validity of the conclusions drawn from the codes.

Caveats and alternatives to 'proving' reliability

Others will argue that the strength of your analysis and the clarity and comprehensiveness of your evidence carry more weight than a measure of reliability. How was the coding system developed? What convinced the team of their conclusions? What were the competing explanations? How were differences resolved? Take your audience through these turning points with the assistance of detailed memos of the processes, decisions, efforts to confirm patterns, and the strategies you used for exploring alternative explanations. These should be supported with evidence from the data. Reliability testing for inter-coder agreement does not, in itself, add to the strength of your conclusions.

Furthermore, in qualitative work, each person brings to the data their own purposes, perspectives, experiences and knowledge. Reliability may be a lower (or non-existent) priority in some research projects where diversity in coding is highly valued. For example:

In a study of African-American girls attending an after-school programme on science, the principal investigator delegated coding of classroom transcripts to two graduate students. One was a self-identified white female, and the other was a self-identified black female. Instead of training these students to code according to an established framework, the principal investigator asked both students to code according to the issues they observed in the data that related to the primary research question: what factors contribute to self-perception as a 'scientist' among the young, African-American girls in the programme? The only directive was to pay attention to the way the identities of the girls may have changed over the course of the study, all of the girls having begun with the self-proclaimed stance that they were not interested in science.

While the white student focused attention on the structure of the course activities and the actions of the innovative instructor (who used collaborative curriculum design, active learning, and unstructured classroom discourse), the black student identified a range of discursive strategies the girls used to experiment with their identities as scientists. While both approaches to coding contributed to answering the research question, they did so from particular, socially constructed vantage points that the principal investigator wanted to leverage in the analysis. This generated a rich interpretation of identity development in the programme and fostered an expansive (rather than narrow) view of the data. Because an expanded, non-standardized view of the data that considered multiple angles was the primary purpose of the research, the approach was well suited to the task.

Comparing coding with the assistance of NVivo

Nevertheless, with the above caveats and alternatives in mind, it is important to acknowledge the reasonableness, in some situations, of expecting some consistency in coding done by different members of a team in a single project (or by the same person across a whole project). In such circumstances, early variation or vagueness in coding is purposefully clarified and 'tidied up' by the time final analyses are undertaken. Additionally, categories developed should 'make sense' to an external observer, to those who provided the data, and/or to those for whom a report is being prepared, with it being evident that data have been fitted appropriately to those categories.

NVivo provides several ways to visualize the coding among the team, and also contains a query designed to compare the coding of two researchers. You will use different strategies, depending on whether you want to:

- see how different coders are working, as a basis for discussion about coding strategies; and/or
- check if there is a sufficiently high level of agreement (inter-coder reliability) between different coders.

Several tools are available to foster both discussion and reliability testing in NVivo.

Using coding stripes

In Chapter 4, we showed you how to examine your coding with coding stripes. If you logged on as different users in the same project or you merged projects, you can also turn on coding stripes according to user. This visualization can facilitate conversations among the team about choice of nodes, the node descriptions, and the coding context selected for particular passages.

View coding by different users

▶ Open a source in *Detail View*.[5]

▶ Select **View** > **Coding Stripes** > **Selected Items** > ☑ **Users**.

You will be shown the equivalent of a coding density bar for each user, allowing you to hover to see what codes each used (if any) for the adjacent passage of text (Figure 12.3).

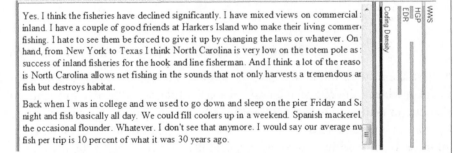

Figure 12.3   Coding stripes showing the work of three coders on a source document

✓ If you are using this method to review or assess commonality of coding strategies, it is critical that you hover over the different users' coding stripes to see what actual nodes have been coded, as the stripe might appear the same but the nodes coded might be different.

---

[5] While you can also compare coding stripes in a node, this is less useful and potentially misleading because the stripes do not necessarily relate to the node and, indeed, a user may be shown who has not coded any text at that node at all (because he or she has coded the same text at other nodes).

Using a coding comparison query

Once you have considered our prior cautions about the unreflective pursuit of coder reliability, and you have established a coding structure, trained research-ers on the coding process, and engaged in some group coding or practice cod-ing, you are ready to pilot a coding comparison query. You will need to identify a source and select a range of data within it (e.g., several pages) that all researchers in the team have coded or will code. We recommend selecting a small portion of the data first, in the event there are problems with the techni-cal process of merging projects or running the query. If things run smoothly, you can do it again on a larger portion of the data.

The coding comparison query

▶ Decide which source(s), node(s) and users you want to compare.
▶ In *Navigation View*, select **Queries**. In *List View* > **Right-click** > **New Query** > **Coding Comparison Query**.
▶ ☑ **Add to project** (if you want to save the query).
▶ Use the **Select** buttons to choose the User or User Group in **A** and **B**.

✓ If you add more than one user for either **A** or **B**, NVivo treats a group of users as though they were a single person. In other words, it aggregates all the coding done by the coders in group **A** and then compares it to the aggregated coding of user group **B**. If you have three or more coders, and you want to compare all of them, you should identify a 'lead' coder and compare the other coders to this leader in separate coding comparison queries.

▶ Change **All Nodes** to **Selected Nodes** and use the **Select** button to identify the node(s) of interest – those that hold interactive coding – otherwise you will also get reports for case nodes, nodes created through auto coding, and results nodes from queries.
▶ Change the **Scope** to **Selected Sources** and use the **Select** button to identify the source(s) of interest, that is, the one(s) that were coded.
▶ Select **Run**.

Statistical output from the query

A portion of the output for a coding comparison query in the *Environmental Change* sample data is shown in Figure 12.4.[6] The coding of Effie (user A) and Wanda (user B) for the single node, *Habitat*, is compared across each of three documents (*Barbara*, *Charles* and *Dorothy*).

(Continued)

---

[6] Node and source details have been edited for clarity of presentation.

(Continued)

Node	Source	Kappa	Agreement (%)	A and B (%)	Not A and Not B (%)	Disagreement (%)	A and Not B (%)	B and Not A (%)
Habitat	Barbara	0.5743	94.47	4.16	90.31	5.53	0.49	5.04
Habitat	Charles	1	100	0	100	0	0	0
Habitat	Dorothy	0	92.51	0	92.51	7.49	0	7.49

Figure 12.4   Statistical output from a coding comparison query

Result columns include:

- *Source size* – total number of units in the source being coded (characters for documents, duration to one-tenth of a second for media files, pixels for images).
- *Kappa* – a value of 1 indicates perfect agreement (identical coding), 0 (or less) indicates no better than chance (or worse than chance).
- *Agreement (%)* – overall level of agreement between coders (a combination of the next two columns).

  ○ *A and B (%)* – the percentage of units in the source coded by both coders.
  ○ *Not A and Not B (%)* – the percentage of units in the source not coded by either coder.

- *Disagreement (%)* – overall level of disagreement between coders (a combination of the next two columns).

  ○ *A and Not B (%)* – the percentage of units in the source coded by A but not coded by B.
  ○ *B and Not A (%)* – the percentage of units in the source coded by B but not coded by A.

Visual output from the query

▶ Double-click on any line in the statistical output. NVivo will take you directly to the source so you can examine the coding stripes for that particular node by those users (Figure 12.5).

▶ Click on a coding stripe to see the exact characters coded. This allows you to see easily and specifically where two people are coding similarly or differently, to provide a basis for discussion.

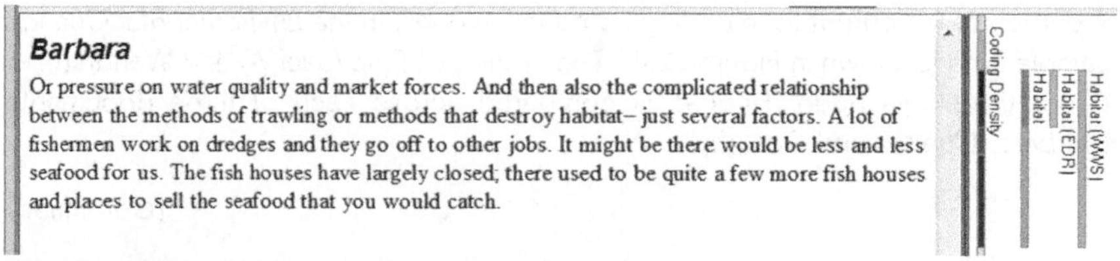

Barbara

Or pressure on water quality and market forces. And then also the complicated relationship between the methods of trawling or methods that destroy habitat– just several factors. A lot of fishermen work on dredges and they go off to other jobs. It might be there would be less and less seafood for us. The fish houses have largely closed; there used to be quite a few more fish houses and places to sell the seafood that you would catch.

Figure 12.5   Comparing the coding detail for two users

To interpret the statistical results, it is important to understand that the unit of measurement for kappa and percentage agreement is the text character (or equivalent small unit in media). Researchers cannot change this default in NVivo (to expand the parameters to a sentence or a paragraph, for instance). This is part of the reason the kappa in Barbara's interview (Figure 12.4) is so low (0.57). To explain both the kappa and the agreement scores, consider the scores from Barbara's data.

The results obtained for Barbara's source lead us to question why the (Cohen's) kappa score is so low, given the high agreement score. While the agreement score is based on a combination of where the coders agreed to apply the node and where they agreed not to apply the node, the kappa only considers data where some coding for the relevant node is present. Because Effie and Wanda, for *Habitat* in Barbara's document, agreed on just over half of the *coded* data for that node across the whole document, the kappa is 0.57 and suggests a failure to achieve a high level of reliability – but 90 per cent of Barbara's document was not coded by either of them, and so they achieved a quite high agreement score.

Apart from difficulties occasioned by the very fine level of assessment (the text character) used in these calculations, there are other difficulties related to the qualitative nature of the data:

- Any particular passage might represent a brief comment or a restatement of what was said earlier – does that mean it should also be coded exactly by both coders?
- The kind of detailed coding differences shown in the statistical output do not necessarily impact the final interpretation of the data, which, as we noted earlier, should depend on patterns across the entire body of data sources.
- If a coding structure contains so many discrete nodes that very few passages from a source are coded to any single node, the agreement score may be artificially high just because of all the text that is *not* coded to the node.
- Coding reliability is a concept borrowed from quantitative research in which only coded data are considered. The idea of including what is not coded as part of a measure is not particularly compatible with this concept.

Finally, to continue agitating these already churning waters, you'll see the coding comparison query does not provide an average agreement (or kappa) across multiple nodes and files, because, unlike quantitative research, at least one key factor makes it difficult to standardize: not all nodes are created equal. Some nodes are much more important to the analysis than others and there's no way to weight the importance of more interpretive nodes versus more descriptive nodes. There's also no way to know during early stages of confirming coder reliability which ones will be more important. Additionally, not all sources are the same size and not all coders do the same amount of work.

? Search Help for *Run a coding comparison query*. This includes a review of the meaning of kappa and methods for and considerations in calculating a global score.

An alternative for the purpose of summarizing the output in the query is to identify the percentage of nodes that fall above or below a certain score. What is more important, however, is to convey how the team revisited the data for the nodes with the lowest scores.

In the end, having considered all this information on the numbers in the coding comparison query, we think using it to review the coding stripes for particular coders for particular nodes and sources is its most appropriate use. Using the query allows researchers to identify potential problem areas but then drill in for further examination to enhance the process of discussing, revising descriptions, and coming up with additional guidelines for coding as a team.

Moving on – further resources

No single book can ever cover the entire range of possibilities with regard to analysis of data, whether with or without a computer. Our hope is simply that the ideas we presented will stimulate you to think about ways of exploring your data (and NVivo), of paying respect to your participants through your handling of their data, and of advancing knowledge that is both relevant and useful. Our further hope is that our guidance helped you understand the principles on which the NVivo software has been built, so you can continue to explore some of its capabilities further on your own. When you face a challenging task for which there are no straightforward instructions, think about what you want to achieve, how the tools in the software work, and be prepared to experiment. (Make sure you save first!) Approach it with the attitude 'There must be a way I can make this program do what I want it to do!' – and indeed, you will often find that there is (although, of course, you must not expect one program to do it all).

If you are looking for further resources, we would be happy to help you. We both thrive on the interesting projects presented to us by researchers around the world. Some have considerable experience with NVivo and require advanced troubleshooting. Others are beginning their journey and want to make sure they start experimenting with tools in the most productive way possible. No single approach is perfect for everyone, so we always focus on the unique blend of your learning style, your preferred approaches to scholarly inquiry, your research questions, your data, and your audience. You can learn more about us and reach us through the following web pages:

- www.researchsupport.com.au – Pat's website has links to articles and resources for qualitative and mixed methods analysis, some involving use of NVivo or computer software more broadly.
- www.queri.com – Kristi's website with training schedules, contact details, and NVivo consulting services in the USA.

In addition, the following sites offer information and resources, and carry links to further sites and resources.

- www.sagepub.co.uk/bazeleynvivo – Here you will find resources specifically to accompany this book, including notes and sample projects, updates to instructions necessitated by new releases, and useful references.
- Access news, tips and videos through the Community section on the NVivo welcome screen.
- www.qsrinternational.com – The developer's site carries updates to the software, teaching resources, links to trainers and consultants in many countries around the world, newsletters with articles about how other researchers are using the software, answers to frequently asked questions (FAQs), and a link to the QSR Forum.
- http://forums.qsrinternational.com – Hosted by QSR International, these forums provide a site where users ask questions, and other users will offer guidance or suggestions to help you. The site includes a searchable archive of previous questions and answers.
- http://caqdas.soc.surrey.ac.uk – The CAQDAS networking project provides practical support, training and information in the use of a range of software programs for use when analysing qualitative data. The information provided includes comparative evaluations, links to developers' websites, and access to trial versions of various software packages.

References

Anderson, R. C., Nguyen-Jahiel, K., McNurlen, B., Archodidou, A., Kim, S.-Y., Reznitskaya, A., Tillmanns, M., & Gilbert, L. (2001). The snowball phenomenon: spread of ways of talking and ways of thinking across groups of children. *Cognition and Instruction, 19*(1), 1–46.

Australian Securities and Investments Commission (ASIC) (2002, June). *Hook, line & sinker: who takes the bait in cold calling scams?* (Report 15). Sydney: ASIC.

Barnett-Page, E., & Thomas, J. (2009). *Methods for the synthesis of qualitative research: a critical review*. NCRM Working Paper Series, 01/09, 1–25. Retrieved 6 February 2012 from http://eprints.ncrm.ac.uk/690/

Bazeley, P. (2006). The contribution of computer software to integrating qualitative and quantitative data and analyses. *Research in the Schools, 13*(1), 63–73.

Bazeley, P. (2007). *Qualitative data analysis with NVivo* (1st edn). London: Sage.

Bazeley, P. (2009). Mixed methods data analysis. In S. Andrew & E. Halcomb (Eds.), *Mixed methods research for nursing and the health sciences* (pp. 84–118). Oxford: Wiley-Blackwell.

Bazeley, P. (2010a). Computer assisted integration of mixed methods data sources and analyses. In A. Tashakkori & C. Teddlie (Eds.), *Handbook of mixed methods research for the social and behavioral sciences* (2nd edn, pp. 431–467). Thousand Oaks, CA: Sage.

Bazeley, P. (2010b). Conceptualising research performance. *Studies in Higher Education, 35*(8), 889–904.

Bazeley, P. (2013). *Qualitative data analysis: practical strategies*. London: Sage.

Bazeley, P., & Kemp, L. (2012). Mosaics, triangles, and DNA: metaphors for integrated analysis in mixed methods research. *Journal of Mixed Methods Research, 6*(1), 55–72.

Bazeley, P., Kemp, L., Stevens, K., Asmar, C., Grbich, C., Marsh, H., & Bhathal, R. (1996). *Waiting in the wings: a study of early career academic researchers in Australia* (National Board of Employment, Education and Training Commissioned Report No. 50). Canberra: Australian Government Publishing Service.

Becker, H. S. (1998). *Tricks of the trade: how to think about your research while you're doing it*. Chicago: University of Chicago Press.

Bernard, H. R., & Ryan, G. W. (2010). *Analyzing qualitative data: systematic approaches*. Thousand Oaks, CA: Sage.

Boote, D. N., & Beile, P. (2005). Scholars before researchers: on the centrality of the dissertation literature review in research preparation. *Educational Researcher, 34*(6), 3–15.

Boyatzis, R. E. (1998). *Transforming qualitative information: thematic analysis and code development*. Thousand Oaks, CA: Sage.

Bringer, J. D., Johnston, L. H., & Brackenridge, C. H. (2006). Using computer-assisted qualitative data analysis software to develop a grounded theory project. *Field Methods, 18*(3), 245–266.

Bryman, A. (2006). Integrating quantitative and qualitative research: how is it done? *Qualitative Research, 6*(1), 97–113.

Bryman, A. (2007). Barriers to integrating quantitative and qualitative research. *Journal of Mixed Methods Research, 1*(1), 8–22.

Caracelli, V. J., & Greene, J. C. (1993). Data analysis strategies for mixed-method evaluation designs. *Educational Evaluation and Policy Analysis, 15*(2), 195–207.

Carvajal, D. (2002). The artisan's tool: critical issues when teaching and learning CAQDAS. *Forum Qualitative Sozialforschung/Forum: Qualitative Social Research*, 3(2), Article 14. Retrieved 1 September 2011, from http://www.qualitativeresearch.net/index.php/fqs/article/view/853

Charmaz, K. (2006). *Constructing grounded theory*. Thousand Oaks, CA: Sage.

Coffey, A., & Atkinson, P. (1996). *Making sense of qualitative data*. Thousand Oaks, CA: Sage.

Coffey, A., Holbrook, B., & Atkinson, P. (1996). Qualitative data analysis: technologies and representations. *Sociological Research Online, 1*(1). Retrieved on 1 September 2011 from http://www.socresonline.org.uk/1/1/4.html

Corbin, J., & Strauss, A. L. (2008). *Basics of qualitative research* (3rd edn). Thousand Oaks, CA: Sage.

Davidson, J., & di Gregorio, S. (2011). Qualitative research and technology: in the midst of a revolution. In N. K. Denzin & Y. S. Lincoln (Eds.), *Handbook of qualitative research* (4th edn, pp. 627–643). Thousand Oaks, CA: Sage.

De Gioia, K. (2003). *Beyond cultural diversity: exploring micro and macro culture in the early childhood setting*. PhD thesis, University of Western Sydney, Sydney.

Dickinson, W. B. (2010). Visual displays for mixed methods findings. In A. Tashakkori & C. Teddlie (Eds.), *Handbook of mixed methods in social and behavioral research* (2nd edn). Thousand Oaks, CA: Sage.

Dixon-Woods, M., Agarwal, S., Jones, D., Young, B., & Sutton, A. (2005). Synthesising qualitative and quantitative evidence: a review of possible methods. *Journal of Health Services Research and Policy, 10*(1), 45–53.

Elliott, J. (2005). *Using narrative in social research: qualitative and quantitative approaches*. London: Sage.

Evers, J. C., Silver, C., Mruck, K., & Peeters, B. (2011). Introduction to the KWALON experiment: discussions on qualitative data analysis software by developers and users. *Forum Qualitative Sozialforschung/Forum: Qualitative Social Research, 12*(1), Article 40. Retrieved 1 September 2011 from http://nbn-resolving.de/urn:nbn:de:0114-fqs1101405

Fielding, N. (2008). The role of computer-assisted qualitative data analysis: impact on emergent methods in qualitative research. In S. Hesse-Biber & P. Leavy (Eds.), *Handbook of emergent methods* (pp. 675–695). New York: Guilford Press.

Fielding, N., & Lee, R. (2007, April). Honouring the past, scoping the future. Plenary paper presented at CAQDAS 07: Advances in Qualitative Computing Conference, Royal Holloway, University of London.

Flick, U. (2007). *Designing qualitative research*. London: Sage.

Flick, U. (2009). *An introduction to qualitative research* (4th edn). London: Sage.

Flyvbjerg, B. (2004). Five misunderstandings about case-study research. In C. Seale, G. Gobo, J. F. Gubrium, & D. Silverman (Eds.), *Qualitative research practice* (pp. 420–434). London: Sage.

Garcia-Horta, J. B., & Guerra-Ramos, M. T. (2009). The use of CAQDAS in educational research: some advantages, limitations and potential risks. *International Journal of Research & Method in Education, 32*(2), 151–165.

Geertz, C. (1973). Thick description: towards an interpretive theory of culture. In C. Geertz (Ed.), *The interpretation of cultures: selected essays* (pp. 3–30). New York: Basic Books.

Gilbert, L. S. (2002). Going the distance: 'closeness' in qualitative data analysis software. *International Journal of Social Research Methodology, 5*(3), 215–228.

Gilbert, L., Jackson, K., & di Gregorio, S. (2013). Tools for analyzing qualitative data: the history and relevance of qualitative data analysis software. In J. M. Spector, M. D. Merrill, J. Elen, & M. J. Bishop (Eds.), *Handbook of research on educational communications and technology* (4th edn). London: Routledge.

Goertz, G. (2006). *Social science concepts: a user's guide*. Princeton, NJ: Princeton University Press.

Guest, G., & McLellan, E. (2003). Distinguishing the trees from the forest: applying cluster analysis to thematic qualitative data. *Field Methods, 15*(2), 186–201.

Happ, M. B., DeVito Dabbs, A., Tate, J., Hricik, A., & Erlen, J. (2006). Exemplars of mixed methods data combination and analysis. *Nursing Research, 55*(2, Supplement 1), S43–S49.

Harden, A., & Thomas, J. (2005). Methodological issues in combining diverse study types in systematic reviews. *International Journal of Social Research Methodology, 8*(3), 257–271.

Hart, C. (1999). *Doing a literature review: releasing the social science research imagination*. London: Sage.

Hume, C., Salmon, J., & Ball, K. (2005). Children's perceptions of their home and neighborhood environments, and their association with objectively measured physical activity: a qualitative and quantitative study. *Health Education Research, 20*(1), 1–13.

Hutchison, A. J., Johnston, L. H., & Breckon, J. D. (2009). Using QSR-NVivo to facilitate the development of a grounded theory project: an account of a worked example. *International Journal of Social Research Methodology, 13*(4), 283–302.

Jackson, K. (2003). Blending technology and methodology: a shift toward creative instruction of qualitative methods with NVivo. *Qualitative Research Journal (Special Issue)*, 96–110.

Jackson, K. (2009, May). Troubling transparency: qualitative data analysis software and the problems of representation. Paper presented at the International Congress of Qualitative Inquiry, Champaign, Illinois.

Jang, E. E., McDougall, D. E., Pollon, D., Herbert, M., & Russell, P. (2008). Integrative mixed methods data analytic strategies in research on school success in challenging circumstances. *Journal of Mixed Methods Research, 2*(3), 221–247.

Johnston, L. H. (2006). Software and method: reflections on teaching and using QSR NVivo in doctoral research. *International Journal of Social Research Methodology, 9*(5), 379–391.

Kaczynski, D., & Kelly, M. (2004, November). Curriculum development for teaching qualitative data analysis online. Paper presented at the International Conference on Qualitative Research in IT & IT in Qualitative Research, Brisbane, Australia.

Kelle, U. (1997). Theory building in qualitative research and computer programs for the management of textual data. *Sociological Research Online, 2*(2).

Kelle, U. (2004). Computer-assisted qualitative data analysis. In C. Seale, G. Gobo, J. F. Gubrium, & D. Silverman (Eds.), *Qualitative research practice* (pp. 473–489). London: Sage.

Kemp, L. (1999). *Charting a parallel course: meeting the community service needs of persons with spinal injuries.* PhD thesis, University of Western Sydney, Sydney.

Kemp, L., Harris, E., McMahon, C., Matthey, S., Vimpani, G., Anderson, T., Schmied, V., Aslam, H., & Zapart, S. (2011). Child and family outcomes of a long-term nurse home visitation program: a randomised controlled trial. *Archives of Disease in Childhood, 96*(6), 533–540.

Kvale, S. (1996). *InterViews: an introduction to qualitative interviewing.* Thousand Oaks, CA: Sage.

Lewins, A., & Silver, C. (2007). *Using software in qualitative research: a step-by-step guide.* Thousand Oaks, CA: Sage.

MacMillan, K., & Koenig, T. (2004). The wow factor: preconceptions and expectations for data analysis software in qualitative research. *Social Science Computer Review, 22*(2), 179–186.

Marshall, H. (2002). What do we do when we code data? *Qualitative Research Journal, 2*(1), 56–70.

Maxwell, J. A. (2013). *Qualitative research design* (3rd edn). Thousand Oaks, CA: Sage.

Maxwell, J. A., & Miller, B. A. (2008). Categorizing and connecting strategies in qualitative data analysis. In P. Leavy & S. N. Hesse-Biber (Eds.), *Handbook of emergent methods* (pp. 461–477). New York: Guilford.

Miles, M. B., & Huberman, A. M. (1994). *Qualitative data analysis: an expanded sourcebook.* Thousand Oaks, CA: Sage.

Mishler, E. G. (1991). Representing discourse: the rhetoric of transcription. *Journal of Narrative and Life History, 1*(4), 255–280.

Mitchell, C. (2011). *Doing visual research.* London: Sage.

Morse, J. M. (1999). Qualitative methods: the state of the art. *Qualitative Health Research, 9*(3), 393–406.

Norman, D. (1998). *The invisible computer.* Cambridge, MA: MIT Press.

Ochs, E. (1979). Transcription as theory. In E. Ochs & B. Shieffelin (Eds.), *Developmental pragmatics* (pp. 43–72). New York: Academic Press.

Ozkan, B. C. (2004). Using NVivo to analyze qualitative classroom data on constructivist learning environments. *The Qualitative Report, 9*(4), 589–603.

Patton, M. Q. (2002). *Qualitative evaluation and research methods* (3rd edn). Thousand Oaks, CA: Sage.

Peräkylä, A. (2004). Conversation analysis. In C. Seale, G. Gobo, J. F. Gubrium, & D. Silverman (Eds.), *Qualitative research practice* (pp. 165–179). London: Sage.

Pink, S. (2001). *Doing visual ethnography.* London: Sage.

Poirier, S., & Ayres, L. (1997). Endings, secrets, and silences: overreading in narrative inquiry. *Research in Nursing & Health, 20,* 551–557.

Rallis, S. F., & Rossman, G. B. (2003). Mixed methods in evaluation contexts: a pragmatic framework. In A. Tashakkori & C. Teddlie (Eds.), *Handbook of mixed methods in social and behavioral research* (pp. 491–512). Thousand Oaks, CA: Sage.

Rich, M., & Patashnick, J. (2002). Narrative research with audiovisual data: video intervention/prevention assessment (VIA) and NVivo. *International Journal of Social Research Methodology, 5*(3), 245–261.

Richards, L. (1998). Closeness to data: the changing goals of qualitative data handling. *Qualitative Health Research, 8*(3), 319–328.

Richards, L. (2002). Rigorous, rapid, reliable and qualitative? Computing in qualitative method. *American Journal of Health Behavior, 26*(6), 425–430.

Richards, L. (2009). *Handling qualitative data* (2nd edn). London: Sage.

Richards, L., & Morse, J. (2012). *Readme first for a user's guide to qualitative methods* (3rd edn). Thousand Oaks, CA: Sage.

Richards, L., & Richards, T. (1994). From filing cabinet to computer. In A. Bryman & R. G. Burgess (Eds.), *Analyzing qualitative data* (pp. 146–172). London: Routledge.

Richards, T. (2002). An intellectual history of NUD*IST and NVivo. *International Journal of Social Research Methodology, 5*(3), 199–214.

Riessman, C. K. (2008). *Narrative methods for the human sciences.* Thousand Oaks, CA: Sage.

Saldaña, J. (2013). *The coding manual for qualitative researchers* (2nd edn). London: Sage.

Sandelowski, M., Voils, C. I., & Knafl, G. (2009). On quantitizing. *Journal of Mixed Methods Research, 3*(3), 208–222.

Schwandt, T. A. (1997). *Qualitative inquiry: a dictionary of terms.* Thousand Oaks, CA: Sage.

Seale, C. (1999). *The quality of qualitative research.* London: Sage.

Seale, C. (2001). Sporting cancer: struggle language in news reports of people with cancer. *Sociology of Health and Illness, 23*(3), 308–329.

Seale, C. (2005). Portrayals of treatment decision-making on popular breast and prostate cancer web sites. *European Journal of Cancer Care, 14*(2), 171–174.

Seale, C., Gobo, G., Gubrium, J. F., & Silverman, D. (2004). Introduction: inside qualitative research. In C. Seale, G. Gobo, J. F. Gubrium, & D. Silverman (Eds.), *Qualitative research practice* (pp. 1–11). London: Sage.

Silver, C., & Patashnick, J. (2011). Finding fidelity: advancing audiovisual analysis using software. *Forum Qualitative Sozialforschung/Forum: Qualitative*

Social Research, 12(1), Article 37. Retrieved 1 September 2011 from http://nbnresolving.de/urn:nbn:de:0114-fqs1101372

Silverman, D. (2010). *Doing qualitative research* (3rd edn). London: Sage.

Sin, C. H. (2007). Using software to open up the 'black box' of qualitative data analysis in evaluations: the experience of a multi-site team using NUD*IST Version 6. *Evaluation, 13*(1), 110–120.

Strauss, A. L. (1987). *Qualitative analysis for social scientists*. Cambridge: Cambridge University Press.

Strauss, A., & Corbin, J. (1998). *Basics of qualitative research* (2nd edn). Thousand Oaks, CA: Sage.

Tesch, R. (1990). *Qualitative research: analysis types and software tools*. London: Falmer.

Ware, C. (2000). *Information visualization: perception for design*. San Francisco: Morgan Kaufmann.

Warr, D. J. (2005). 'It was fun...but we don't usually talk about these things': Analyzing sociable interaction in focus groups. *Qualitative Inquiry, 11*(2), 200–225.

Weitzman, E., & Miles, M. (1995). *Computer programs for qualitative data analysis*. Thousand Oaks, CA: Sage.

Wickham, M., & Woods, M. (2005). Reflecting on the strategic use of CAQDAS to manage and report on the qualitative research process. *The Qualitative Report, 10*(4), 687–702.

Willig, C. (2003). Discourse analysis. In J. A. Smith (Ed.), *Qualitative psychology* (pp. 159–183). London: Sage.

Wodak, R. (2004). Critical discourse analysis. In C. Seale, G. Gobo, J. F. Gubrium, & D. Silverman (Eds.), *Qualitative research practice* (pp. 197–213). London: Sage.

Yin, R. K. (2003). *Case study research: design and methods* (3rd edn). Thousand Oaks, CA: Sage.

Yuen, H. K., & Richards, T. J. (1994). Knowledge representation for grounded theory construction in qualitative data analysis. *Journal of Mathematical Sociology 19*(4), 279–298.

Index